Bloom's Modern Critical Interpretations

George Eliot's
SILAS MARNER

Edited and with an introduction by
Harold Bloom
Sterling Professor of the Humanities
Yale University

D0209799

CHELSEA HOUSE
PUBLISHERS
An imprint of Infobase Publishing

Bloom's Modern Critical Interpretations: Silas Marner

© 2003 by Infobase Publishing
Introduction © 2003 by Harold Bloom

Chelsea House
An imprint of Infobase Publishing
132 West 31st Street
New York NY 10001

Library of Congress Cataloging-in-Publication Data
George Eliot's Silas Marner / edited and with an introduction by Harold Bloom.
        p. cm.—(Modern critical interpretations)
   Includes bibliographical references and index.
     ISBN 0-7910-7045-X
   1. Eliot, George, 1819–1880. Silas Marner. I. Bloom, Harold. II. Series.
   PR4670.G46 2002
   823'.8dc21   2002009106

Chelsea House books are available at special discounts when purchased in bulk quantities for businesses, associations, institutions, or sales promotions. Please call our Special Sales Department in New York at (212) 967-8800 or (800) 322-8755.

You can find Chelsea House on the World Wide Web at
http://www.chelseahouse.com

Contributing Editor: Pamela Loos
Cover design by Terry Mallon
Cover: © Christie's Images/CORBIS

Printed in the United States of America

Lake EJB 10 9 8 7 6 5 4 3 2

This book is printed on acid-free paper.

Bloom's Modern Critical Interpretations

Contents

Editor's Note

My Introduction briefly contemplates the crucial epiphany in which Silas Marner first encounters Eppie and, for a moment, thinks her his lost gold.

Philip Fisher shrewdly finds in the novel a dialectic of harsh substance and sentimental surface. The role of metaphor in *Silas Marner* is explored by Meri-Jane Rochelson, while Elizabeth Deeds Ermarth analyzes George Eliot's idea of sympathy.

Harold Fisch finds the style of Biblical realism in the novel after which Angus Easson evokes the Wordsworthian influence.

Kerry McSweeney sensitively prefers *Silas Marner* to *Adam Bede*, while Patrick Swinden admits that Part 2 of the book does little new with Eppie and Silas, but points out it is essential for understanding Godfrey Cass.

In Terence Dawson's analysis, Silas contrasts interestingly with Nancy, since they share "feminine" characteristics.

The context of George Eliot's shorter fiction is invoked by Alan W. Bellringer, after which Henry Alley sees the book as blending fatherhood and motherhood into an "anonymous heroism of parenthood."

In this volume's final essay, Efraim Sicher finds an ethics of cohesion in *Silas Marner*, founded upon the bond of feeling, both common and communal.

Introduction

S*ilas Marner: The Weaver of Raveloe* remains a beautiful and highly readable book, still immensely popular 140 years after its initial publication. It is not quite of the aesthetic eminence of George Eliot's masterwork, *Middlemarch*, but only because it is much the less ambitious novel, far shorter and confined as it is to a small village in the Midlands. Its protagonists are simple people, seen against a background in which the common folk of the countryside and the natural world itself are so interpenetrated that we feel we might be reading a narrative poem by William Wordsworth, whose spirit hovers everywhere. Henry James, writing about *Silas Marner*, and the early *Adam Bede*, George Eliot's first full-length novel, said "her perception was a perception of nature much more than of art," by which he meant that both books thus displayed an artistic weakness. James was not much interested in country folk, and *Silas Marner* is very much a pastoral novel, prophesying Thomas Hardy. We learn to read *Silas Marner* as we read the Book of Ruth in the Bible, or as we mull over Wordsworth's *The Ruined Cottage* or Hardy's *The Return of the Native*. A vision of nature and its processes is as much a part of such pastoral stories as the leading characters are, and Henry James's distinction between a perception of nature and a perception of art fades away in great writings of this kind.

F.R. Leavis sensibly compares *Silas Marner* to Charles Dickens's *Hard Times*, pointing out that both were "moral fables." A moral fable presumably allows for somewhat different standards of probability than a wholly naturalistic fiction could sustain. Silas is truly a rather unlikely prospect, being a half-mad solitary, to have a deserted child deposited upon his hearth, but within the aesthetic borders of what is almost a fairy story (as Leavis observed) the substitution of the little Eppie for Silas's stolen gold and dead sister is wonderfully persuasive:

> When Marner's sensibility returned, he continued the action which had been arrested, and closed his door, unaware of the chasm in his consciousness, unaware of any intermediate change, except that the light had grown dim, and that he was chilled and faint. He thought he had been too long standing at the door and looking out. Turning towards the hearth where the two logs had fallen apart, and sent forth only a red uncertain glimmer, he seated himself on his fireside chair, and was stooping to push his logs together, when, to his blurred vision, it seemed as if there were on the floor in front of the hearth. Gold!—his own gold!—brought back to him as mysteriously as it had been taken away! He felt his heart beginning to beat violently, and for a few moments he was unable to stretch out his hand and grasp the restored treasure. The heap of gold seemed to glow and get larger beneath his agitated gaze. He leaned forward at last, and stretched forth his hand; but instead of the hard coin with the familiar resisting outline, his fingers encountered soft warm curls. In utter amazement, Silas fell on his knees and bent his head low to examine the marvel: it was a sleeping child—a round, fair thing, with soft yellow rings all over its head. Could this be his little sister come back to him in a dream—his little sister whom he carried about in his arms for a year before she died, when he was a small boy without shoes or stockings? That was the first thought that darted across Silas's blank wonderment. *Was* it a dream? He rose to his feet again, pushed his logs together, and, throwing on some dried leaves and sticks, raised a flame; but the flame did not disperse the vision—it only lit up more distinctly the little round form of the child and its shabby clothing. It was very much like his little sister.

In a fable of regeneration, like Silas Marner, this epiphany has extraordinary plangency and force. George Eliot's art, throughout the book, is almost flawless in its patience. The narrator's stance is one of Wordsworthian "wise passivity"; it is nature and community working slowly and silently together that regenerate Silas and that punish both the Cass brothers, each in proportion to his hardness of heart. It is the same spirit, of what might be called the natural, simple heart, that is manifested by Eppie when she chooses to stay with Silas rather than return to the wealthy father who abandoned her:

'Thank you, ma'am—thank you, sir, for your offers—they're very great, and far above my wish. For I should have no delight i' life any more if I was forced to go away from my father, and knew he was sitting at home, a-thinking of me and feeling lone. We've been used to be happy together every day, and I can't think o' no happiness without him. And he says he'd nobody i' the world till I was sent to him, and he'd have nothing when I was gone. And he's took care of me and loved me from the first, and I'll cleave to him as long as he lives, and nobody shall ever come between him and me.'

"Cleaving" is the Biblical metaphor there and throughout *Silas Marner*. Most moral fables in literature fall away into an Abstract harshness, and become rather bad books. George Eliot's genius vitalizes he fairy story or fabulistic aspect of *Silas Marner*, because of her uncanny power of humanizing all concerns of morality. In a letter to her publisher, she remarked upon "the remedial influence of pure, natural human relations," as she had sought to portray them, and then added a fine, afterthought: "The Nemesis is a very mild one."

PHILIP FISHER

Silas Marner

Like the Book of Job, *Silas Marner* takes the form of a process of subtraction and loss that plunges to an absolute nadir, a just-above-zero of the human condition, and then recovers by a process of addition until the end restates the beginning. Whether Job or Marner, there is an unreality, a gratuitous quality about the "recovery" quite different from the equally arbitrary fall. The accident that brings the thief to Marner's door is of a different order from the one that brings the tiny infant crawling through the snow. Loss at an accelerating rate we can believe in, as we do in avalanches, but no one has seen the rocks rise back up the mountain. In certain moods everyone believes in a kind of law of gravity in life as well as stones; one of the motifs of *Ulysses* is the phrase "32 ft. per second per second," the law of falling bodies.

The optimism of Job or *Silas Marner* is of a kind in which we hope rather than believe. In reading either book, we are closer to those stories of subtraction without end, *King Lear* or Wordsworth's "The Ruined Cottage," than we are to genuinely confident works. We do not believe in the recovery because we know that a man never sits in his chair with the same ease after he has once been sold up. So much of happiness is the confidence that it will not disappear in the blink of an eye, and the man wasted once by arbitrary events will never live without the anxiety that what he has might be gone by

From *Making Up Society: The Novels of George Eliot.* © 1981 by the University of Pittsburgh Press.

morning. While the end of the Book of Job or *Silas Marner* resembles the beginning, it does so only on the surface of events, in the numbers of friends and sheep. Job knows what no happy man ever considers: that the ground he walks on is thin paper over a gulf.

A look at the specific form of the recovery provides even more reason to place it in quotation marks. With a knot, it is true that to return to the beginning, you must exactly reverse the steps that led to the complexity. People after a disaster often fasten on the sequence and imagine that by repeating every step of it in reverse order, they will return from the predicament. This habit is pure fantasy in history or psychology. When thinkers realized in the nineteenth century how religion had taken on an economic vocabulary under the rise of capitalism, until it gave way to an economic image of man, many saw the antidote in attempts at religious revival. But sequences do not reverse in history.

To take the central example in *Silas Marner*, one of Eliot's absolutely correct insights was the growing importance of things, of hoarded goods in which one's value was recorded. In *Adam Bede* and *The Mill on the Floss*, these goods are a key to the new society, an intense center of life and self-recognition. The hoard of goods, along with reputation, states one's place and identity. It replaces the relations of station in the earlier society, relations to those above and beneath one, and equally it replaces the web of tasks that spoke one's place. When the community and round of duties no longer articulate the self, the relation to these gives way to a relation of things. And these things speak out in public to declare "what one is." The process is in one direction. But, like those who imagined religion as the cure for the condition it had been unable to prevent, Eliot pictures in *Silas Marner* the mirror image of the true history: she shows the gold hoard giving way to the child and, through the child, to the web of community.

In other words, the cure is only the catastrophe run backward; to imagine rescue is only to imagine the disaster in reverse. What offers itself as optimism is historically and psychologically the equivalent of a pessimism so hopelessly evocative of the problem that it can see no solution but the vanishing of the conditions that caused it.

For this reason, the story of Marner stands alongside that other fable of a weaver, Wordsworth's "Ruined Cottage." Both are tales of destruction, first of community, then of life itself. Weaving was the single most important English industry in the period of transition to capitalism. Just as Melville chose whaling, that first New England industry, so Wordsworth and Eliot chose weaving to create a generalized statement. When she wrote to her publisher about *Silas Marner*, Eliot mentioned Wordsworth and imagined her story was of a kind no one would like now that the old poet was dead.

The poem offers its bleak images in simple chronicle without the surface of sentimental reassurance and facile hope. But *Silas Marner*, too, is made of these images and tells in parallel of a double destruction.

The community of the Lantern Yard is shattered by treachery that grows out of a sexual attraction. Marner's fiancée and his best friend fall secretly in love. Sarah cannot break the engagement. "Their engagement was known to the church, and had been recognized in the prayer-meetings; it could not be broken off without strict investigation, and Sarah could render no reason that would be sanctioned by the feeling of the community" (p. 222). In the control through the public notice that the community takes of private feeling lies the strict demand that all life be social life. Sarah and Vane conspire to disgrace Silas through an accusation of robbery: they accuse him of the crime they commit against him. The community never appears except in the tragic injustice of Silas's trial. From the trial of Hetty to that of the witch to that of Silas there is a direct line. Silas is tried by an appeal to chance, by the drawing of lots that declares him guilty.

Silas accuses his friend, breaks with him, finds his engagement ended, blasphemes against God, renounces his faith, and leaves the Lantern Yard to appear in Raveloe, a mysterious stranger. A weaver, he relates to others only through his industry; otherwise he is as unfathomable to them as a witch. He is credited with powers to cure or blight. Men like Marner "were to the last regarded as aliens by their rustic neighbors, and usually contracted the eccentric habits which belong to a state of loneliness" (p. 216). The neighbors' suspicion finally produces oddities that it can use to justify its originally groundless fear. In describing the effect on Silas himself, Eliot makes the most direct statement in all her work of the relationship of a sense of self to a sense of community and familiarity.

> Even people whose lives have been made various by learning, sometimes find it hard to keep a fast hold on their habitual views of life, on their faith in the Invisible, nay on the sense that their past joys and sorrows are a real experience, when they are suddenly transported to a new land, where the beings around them know nothing of their history, and share none of their ideas—where their mother earth shows another lap, and human life has other forms than those on which their souls have been nourished. Minds that have been unhinged from their old faith and love, have perhaps sought this Lethean influence of exile, in which the past becomes dreamy because its symbols have vanished, and the present too is dreamy because it is linked with no memories. (P. 226)

At last even the present is dreamy—a mere sensation—in the absence
of echoing experience, the texture of memories and objects and known
relationships in which every thread leads to another, every event defines itself
against other events.

Marner in Raveloe is reduced to that position from which so many later
novels begin. "In this strange world, made a hopeless riddle to him, he might,
if he had had a less intense nature, have sat weaving—looking towards the
end of his pattern, or towards the end of his web, till he forgot the riddle, and
everything else but his immediate sensations" (p. 231). The words are similar
to Pater's in the conclusion to *The Renaissance*. "Experience, already reduced
to a swarm of impressions, is ringed round for each one of us by that thick
wall of personality through which no real voice has ever pierced on its way
to us, or from us to that which we can only conjecture to be without."[1] To
try to untangle Marner's riddle, as so many novels of investigation do in the
next generation; or to create a miniature rational world of work and patterns
that, with our shortsightedness, we can contemplate instead of the riddle; or
to begin to take pleasure in atomized, immediate sensation as those after
Pater did—all three are in bondage to the same reading of life, the same
incomprehensibility of social, and, in consequence, individual existence.

Marner's is the solution by work. Reducing life to a closed universe
where one is absolutely in control—a self-made universe—he cannot see
beyond the cycles of project and payment, work promised and work
delivered, money owed and money paid. The world makes sense because it
is empty. Only two elements exist, the loom and the hoard of gold. Like
Hetty, Marner in the evening ritualizes his sensuality into a relationship with
his hoard. He enjoys the "companionship" (p. 232) of his money, the society
of inanimate things.

Three of the great mythic figures of the mid-nineteenth-century novel
are misers: Dickens's Scrooge, Balzac's Grandet, and Eliot's Marner. Avarice
is the essential deadly sin in an age of individualism. In de Tocqueville's
description, the social energies are hoarded, and capitalism is a public form
of hoarding, capital accumulation. Behind the self-made man stand two
mythic figures: the monster and the miser, Frankenstein's creation and
Scrooge.

Paradoxically, the miser, man totally in isolation, always hoards goods
that have only social value—money, diamonds, jewelry. No miser hoards
what he needs to live. Hetty, when most alone, was most intensely involved
in social fantasies. The miser accumulates what a change of social forms can
turn to junk, like those Indian graves filled with treasures of beads. The miser
lives in a theater of the imagination, as Eliot called it, a make-believe society
that seems solid and ultimate in its simplicity, but is as fragile as the society
of riddles it has replaced.

Although everyone guesses Silas has gold hidden in his cottage, no one can steal it. Legibility and community create one another. "How could they have spent the money in their own village without betraying themselves? They would be obliged to 'run away'—a course as dark and dubious as a balloon journey" (p. 232). After the theft Marner accuses Jem Rodney, whose defense cannot be questioned. "'What could I ha' done with his money? I could as easy steal the parson's surplice and wear it' " (p. 270). The money is stolen by those who could never be suspected of needing it, the rich, and Marner reaches the bottom. The theft proves that even a miser is still in society. The man most isolated remains part of the intentions of those around him, part of their imaginations if nothing else. In the Victorian novel, there is often a grim proof that society exists whether we will it or not. The agents of this proof are crime, illegitimacy, and contagious diseases. In *Bleak House*, the most distant corners of society are shown connected by their ability to ravage one another. Jo carries the disease; Esther's illegitimate parentage binds high and low; crime is woven through the whole. Society exists at least enough for everyone to stalemate one another at law while the inheritance that should be shared by all vanishes.

When Dunstan Cass enters Marner's cottage and when Godfrey's child crawls through the open door, society still exists in this minimal, negative sense. The opium addict dies in Marner's front yard on her way to disgrace Godfrey by revealing that she is his wife. The childlessness of Godfrey's marriage to Nancy is symbolically a result of the earlier marriage. Had the prudery of the time not enforced silence, Eliot might have openly stated that the childlessness was the result of venereal disease.

Only twice are high and low connected in the novel. The first time is when Dunstan Cass enters to steal the gold. It is a startling moment because only the rich can steal this money, since only they don't need it. The second event is the visit of Godfrey to steal Eppie, to reclaim her. United by catastrophe, by their ability to damage each other, the extremes of rich and poor never meet otherwise. No society includes them. The characters of the novel are individuals who enter relationships with one another, who make up their lives with one another; no network exists into which they find themselves integrated at birth.

Silas Marner is the first of Eliot's novels that critics speak of by parts, a Marner half connected only at flash points with a Cass half. Each novel that follows can be divided similarly. Nothing unites the parts but events. Yet nothing is more essential and at the same time more hopeless in Eliot's ambition than the demand that experience must have its meaning in terms of a wider frame than that of individual history. Biography seems the obvious form for her to work in, but it is the one form that is most untrue to what she knows as the truth of events. If experience is legible through the context of individual history—as it is for Freud, who finds the complete meaning of an event within the absolute vacuum of the patient's memory—then the self is the one reference point for motive and the one goal of action.

Looking back at Adam's life or Maggie's, we can see that the most important changes were not willed and could not be understood with only their lives as contexts. The love affair between Hetty and Arthur indirectly gives the critical turn to Adam's life. Her father's feud with Wakem and the family bankruptcy do the same for Maggie. Silas's whole life is altered by the love between his fiancée and his friend. None of these lives makes sense as a project; none can be talked of in the language of Mr. Deane, where a man can be anything he wants to be. Mr. Deane's is the language of the biographical form, the motto of which is "Be yourself." Dozens of later novels follow the pattern of Joyce's *Portrait of the Artist As a Young Man* and base themselves on the sensitive, isolated hero, often an artist, surrounded by others who are completely different from him and who affect him mainly by temporarily preventing him from "finding himself," and then from "being himself." This self is harmonious and complete; each part has meaning through the others; each is in focus when seen against the whole of the self. But this self that is like a work of art, because it has complete meaning in itself, is self-explanatory but not self-sufficient. It is in exile.

Where the biographical form is accepted, the values of will, energy, and the imagination to project the self in a daring and novel way follow. The form can be used against the grain: Dickens did so in *Great Expectations*. Pip's life is like that of a puppet at the end of strings so long that they pass out of sight. Practically without will, he is here, then moved there, claimed and reclaimed. But the use of a form against itself is like a temperance speech in a tavern. Eliot combines lives because she must, in order to keep the legibility of lives that, as she shows, only make sense in the wider context of other lives.

At the same time, she is detailing the disappearance of society, the natural context of wider meaning. Family and society, the Tullivers and the village of Hayslope, make the magic circle James spoke of. "Really, universally, relations stop nowhere, and the exquisite problem of the artist is eternally but to draw, by a geometry of his own, the circle within which they shall happily appear to do so."[2] James is wrong in assuming there is no natural circle; Hayslope and the family life of the Tullivers are natural circles, those of continuous existence: the same people in the same place through time. An image from Marner indicates the challenge to the novel from the new society in which circles do only "appear" final. Marner, an outsider even after fifteen years in Raveloe, appears like a ghost at the Casses' New Year's Eve party. In his arms he holds an unknown child. He is an outsider holding a stranger. By the laws of melodrama, he has brought the child to its home and into the sight of its father, who is married secretly in another town. The secrecy of Godfrey's life carries further, by willing it, the type of discontinuity thrust on Marner. The natural circle does not exist. Only the circle of art makes sense of this moment in the doorway. Marner knows a fraction, Godfrey a little more, the rest of the party know nothing, and never will: the reader knows it all.

A more extreme example is the group that assembles in the first chapters of James's *Portrait of a Lady*: Daniel Touchett, Ralph, Mrs. Touchett, Isabel, Lord Warburton, and Mme. Merle. In life, as James knows it, in rootless life, real relations end nowhere. In Hayslope they do end; Raveloe is halfway between Hayslope and Gardencourt, between community and collection. Where art closes the circle, as it does in Raveloe, it stands as an illusory barrier to incomprehensibility. There is only a step between those circles closed by art and those closed by the imagination, whether sane or insane—between the circles in James's *Sacred Fount* or Faulkner's *Absalom, Absalom!*

The narratives we see divided in parts are only the first of the synthetic replacements Eliot found for the community she lost. The form of the social novel was lost along with the community. To the extent that family was at least a miniature community in *The Mill on the Floss*, the first two of her novels showed the disintegration in process. *Silas Marner* is the first of her works after the fall. The Cass half of the novel is the context for our comprehension—but not his own—of Marner's life. Like Maggie and Adam, he is shaped by life. The keys to his life are outside: the betrayal by his friend, the robbery, the appearance of the child. He responds but does not initiate. Passivity, resignation, and acceptance are the inversions of the initiative, imagination, and energy of the self-made man. The virtues are those of characters made by catastrophes they could not even foresee, let alone prevent.

Within the Cass chapters, the novel outlines a grammar of inverted appearances and truths. Three families exist: the squire and his sons; Godfrey's first marriage with Molly and the child that results; and Godfrey's second, childless marriage with Nancy. Each family is seen only in glimpses of moments when it is acting out the truth of the relationship, a truth that is always a savage reversal of the public meaning of the tie. Godfrey lies out of necessity, Dunstan for pleasure. In the first family, one brother is blackmailing the other, and both rob the father. When any two meet, they argue, and when Dunstan disappears no one misses him, no search is made. Godfrey would be pleased to learn of his brother's death.

The second family exists only in Molly's journey through the snow to disgrace her husband, the dishonor him at the party by revealing the marriage. She falls asleep from the opium and dies. Godfrey arrives only to make sure she is dead. Again bonds are inverted; twice Godfrey is best served by the deaths of those he is most closely related to.

The single great moment in the novel is the final reversal of what Eliot would call natural human bonds. The scene is the exact equivalent of Hetty's murder of her child. A contrast of the two scenes shows the extent to which psychology and internal action have replaced public events in Eliot's work. Melodrama gives way to the subtleties of the modern social novel where action is invisible or inscrutable or both. Godfrey stands in Marner's cottage after he has been assured that the woman to whom he is secretly married is dead. One danger remains: the child. If the child didn't exist, he would be free of the past—something he is forced, by inversion, to desire. Only one last detail to erase, and the previous years will be a blank. He looks at the child. "The wide-open blue eyes looked up at Godfrey's without any uneasiness or sign of recognition: the child could make no audible claim on its father; and the father felt a strange mixture of feelings, a conflict of regret and joy, that the pulse of that little heart had no response for the half-jealous yearning in his own, when the blue eyes turned away from him slowly and fixed themselves on the weaver's queer face" (p. 337). In the joy he feels that the child treats him as a stranger, he has reached a point equivalent to Hetty's.

Godfrey's third family is likewise in sight only at a moment of paradox. The fifteen years skipped pass over what happiness he and Nancy had. We see only his confession of his earlier marriage. The two try to recover Eppie and fail. The crisis of this part of the novel concerns Eppie's choice. Will she live with her legal father, her father in fact, or stay with Silas? Godfrey's claim would be recognized by society; any court would award him custody. But Silas is the father in supplying the recognition Godfrey denied her.

The ties are concealed or denied or perverted until they are unrecognizable. Brother, father, family—none has reality, all conceal the true bonds that are independent of the formal relationships. Before disappearing, the society is distorted into grotesque variants on what it was to be. It is the rich that rob the poor.

The harsh substance of the book provides the motive for the compensating surface of sentimentality. The marriage that concludes the book, the symbolic holy family (in which there is more of true family feeling than in any of the actual families of the novel) made up of Silas, Dolly Winthrop, and Eppie, does not weigh against the treachery and paradox that have destroyed both communities, that of the Lantern Yard and that of Raveloe. The neat satisfactions of justice in the novel are deceptive: the fog that allows the robbery conceals the stone pits that punish the thief. Godfrey, who denies his child, must stay childless for the rest of his life. In the end, the gold Silas seemed to have lost in order to gain the golden child reappears as though to say he couldn't have blessings enough.

The state of life that is recovered is not at all like Job's—the literal return of what was lost. Instead of the fiancée and friend of the Lantern Yard, Marner, an old man now, has the sexless family in which the single emotional tie is the child. His life is lost and he has only a simulation that, like the metaphor of gold and golden hair, is true only on the plane of the imagination.

NOTES

1. Walter Pater, *The Renaissance* (1873; reprint ed., New York: Mentor Books, 1960), p. 157.
2. Henry James, *The Art of Fiction*, ed. R. P. Blackmur (New York: Scribner's, 1934), p. 5.

MERI-JANE ROCHELSON

The Weaver of Raveloe:
Metaphor as Narrative Persuasion in Silas Marner

The strong presence of the narrator in George Eliot's novels and the extensive use of metaphor within their texts are both significant characteristics of Eliot's art, and both have received a great deal of critical attention. For the most part, previous studies have focused on either the narrator alone,[1] or on the imagistic content of metaphors without reference to the narrator.[2] A few writers on George Eliot's metaphors, however, have gone beyond the tracing of images in relation to theme, and have begun to look at some of their more rhetorical functions.[3] My study proceeds from the belief that metaphors in fiction contribute to meaning not only by illuminating the ideas in a novel, but also by helping to create the narrator who must make the reader understand, and believe in, those ideas.

This discussion of how the narrator of *Silas Marner* is created, in part, by the metaphors she[4] makes is based on Aristotle's notion of the "ethos" of a speaker. In the *Rhetoric*, Aristotle asserts that ethos, or "moral character... constitutes the most effective means of proof," and that a speaker "persuades by moral character when his speech is delivered in such a manner as to render him worthy of confidence."[5] While the persuasive power required by a writer of fiction is of a subtler kind than that expected of a political orator, still the need for persuasion exists. Before any narrative meaning can proceed from author to reader, the reader must be persuaded that he wants to keep

From *Studies in the Novel* XV, no. 1 (Spring 1983). © 1983 by North Texas State University.

on reading, that what he can obtain from the reading experience will be worth the having. By creating a narrator to whom the reader wants to listen—whose personal qualities, character, and values are such that the reader is willing to join him through the novel—the author brings about the most important relationship in the narrative. If the ethos of the narrator is right, then the bond will be created; the reader will go on reading and, under the guidance of the narrator, will come to understand the fictional world in the way the author wants him to. If the ethos is wrong, however, and the reader does not develop just the right amount of trust or distrust in his narrative guide, or if he misses cues for questioning or accepting or pondering because he is alienated, confused, or—as might happen in some modern fiction—inappropriately engaged, then the effect of the entire novel will be lost.

By examining the use of metaphor in George Eliot's novels, one can learn a great deal about the ethos of that narrator whose presence is so substantial in her works, and about the ways Eliot's narrative method itself helps convey the world-view that underlies her fiction. I have chosen to focus my discussion first on a close reading of a passage of overt narrative commentary in *Silas Marner*, to see how metaphor interacts with other forms of persuasion to create the essential bond when the narrator speaks directly to the reader. Later I will deal with the use of metaphor in the presentation of characters, to see how the narrator employs metaphor—in one case quite effectively, in another less so—to shape the reader's response to persons in the novel. By taking three somewhat different perspectives toward the analysis of metaphor as narrative persuasion in *Silas Marner*, I hope to suggest the range of potential in this approach for adding to our understanding of George Eliot's art.

A passage early in Chapter 2 illustrates how the narrator of *Silas Marner* uses metaphor to bring the reader into the world of the novel, as she explains to the reader Silas's growing alienation from God. Many critics have commented on the way Eliot frequently shifts the perspective of her narrative, like the changing or refocusing of a lens,[6] and she does so in the following passage early in *Silas Marner*. The narrator begins at a medium distance: "And what could be more unlike that Lantern Yard world than the world in Raveloe?—orchards looking lazy with neglected plenty; the large church in the wide churchyard, which men gazed at lounging at their own doors in service-time; the purple-faced farmers jogging along the lanes or turning in at the Rainbow; homesteads, where men supped heavily and slept in the light of the evening hearth, and where women seemed to be laying up a stock of linen for the life to come."[7] The narrator describes Raveloe as an objective traveler might, surveying its landscape and inhabitants from sufficiently near to infer its complacent abundance, but at a distance that still prevents intimate acquaintance. The picture is in many ways inviting, but the remote perspective suggests a coolness or aloofness which is, in fact, confirmed in the second sentence: "There were no lips in Raveloe from which a word could fall that would stir Silas Marner's benumbed faith to a sense of pain." The narrator's view moves closer in, to Silas, and we see that his soul remains untouched by the bounty and activity around him.

There has not been much metaphor in this section so far, so that when it does appear—in the reference to a word that might "stir ... benumbed faith"—its effect is the more dramatic. Analogies have appeared in the paragraph to this point: the orchards "look" lazy, and the women only "seem to be" storing linen for the afterlife. These comparisons help assure the reader of the narrator's perceptive eye, and the content of the second is appropriate to the discussion of faith and varieties of belief that make up the subject of the passage. But that they are straightforward analogies, drawing attention through their form to the fact that the narrator is creating them and that the reality they illuminate is quite ordinary reality, makes one feel, too, how strongly the narrator is in control. This feeling that one is being led along by a calm, perceptive, controlled narrator contributes as much to one's sense of the comfort of Raveloe as the actual images themselves. It is thus not only the shift in perspective, but also the shift to metaphor, that accounts for the discomfort produced by the sentence about Silas. His faith does not "seem" numb, it *is* numb, and it must be awakened to pain when it begins to feel.

Many theories have been advanced as to what makes up the rhetorical difference between similes and metaphors. Aristotle found simile "less pleasant" than metaphor because, since it contains a word that points out the comparison, simile deprives the listener of making the connection for himself.[8] More recent theorists, such as Max Black, find the difference between metaphor and simile to lie in the complexity of meaning produced by each, the simile presenting a static, clearly defined comparison, while the metaphor calls into play systems of implications and connotations, changing the meanings of both "principal" and "subsidiary" terms.[9] But similes and analogies, as George Eliot's own works show, can be quite as rich and suggestive in meaning as metaphors. The difference in effect lies, then, not only in the difference in content between the two types of expressions or in how much effort the reader must expend to understand that content, but also in the difference in relation between narrator and reader that the simile and the metaphor create. In the passage under discussion, the narrator, previously guiding and explaining, now asserts a comparison to the reader as a truth, assuming the reader no longer needs to be led by the hand but can apprehend the point of the comparison at once. At the same moment, the reader is both challenged by the narrator and accepted by her as an equal. Since the preceding analogies have helped establish the narrator as intelligent and perceptive, one willingly accepts the offer of equality and partnership. The bond between reader and narrator is thus subtly strengthened, throughout the novel, by shifts such as this one.

The movement from one means of explanation to another conveys the earnestness of the narrator's desire to explain, and at the same time suggests that nothing can be explained through only a simple presentation of the data. The narrator then makes clear that the shift in perspective (from Raveloe to Silas, from survey of community to analysis of character) and the shift in rhetoric (from literal speech, to analogy, to metaphor) are still not enough to make the reader understand just what Silas Marner is experiencing. The sentence about Silas's benumbed faith is therefore followed by another shift in perspective: "In the early ages of the world, we know, it was believed that each territory was inhabited and ruled by its own divinities, so that a man could cross the bordering heights and be out of the reach of his native gods, whose presence was confined to the streams and the groves and the hills among which he had lived from his birth. And poor Silas was vaguely conscious of something not unlike the feeling of primitive men, when they fled thus, in fear or in sullenness, from the face of an unpropitious deity."

The wider view provides a comparison between Silas's plight and the lives of "primitive men," and results from the same philosophical impulse as the employment of analogy and metaphor. What the narrator suggests is that fullness of understanding can only be approached if one compares the situation at hand to other situations like it. At base is the idea that all things can be related; as readers, we feel the narrator to be someone who sees in the world a unity between the petty details of life and the cosmic beliefs of ancient men, who cannot tell the story of one weaver without joining it to the lives of all people in all time.[10] We also sense the narrator's erudition in the fact that she knows about primitive men and their gods; our faith in her reliability as guide and interpreter increases as we appreciate her wisdom. We are impressed by her compassion in going to such lengths to make sure we understand what she is saying, and we are flattered that this wise, all-seeing narrator assumes "we know," as she does, all about ancient religion.

The brief explanation of local deities is presented as a simple, literal, matter of fact. Having already established her own reliability, the narrator thus places the reader in an attitude of respect toward something he might otherwise have treated with some scorn. He is then prepared to sympathize with Silas in his loss of faith. But in a subtle way this particular analogy also prepares the reader to reject, along with the primitive superstitions, certain

forms of Christian belief which Eliot is to supplant in the novel with a
religion of human compassion. The images of primitive gods take their place
beside the lots-drawing of Lantern Yard in a system of references throughout
the novel to superstitious faiths whose foundations may be false but whose
believers are sincere.

The comparison between Silas and the early believers is stated
explicitly, and as the paragraph ends the narrator reminds us of the more
immediate comparison with which it began, the contrast between Raveloe
and Lantern Yard: "It seemed to him that the Power he had vainly trusted in
among the streets and at the prayer-meetings, was very far away from this
land in which he had taken refuge, where men lived in careless abundance,
knowing and needing nothing of that trust, which, for him, had been turned
to bitterness." All the strands of explanation gradually come together here,
in a powerful, simple metaphor. The sense of the whole paragraph is finally
epitomized in the last sentence of the passage, an example of the "summary
metaphor" that characterizes Eliot's narrator's rhetoric. By its very existence
as metaphor, this statement adds something to the narration that could not
have been rendered exactly any other way: "The little light he possessed
spread its beams so narrowly, that frustrated belief was a curtain broad
enough to create for him the blackness of night."

This sentence moves from light to darkness as the chapter so far has
moved from the spiritual brightness of Silas's early life to the blankness of his
later existence. In the "blackness of night" we have the clearest presentation
yet of just how desolate his spiritual state is. With the metaphor, a "curtain"
comes down on the bright and active scene of Raveloe life; it is blotted out
for the reader just as, for Silas, the benevolent possibilities of that life are
made invisible by his disillusionment. It is as if the narrator knows the reader
cannot truly understand Silas's plight unless he has all the facts, and through
every possible means. If we understand the narrowness of his "light," we will
not be too impatient with Silas when frustration removes it completely. And
in taking such a well-worn metaphor as the "light of faith" and transforming
it into a physical light one may possess—a feeble, useless light, at that—the
narrator reveals the pathos of Silas Marner's situation while at the same time
suggesting the homely, personal quality of faith. We are led to speculate as to
the solace a faith might provide, were its light only wide enough.

To this point I have been concerned with the ways George Eliot uses
metaphor in overt narrative commentary, both as part of the process of
explanation, and in allying the reader with the narrator in that process. But
although a reader's sense of "who the narrator is" may come first through
such direct intrusions of the narrator's voice, the values of a narrator in any
work are in fact presented all through the narrative, even in sections of free

indirect speech, which are intended most closely to reflect the thoughts of characters. In *Silas Marner*, as we have seen, the ability to create metaphors reveals the narrator's generous, farseeing moral nature, and this connection between metaphor-making and character appears, as well, when she narrates her characters' ruminations in free indirect discourse.[11] When Godfrey Cass shrinks from confessing to his father the fact of his secret marriage, the narrator traces his reasoning as follows:

> Why, after all, should he *cut off the hope* of them [favorable chances] by his own act? He had seen the matter *in a wrong light* yesterday. He had been in a rage with Dunstan, and had thought of nothing but a *thorough break-up* of their mutual understanding; but what it would really be wisest for him to do, was to try and *soften* his father's anger against Dunsey, and keep things as nearly as possible in their old condition. If Dunsey did not come back for a few days, ... *everything might blow over*. (8:119-20, emphasis mine)

Godfrey's desperate rationalization is expressed in a series of metaphors so overworked they are clichés. Developed individually most of these metaphors could be reinfused with their original power; we have already seen what Eliot is able to do with the "light of faith." But piled one upon the other as they are here, these hackneyed phrases indicate only the barrenness of Godfrey's verbal and moral resources, as well as the emptiness of his excuses. By ending the chapter with the feeble phrase, "everything might blow over," the narrator emphasizes the futility of all Godfrey's ill-expressed hopes. If we try to imagine the kinds of metaphors the narrator might use to comment on a situation of such moral complexity, we see the difference in ethos that can be revealed through metaphor. It is significant that when Godfrey finally confesses his guilt, but is prevented from easily "making things right," he expresses his resignation by turning around a cliché: "it is too late to mend some things, say what they will" (20: 237). Growth of understanding, for Godfrey, takes the form of seeing the limitations in metaphors made lightly.

For the most part George Eliot's touch is sure. In the narrator of *Silas Marner* she has created a wise, compassionate, earnest guide whom the reader willingly joins and follows. As presented by this narrator, the characters in the novel attain a reality which encourages the reader's concern for their fates. There is one case, however, in which characterization falls short of success, to a large extent because of an inappropriate use of metaphor and symbol. This is what we find in the treatment of Eppie.

Part of the problem stems from the novel's insistence on Eppie as Silas's new treasure, the replacement for his lost gold. She is introduced as an agent in the fairy tale plot,[12] her symbolic function noted by both narrator and characters. In the descriptions of Eppie's childhood, the narrator's attempts to portray infantile reality through her mischievous behavior are overshadowed by Eppie's symbolic presence as the replacement for the gold and the agent of Silas's regeneration. And although the reader may well sympathize with the process Eppie brings about, this sympathetic involvement is won more by the narrator's comments and generalizations than by her actual depiction of Eppie as Silas's child. Since none of the other characters in the novel have such a purely symbolic presentation, the child Eppie stands out as an anomaly.

Part Two of the novel presents greater difficulties. Eppie, grown to young womanhood, has already helped reintegrate Silas into the human community. She still must serve to effect Godfrey Cass's chastening, but she carries out this function not much differently from the ways in which other, less symbolic, characters perform theirs. Thus, although the identification of Eppie with the gold remains strong (the section begins "sixteen years after Silas Marner had found his new treasure on the hearth"), the reader is also invited to view Eppie as a "rounder" character, with her own emotions, decisions, and individual destiny. The narrator's metaphors, however, interfere with one's acceptance of Eppie in this light.

Specific metaphors, as well as more indirect images, depict Eppie as something of a playful animal. She jokes about Aaron Winthrop, "laughing and frisking" (16:199), and is shown in affectionate communication with the animals around her home, including "a meek donkey, not scornfully critical of human trivialities," and various dogs and kittens with other human attributes. Personification is used quite effectively in other places by the narrator as in the ironic allegorization of "inquiry" that starts Chapter 10, and the "importunate companion, Anxiety," who appears at its end. But in these cases the more abstract metaphors are appropriate where they appear, and consistent with the ethos of the narrator that has been established. The personifications of domestic animals do not seem to fit in their context, because a conflict exists between the content and rhetoric of these metaphors and the implications inherent in other equally strong images.

Max Black has suggested that the best way to help a child understand what metaphor is would be to give him examples of personification.[13] This does not mean that all personifications are childlike, but it does suggest that they can be particularly accessible to children. If we are to accept that the narrator, through her choice of metaphors, creates an ethos that embodies for the reader a mode of explanation, then the ethos presented in this section to some extent alienates the reader. Both the form and content of the metaphors present a mode of seeing associated with children, who as readers would certainly not have responded properly to the narrator as previously developed. The reader may justly ask why he is now appealed to in this childlike way, and who, in fact, is making the appeal.

What one seems to experience in this part of the narrative is an indirect presentation of Eppie's childlike ethos. The problem, of course, is that Eppie is not a child, but a young woman about to be married. The "playful animal" has another side; Eppie's sexuality is suggested repeatedly in the image of her garden,[14] in the unruliness of her hair, and even in her exuberant behavior. That married life is so strongly symbolized by Eppie's garden suggests that the narrator intends sexual awakening to be seen as part of Eppie's fulfilment. But the childish innocence that may also be meant to show the success of Eppie's upbringing does not fit. The metaphors conveying a childlike view of the world are at war with the notion of Eppie as a woman, and finally they overpower it.

It may be that Eppie's innocence is essential to the happy ending the fairy tale plot requires. But Eliot has trouble with happy endings; they tend to become, in her work, too happy, too conventional. Perhaps it is because she believes, with the narrator of *Silas Marner*, "that life never *can* be thoroughly joyous" (17: 220). Straining for the conventions of peaceful contentment, in the portrait of Eppie the narrator fails to reconcile happiness with the complexity of human fates on which the rest of the novel insists.

The relative failure of Eppie's characterization is, however, only the exception that proves the rule. Looking at metaphor as part of a narrator's rhetoric provides an additional dimension to one's understanding of how meaning is conveyed to the reader of a novel. The extent to which a narrator uses metaphor, as well as when and how he uses it, affects the way a reader responds to him—and thus to the narrative—at each point. In *Silas Marner*, the narrator's use of analogy and metaphor allies the reader with her in the process of explanation; at the same time it reveals her own sense of how difficult any explanation is. The moments at which she chooses to employ metaphor, and the kinds of metaphors she chooses, help so strongly to shape one's views of characters and events that at least once the narrator's metaphors produce a response in conflict with what the author seems to have desired.

In *Silas Marner* the use of analogy in narration also has a strong thematic appropriateness. Silas is the "weaver of Raveloe" in more than the literal sense; his misfortune unites his neighbors to him in sympathy just as Eppie reawakens his own sense of ties to the community. The raveled threads of the village are woven into a fabric as Silas and his neighbors each come to see how, despite their first feelings of strangeness from each other, they are in fact mutually connected. By using analogy and metaphor as her predominant means of explanation, the narrator allows the reader similarly to see relationships among apparently disparate phenomena. The theme of universal interconnectedness, which in some way underlies all Eliot's novels, is thus presented through the method of narration, itself, based in the idea that things can best be understood when viewed "in the light of" each other.

NOTES

1. Also known, for much of the twentieth century, as the "intrusive narrator." In "George Eliot and the Omniscient Author Convention," *Nineteenth-Century Fiction*, 13 (1958), 81-108, and in his chapter on the omniscient narrator in *The Art of George Eliot* (London: Chatto & Windus, 1961), W. J. Harvey summarizes and refutes the arguments of its detractors.

2. Among these are—to list only a few—Reva Stump's full-length study of *Movement and Vision in George Eliot's Novels* (1959; reissued New York: Russell & Russell, 1973); articles on one image traced through one novel, such as Clyde de L. Ryals's "The Thorn Imagery in *Adam Bede*," *Victorian Newsletter*, No. 22 (Fall 1962), 12-13; on one image traced throughout the novels, as Barbara Hardy's "The Moment of Disenchantment in George Eliot's Novels," *Review of English Studies*, NS 5 (1954), 256-64; and on patterns of imagery within one novel, as William R. Steinhoff's "The Metaphorical Texture of *Daniel Deronda*," *Books Abroad*, 35 (1961), 220-24.

3. See, for example, John Holloway's chapter on Eliot in *The Victorian Sage: Studies in Argument* (London: Macmillan, 1953), and Janet K. Gezari, "The Metaphorical Imagination of George Eliot," *ELH*, 45 (1978), 93-106. Two early essays which concern the structuring function of imagery, but which also suggest the role metaphors play in uniting author and reader, are Mark Schorer's "Fiction and the 'Matrix of Analogy,' " *Kenyon Review*, 11 (1949), 539-60, and Barbara Hardy's "Imagery in George Eliot's Last Novels," *MLR*, 50 (1955), 6-14, later incorporated, with slight revision, into Chapter 11 of *The Novels of George Eliot: A Study in Form* (London: Athlone Press, 1959). Carol Howe Spady, in her essay, "The Dynamics of Reader Response in *Middlemarch*," *Rackham Literary Studies*, No. 9 (Spring 1978), 64-75, examines how metaphors "humanize" the reader of the novel. Spady's essay, which only recently came to my attention, is similar to mine in its analytical approach. Finally, an important but controversial contribution to the study of metaphor in Eliot's narrative method is J. Hillis Miller's "Optic and

Semiotic in *Middlemarch*," in *The Worlds of Victorian Fiction*, ed. Jerome
H. Buckley, Harvard English Studies, 6 (Cambridge: Harvard Univ.
Press, 1975), pp. 125-45. In brief, Miller finds the models of totalization
in *Middlemarch* to be in combat with incompatible metaphors of vision.
He concludes that the narrator is finally "entangled and trapped" in this
"web of interpretative figures," the coherence of the novel shattered on
a "battleground of conflicting metaphors" (p. 144). Although *Silas
Marner* is a less complex novel than *Middlemarch*, my own analysis
should suggest the more positive conclusions that may be drawn from
Eliot's use of multiple metaphoric models.

4. K. M. Newton, in "The Role of the Narrator in George Eliot's Novels,"
Journal of Narrative Technique, 3 (1973), 97-107, argues that Eliot
intended her narrator to be seen as male, and at least never explicitly said
anything to the contrary. Newton prefers to use the masculine pronoun
for the narrator, to underscore the fact that narrator and historical
author are not the same (p. 98; J. Hillis Miller makes a similar point in
"Optic and Semiotic," p. 130, n. 5). No critic, as far as I know, however,
has ever used the feminine pronoun to refer to the narrator of a male
author's work simply in order to preserve this distinction. The narrator
of George Eliot's novels strongly invites identification with an authorial
voice, and to all readers after 1859, the author in question was known to
be a woman. Except in discussions of *Scenes of Clerical Life* or "The Lifted
Veil" (the "masculine" references in other novels are problematic), the
narrators in George Eliot's fiction may justifiably be referred to as
female. This does not imply that the narrator *is* George Eliot (or Marian
Evans Lewes), but simply that the reader hears a female voice in the
narrator's control and omniscience.

5. Aristotle, *The "Art" of Rhetoric*, trans. John Henry Freese, Loeb Classical
Library (Cambridge: Harvard Univ. Press; London: Heinemann, 1926;
rpt. 1967), p. 17 (I, ii, 4). The issue of metaphor and the ethos of the
narrator in fiction is discussed by Wayne C. Booth in "Metaphor as
Rhetoric: The Problem of Evaluation," *Critical Inquiry*, 5 (1978), 49-72.

6. An especially perceptive analysis of the technique may be found in
Elizabeth Ermarth's essay, "Method and Moral in George Eliot's
Narrative," *Victorian Newsletter*, No. 47 (Spring 1975), 4-7.

7. George Eliot, *Silas Marner: The Weaver of Raveloe*, ed. Q. D. Leavis
(Harmondsworth: Penguin, 1967), Chapter II, pp. 63-64. All subsequent
references in text are to this edition.

8. Aristotle, p. 397 (III, x, 3).

9. Max Black, "Metaphor" (1954), in his *Models and Metaphors* (Ithaca, N. Y.:
Cornell Univ. Press, 1962), pp. 25-47.

10. This belief in analogy as the basis for understanding finds support in George Eliot's essays as well as in her novels. In "The Future of German Philosophy," a review of Otto Friedrich Gruppe's *Gegenwart und Zukunft der Philosophie in Deutschland*, Eliot affirmed her agreement with Gruppe that abstract ideas must be attained "by an ascent from positive particulars." Abstractions arise from perceptions or judgments, she writes, and "every judgment exhibits itself as a comparison, or perception of likeness in the midst of difference: the metaphor is no mere ornament of speech, but belongs to its essence" (*Leader*, 6 [1855], 723-24; rpt. in *Essays of George Eliot*, ed. Thomas Pinney [New York: Columbia Univ. Press, 1963], pp. 152, 151).

11. Gezari notes this relationship between "metaphorical capacity and moral capacity" in Eliot's novels (p. 103).

12. As Jerome Thale points out, "the Godfrey story... is realistic where the Silas story is pastoral and fairy-tale-like" (*The Novels of George Eliot* [New York: Columbia Univ. Press, 1959], p. 59). The treatment of characters within both stories is, however, largely realistic.

13. Black, p. 26.

14. This sexual connotation holds, I believe, even if the garden is viewed as an image of Eden, as Joseph Wiesenfarth suggests in "Demythologizing *Silas Marner*," *ELH*, 37 (1970), 243-44.

ELIZABETH DEEDS ERMARTH

George Eliot's Conception of Sympathy

For George Eliot sympathy lies near the heart of moral life. Her particular view of sympathy, one that sometimes has eluded her modern critics, has little to do with selfless benevolence. "We should distrust a man," she wrote, "who set up shop purely for the good of the community." Such "disinterested officiousness,"[1] as she termed it, stands opposed to true acts of sympathy that involve a difficult psychic negotiation between self and other. Though sympathy is a crucial concern to George Eliot throughout her career, it has a special meaning in the fiction of her mid-career (*Romola, Silas Marner*, and *Felix Holt*) because here her concern about sympathy begins to transform her entire treatment of social and moral problems. In her work sympathy depends absolutely upon a division in the psyche, a split in consciousness that permits two conflicting views to exist simultaneously. This mental division is the material of conscience. Her early novels treat sympathy mainly in terms of the relations between well-acquainted individuals, usually members of the same family or small community. The two middle novels, together with a short tale written during the same period, effect an important shift to the concern with sympathy between people more casually related: a concern central in the late novels. Although the first two novels (*Adam Bede* and *The Mill on the Floss*) and the last two (*Middlemarch* and *Daniel Deronda*) have been considered her best fiction, all the novels have been measured by standards

From *Nineteenth-Century Fiction* 40, no. 1 (June 1985). © 1985 by the regents of the University of California.

that need revision. The three middle works under discussion here represent a considerable achievement and, in the presentation of sympathy, an achievement well beyond the first novels and preparatory to the finest accomplishments of the last.

A glance at Feuerbach's *Essence of Christianity* will help to suggest the psychic conditions for sympathy. This work influenced George Eliot directly and, through her translation of it, influenced many of her contemporaries as well. Both she and Feuerbach stress the therapeutic and liberating value of a double consciousness; both suggest its moral and even "sacred" function. In the relevant passage of *The Essence of Christianity* Feuerbach's immediate subject is prayer. As always in the Feuerbachian equation, mankind replaces God. This transposition between God and the human species is wholly congenial to George Eliot, who believed, as she explained it to a friend, that "the idea of God, so far as it has been a high spiritual influence, is the ideal of a goodness entirely human (i.e., an exaltation of the human)."[2] This is what Feuerbach has to say about prayer.

> In prayer, man addresses God with the word of intimate affection—*Thou*; he thus declares articulately that God is his *alter ego*; he confesses to God, as the being nearest to him, his most secret thoughts, his deepest wishes, which otherwise he shrinks from uttering.... Prayer is the self-division of man into two beings,—a dialogue of man with himself, with his heart.... he makes his heart objective.... The other is my *thou*,—the relation being reciprocal,—my *alter ego*, man objective to me, the revelation of my own nature, the eye seeing itself.[3]

This self-division signals at once a recognition of personal limitation and an effort to reach beyond that limit. The attitude of prayer, then, is one in which the mind, by recognizing its limitations, passes beyond them toward infinite possibilities of the species. It passes, furthermore, not to a single supernatural Father but to a different kind of divine other—the multiple being of humanity as a whole, that is, of the human species. In it the individual finds the divine echo.

This view of other human beings radically changes an individual's relation to others from what it was in a Christian framework. When fellow creatures replace divinity, they cease to be enemies and become, in the sheer fact of their difference, an infinitely valuable resource. Feuerbach cherishes the "qualitative, critical difference between men," and he faults Christianity because it "extinguishes this qualitative distinction; it sets the same stamp on all men alike." Such carelessness about individual differences creates an "exaggerated subjectivity" that cripples moral life.

> If ... no qualitatively different men exist, or, which is the same
> thing, if there is no distinction between me and others, if we are
> all perfectly alike, if my sins are not neutralised by the opposite
> qualities of other men: then assuredly my sin is a blot of shame
> which cries up to heaven; a revolting horror which can be
> exterminated only by extraordinary, superhuman, miraculous
> means. Happily, however, there *is* a natural reconciliation. My
> fellow-man is *per se* the mediator between me and the sacred idea
> of the species.... My sin is made to shrink within its limits, is
> thrust back into its nothingness, by the fact that it is only mine,
> and not that of my fellows.[4]

In other words, the differences between me and my fellow creatures establish
both the limits of my own failings and also the marvelous possibilities
available to me as a human being. They confirm my possibilities and limit my
failures. In this reciprocal relation one individual extends and completes the
best possibilities of the other.

    This model of individual relationship closely resembles George Eliot's
idea of sympathy. In her novels any constructive action must be preceded by
the recognition of difference: between oneself and another, or between the
differing impulses of one's own complex motivation. The capacity to vacillate
in itself does no harm and in fact establishes the possibility for creative
action. In *Adam Bede* the fact that Arthur Donnithorne vacillates, for
example, does not destroy him; his nemesis is rather a weakness of will in
heeding the voice that counsels restraint. It could be said fairly that he does
not vacillate enough. Adam Bede's character improves, developing a new
sympathy, when he begins to experience inner struggles with himself. Single-
minded characters in George Eliot usually resemble, not the virtuous Adam,
but Tom Tulliver in *The Mill on the Floss*, or Tito Melema in *Romola*, or
Jermyn in *Felix Holt*, characters who are strong by negation and whose very
single-mindedness becomes a nemesis. Private imperatives always exist in
context for George Eliot and must come to terms with actual cases however
much they may differ from the projected ideal. To act in well-meaning
ignorance, as Harold Transome does in *Felix Holt*, means to act in a dream,
which hard, unaccommodating actuality will bring crashing down.

    In George Eliot, as in Feuerbach, sympathy is the first step of a double
imperative: first, to accept unruly circumstances, especially those embodied
in neighbors and friends; and second, to act on the basis of this acceptance
for some particular end. George Eliot was fond of quoting Comte to the
effect that our true destiny is composed of *resignation* and *activity*; of
acceptance and knowledge of what cannot be changed regardless of our
wishes, and the occupation that consists in building on this foundation.[5] Any

vision that disregards the hard, unaccommodating actual is an unsympathetic vision and one that usually turns destructive. Only vision that respects actuality can create order and form. George Eliot's idea of sympathy, therefore, has close affinities with her idea of art; in fact, as I have suggested elsewhere, for her life *is* art. "Form, as an element of human experience, must begin with the perception of separateness," she writes in her "Notes on Form in Art (1868)."[6] Separateness, difference necessarily precedes unity since what does not differ cannot be joined. It is true of life and art alike that "every difference is form." True, there are risks in emphasizing differences because some are not reconcilable in immediate or satisfactory ways. But this risk notwithstanding, George Eliot commends to her readers the double action of differentiation and unification, of sympathy and self-expression as the supremely moral act.

George Eliot's characteristic treatment of sympathy is fully evident in her third novel, *Romola* (1863), which is set in fifteenth-century Florence during a crucial period of transition between feudal and modern society. In her extensive research on Renaissance Florentine culture George Eliot attended to every feature of its life, its manners, its customs and slang, its dress, its religious, political, and artistic developments. She made two trips to Italy for these investigations and kept notebook records of everything from theological doctrine to domestic detail. Sometimes this preparation seems to interfere with the naturalness of the descriptions, the contrivances sounding rather too audibly in the background. But by far the most common effect of this novel—an effect intensified by rereadings—is one of breathtaking audacity both in scope and in conception. The metamorphoses of the Proem introduce a novel of extraordinary philosophical resonance and range. George Eliot's powerful grasp of the psychological corollaries of political traditions, the knowledge that supports her association of liberal traditions with humanist learning, her investigation of the dangerous gaps between intention and act—such concerns make *Romola* one of George Eliot's most interesting novels. Years after its publication she wrote to her editor, "there is no book of mine about which I more thoroughly feel that I could swear by every sentence as having been written with my best blood, such as it is, and with the most ardent care for veracity of which my nature is capable."[7]

Romola's private story concerns the disillusionment of an idealistic girl. The crises of this personal history, however, stem from political developments in a turbulent period of Florentine history. George Eliot shows how the public struggle between political and religious authority reaches into the private history of her heroine. The man Romola marries, Tito Melema, a stranger in the city, insinuates himself into various positions by making himself useful, first to Romola's father, Bardo, a well-born scholar, and then to various factions vying for political power. Tito has betrayed his adoptive father, a scholar who was held for ransom and whom Tito abandoned to slavery, preferring the money to the parent. No sooner does he arrive in Medicean Florence than he sets up as a power broker, intriguing among the various factions of that city-state. Tito, the complete political functionary, consults nothing but his own self-interest, and the results do not recommend his procedure. On the unenlightened nature of Tito's self-promotion, the following comment is telling, especially because it comes from a historical personage who occasionally appears in the margins of the story and who cannot be faulted for dreamy idealism: "'It is a pity his falsehoods were not all of a wise sort,' said Macchiavelli, with a melancholy shrug. 'With the times so much on his side as they are about Church affairs, he might have done something great.'"[8] Tito makes betrayal a profession—first of his adoptive father, then his father-in-law, then his wife, then even of more powerful men, and finally himself.

Tito's undoing lies in a kind of self-betrayal that intrigues George Eliot. He cannot trust others, it is clear, because he cannot trust himself; consequently, others cannot trust him. Circumstances often catch Tito by surprise because he consults not circumstances but his own inclinations, and inclinations turn out to be inadequate guides to action. He shifts allegiance from one political faction to another until he is trusted by no one—not because the politics of Medicean Florence are so pure but because his own lawlessness becomes increasingly evident. At one crisis "he was at one of those lawless moments which come to us all if we have no guide but desire, and if the pathway where desire leads us seems suddenly closed; he was ready to follow any beckoning that offered him an immediate purpose" (p. 191). George Eliot traces this weakness directly back to his inability to question himself: "It belongs to every large nature, when it is not under the immediate power of some strong unquestioning emotion, to suspect itself, and doubt the truth of its own impressions, conscious of possibilities beyond its own horizon" (p. 309). This description would serve as a good definition of sympathy as George Eliot understands it. Wholly absorbed in his plans for personal success, Tito lacks that capacity to see choices which would enable him to take the necessary risks for success. Confronted with an opportunity to save his benefactor from slavery, he has one "colloquy with himself" (p. 149), but his love of ease triumphs. Under the mistaken impression that such inaction is the same as doing nothing, Tito does not act, and "the little rills of selfishness" that had formerly been scattered "had united and made a channel, so that they could never again meet with the same resistance" (p. 151): Such is a splendid case of the banality of evil. In Tito, George Eliot gives a brilliant portrait of the circumstantial man: his secretiveness, his urge to be "safe," his instinct for mastery, and, ultimately, his self-destruction.

Despite her difficulties, despite her faltering, Romola has what Tito lacks: the power to question herself, the ability to acknowledge mistakes, and the capacity to recognize validity in claims inconsistent with her own. These powers necessarily entail risks to her independence. Alternatively submissive and rebellious, Romola seems to vacillate continuously without finding a way of her own. Her two flights into exile and her two returns dramatize in an extreme form her need for a center of self equivalent to those around her. When she flares up at Tito for having betrayed her dead father's trust by selling his unique library, she expresses her self-abnegation: "What else did I live for but for him and you?" (p. 354). With nothing to live for but two self-absorbed men, Romola first submits to them wholly, and, then, when they inevitably fail her ideal of them, runs away. Locking away the symbols of her marriage, she rebels against her life and sets out to begin a "new life," one of "loneliness and endurance, but of freedom." Once on the road she feels "free and alone" (pp. 400, 401). Because she has confused submission with sympathy Romola finds her personal resources diminished by her efforts, and so attempts to find freedom in solitude. But she is stopped in the act of flight by the controversial religious leader Savonarola, who turns her back to a life of duty. "Live for Florence" is his advice, and Romola submits again. "Father, I will be guided," she says reverentially, and "almost unconsciously she sank on her knees" (p. 436). Romola, like Maggie Tulliver, understands the importance of trusting others; she also likes to submit.

For a while she maintains this "enthusiasm of sympathy with the general life"—a very abstract form of sympathy—because she trusts to Savonarola's guidance. Eventually he too betrays her absolute trust, allowing Romola's godfather, an innocent man, to go to the scaffold for the sake of political expediency. When Romola appeals to him to put God's justice over the claims of party, Savonarola replies, "The cause of my party *is* the cause of God's kingdom." "I do not believe it!" Romola protests. "The two faces were lit up," we are told, "each with an opposite emotion, each with an opposite certitude" (p. 578). The claim of each, then, is partially valid, yet the greater mistake clearly lies in Savonarola's sacrifice of human considerations for his view of superhuman ones. Whatever his provocations—and they are many— Savonarola's association of one ideology with Truth is a position that, in George Eliot's work, verges on blasphemy. Even one unbeliever, one individual with a different view, qualifies the absolute claim of any position, and perhaps especially a position claiming God as an ally.

Once again Romola runs from conflict. This time she knows submission can never again be an option—"all clinging was at an end for her" (p. 585)—but she still confuses "clinging" with any social contact and gives both up together. This time she meets no one who returns her to the city, and she soon discovers that giving up on others means giving up on herself as well. "She was alone now: she had freed herself from all claims" and from saving occupation as well. "Romola felt orphaned in those wide spaces of sea and sky. She read no message of love for her in that far-off symbolic writing of the heavens, and with a great sob she wished that she might be gliding into death" (p. 590). She has confused resignation with submission, and she has confused activity with rebellion. Accident saves her from this confusion but not before she feels the deadly threat of total solitude. Neither in society nor in solitude does she find it possible to live.

And yet she does live. The process of vacillation itself produces growth and change in Romola. Precisely because she can vacillate between commitment and isolation, Romola learns how to trust herself and how to find a center of self that makes possible engagement with others. Her lesson resembles the more explicit one of Dorothea Brooke in *Middlemarch*, whose dark night teaches her, not the claims of others, but the claims of her own heart. Only with this knowledge can Dorothea occupy her place, and her flights, like Romola's from the city, are from the pain and engagement of that ultimately personal commitment. The ego as well as the other, the I as well as the Thou, are required participants in the life of sympathy. In her efforts to escape commitment Romola resembles Tito to the extent that she confuses being "free" with being "alone." The hard lesson, the one Tito never learns, is that personal freedom can be found only in relation to others and not in opposition to them or in isolation from them.

Rebellion and submission are two sides of the same coin, both in personal relationships and in politics more broadly conceived. Romola's confusion as she vacillates between self-assertion and self-suppression at least maintains the conditions of growth, whereas Tito's single-minded self-interest does not. The ability to accommodate views different from her own gives Romola her strength and it is in distinction from those views, in dialogue with those alter egos, that she finds her own view and her own voice. Without her own voice she pursues a kind of abstract, altruistic zeal, unchecked by feeling and experience. Romola's story confirms a Feuerbachian view of human possibility. The Christian soul would find a message of love in the sky, but Romola only finds such answering messages in human society.

Although *Silas Marner* (1861) was published before *Romola*, I consider it after *Romola* for two reasons: George Eliot had begun work on her Italian novel before she wrote the shorter tale, and the latter, *Silas Marner*, anticipates the structural originality of the last novels. The story was, as she wrote Charles Bray, "quite a sudden inspiration that came across me in the

midst of altogether different meditations." In her journal she describes it as
a story that "has thrust itself between me and the other book I was
meditating."9 This elegant little tale, sometimes inflicted upon school
children too young to grasp its depth, has more to it than an obvious moral
about the superiority of love to money. An extended reflection on the
problem of relationship, *Silas Marner* tells a double story about isolation and
community.

The plot connects two separate stories, that of Silas Marner and that of
Godfrey Cass, and within each story a problem exists about connection
between past and present and, consequently, between the central character
and others. In Silas's story the central problem of community begins with
betrayal. As a member of a narrow religious sect in an industrial city, Silas
resembles his brethren in almost everything except in one particular—his
tendency to fall into cataleptic trances. These "fits" the brethren accept
sympathetically as Silas's unique gift until his best friend turns the gift against
him. Disillusioned by this betrayal, Silas withdraws from Lantern Yard and
from society almost altogether, moving to Raveloe, where he knows no one
and where he can weave at his loom, hoard his earnings, and forget his past.
George Eliot describes this retreat with metaphors of isolating enclosure.
The sect of Lantern Yard is a "little hidden world" withdrawn from the city
and world affairs. From this Silas withdraws to his "hard isolation" in
Raveloe, a place "hidden even from the heavens."10 Inside his isolated
cottage Silas hides from his neighbors, and under his floor in a hole he hides
his growing hoard of gold. His only gestures of affectionate response are
made towards this gold, the product of his own activity. Like an insect
spinning its means out of itself, with only the slenderest connection to the
surrounding world and with only the slenderest nourishment, Silas regresses
to the margins of humanity, his best faculties dormant for lack of exercise.

Counterpointing these metaphors of enclosure are metaphors of
mysterious openings and of thresholds: the threshold between Silas and his
neighbors, which few ever pass; the threshold between past and present,
which Silas himself avoids crossing; and the threshold of consciousness,
represented by his cataleptic trances. In crossing these thresholds Silas
begins the labor of reviving his connections to humanity. He begins directly
after yet another betrayal, one to which even his minimal needs leave him
vulnerable. One night, when he has left the cottage momentarily for water, a
thief steals the unguarded gold, violating the secret life and forcing Silas into
company.

> Formerly, his heart had been as a locked casket with its treasure
> inside; but now the casket was empty, and the lock was broken.

Left groping in darkness, with his prop utterly gone, Silas had
inevitably a sense, though a dull and half-despairing one, that if
any help came to him it must come from without; and there was
a slight stirring of expectation at the sight of his fellow-men, a
faint consciousness of dependence on their goodwill. He opened
the door wide to admit Dolly. (pp. 134–35)

The half-open door which offers admittance both to providers and to thieves
emblematizes the risk and the opportunity of such openness, the need to
control it, and the importance of that threshold between the private security
and the public circumstance.

Silas's trances function for good and ill in a similarly ambiguous way.
As he stands at his cottage door one night, handle in hand, a fit overtakes
him, and while he momentarily departs from consciousness into some other
state, a child crawls past him through the half-open door. The special gift
that was once an occasion for betrayal now proves a mysterious opening into
a new life. The remainder of Silas's story mainly concerns his difficulties in
raising the child he calls Eppie, and the necessity, brought on him by her
surprising infant habits, for more recourse to his neighbors for advice.

Meanwhile, the tale of Godfrey Cass concerns a different kind of
tension between a man and his community. Godfrey's heart is divided
between his established role as landowner and bachelor and the secret life
which has already made him a husband and father. Like the locked casket and
the closed heart of Silas Marner, the sealed lips of Godfrey Cass isolate him
and cut him off from nourishment. The barrenness of his second marriage
embitters him particularly because he has left his own child unclaimed. The
kinship that Godfrey secretly renounces Silas takes up, unknowingly
replacing Godfrey as the father of the apparently orphaned infant. But Cass's
secret eventually comes to light, as secrets always do in George Eliot's
fiction, through the intricate weblike interrelations of social life; and the plot
concerns the nature and consequences of this secret's eventual revelation.

The patterns of similarity and difference between these two stories
have enormous richness and complexity only suggested by this brief sketch.
The relation of these plots has been developed elsewhere; what deserves
notice here is the importance of this story in George Eliot's development.
Her most mature work characteristically directs our attention to the points
of contact between people who are only casually related. The development
in *Silas Marner* of two apparently separate stories to a point of accidental
connection anticipates the last novels. The central characters in *Silas Marner*
are linked, not by blood ties or legal ties as they are in the first two novels,
but by accidents of neighborhood, accidents that become important at

critical moments in *Romola* and in *Felix Holt*, and that become continuously important in *Middlemarch* and in *Daniel Deronda*. The mutual dependence of strangers comes home in this short tale as it has not in the previous novels and introduces a theme central to the form of George Eliot's greatest work.

The reader sees influence between strangers clearly in this tale, even though the characters themselves make little of it. By focusing on the convergence of separate histories George Eliot emphasizes the importance of trust in dealing with conflicting claims. To perceive another's opposition as a resource requires, as Romola's experience demonstrates, a certain strength of character. Romola's trust in Tito makes her vulnerable to bitter disappointment; she finally despairs of her marriage when she realizes that there is a "terrible flaw in the trust." Silas's "trusting simplicity" likewise makes him vulnerable to a rapacious friend (p. 57). But while that trust creates vulnerability, it also binds these characters to life and change in spite of their efforts to escape. The homely wisdom of Dolly Winthrop puts it to Silas directly: "If anything looks hard to me, it's because there's things I don't know on; and for the matter o' that, there may be plenty o' things I don't know on, for it's little as I know—that it is.... And all as we've got to do is to trusten, Master Marner—to do the right thing as fur as we know, and to trusten" (p. 204). The matter of "right" and "wrong" here becomes tolerably confused, as it should in a universe with few moral absolutes. Dolly's advice places in the simplest terms that negative capability which for George Eliot makes sympathy possible. The "right" of any view is always qualified, used in a hypothetical way, understood in practical not dogmatic terms.

What comes gradually to Romola and Silas is a kind of resignation that is the opposite of losing the self. By acknowledging the difference between themselves and others, by accepting the gaps between their desires and their abilities, both Silas and Romola validate their individual experience and locate it in relation to others. "What if ... ," Romola reflects, "What if the life of Florence was a web of inconsistencies? Was she, then, something higher, that she should shake the dust from off her feet, and say, 'This world is not good enough for me'? If she had been really higher, she would not so easily have lost all her trust" (p. 652). The ability to sustain conflict without irritably reaching for certainty holds open the possibility for change and growth. Will Ladislaw in *Middlemarch* sums up the proper attitude best. "I have not given up doing as I like, but I can very seldom do it."[11]

Without sympathy and trust in the possibilities of others, characters like Godfrey Cass and Tito demonstrate the alternative experience of enmity and suspicion. Hostage to their secrets, these characters remain alone even in company. They remain on guard, defensive, fearful of discovery when discovery alone would save them. One of George Eliot's favorite metaphors for this destructive instinct is gambling. The metaphor first appears clearly developed in *Silas Marner*, and it reappears with special definition in *Felix Holt* and in *Daniel Deronda*. Often associated with cramped spaces and with narcotic influences, gambling is a kind of unholy opposite to sympathetic relationship because it pits individuals against each other and reduces the importance of their personal, individualizing differences. For example, *Daniel Deronda* opens at the roulette table in a continental gambling casino, with an international company:

> Livonian and Spanish, Graeco-Italian and miscellaneous German, English aristocratic and English plebian. Here certainly was a striking admission of human equality.... where else would her ladyship have graciously consented to sit by that dry-lipped feminine figure prematurely old, withered after short bloom like her artificial flowers, holding a shabby velvet reticule before her, and occasionally putting in her mouth the point with which she pricked her card?[12]

The atmosphere of "dull, gas-poisoned absorption" suspends spontaneous activity and personal differences for the sake of the mechanical wheel. "'Faites votre jeu, mesdames et messieurs,' said the automatic voice of destiny." The "uniform negativeness" of the players' expressions, has the "effect of a mask" (pp. 37, 39), reducing to monotonous likeness all the differences implied by the description. *Silas Marner* anticipates the last novel in several ways, and most strikingly in its attention to this metaphor.

Silas's history, too, opens with a form of gambling, one literally elevated into a religious program. The worshippers of Lantern Yard venerate "Favorable Chance," also the god of Godfrey Cass and "of all men who follow their own devices instead of obeying a law they believe in" (p. 126). These worshippers actually gamble for salvation by putting moral questions to a lottery. In Silas's case the lottery decides the guilt of an innocent man and benefits his betrayer. Gamblers, these and others, rely on chance to protect them from ordinary probabilities and to fulfill their desires by some magic. This converts life into "a hideous lottery, where every day may turn up a blank."[13] Mrs. Transome in *Felix Holt*, of whom this observation is made, is one of George Eliot's losing gamblers. Without abandoning her establishment, Mrs. Transome attempts to live apart from the codes and obligations of her society, as if she could escape by an act of will from any hindrance to her inclination. The novel dramatizes the consequences: "There is no private life," says the narrator of *Felix Holt*, "which has not been determined by a wider public life, from the time when the primeval milkmaid had to wander with the wanderings of her clan, because the cow she milked was one of a herd which had made the pastures bare" (p. 51). Ignoring the determinate givens of experience is the most desperate gamble because, as Romola knew, it involves a withdrawal from opportunity as well as from limitation.

In *Felix Holt, The Radical* (1866) George Eliot considers the social "web of inconsistencies" in a way that consolidates the gains she made in *Silas Marner* and shifts the balance in her fiction toward a new focus of attention. Like the novel preceding it, *Felix Holt* sets a courtship and marriage against a background of political and legal affairs, this time the affairs of England just preceding the Reform Bill of 1832. But neither the private history of Esther Lyons' marriage to Felix Holt nor the public life represented by politics and legalities holds center stage in this novel. *Felix Holt* magnifies the pattern found in *Silas Marner* of accidental conjunction between separate groups. Such meetings become the center of attention: not merely the relations within families or the relations between one family and its general social background, but rather the relations between different families. In previous novels there is an important gap between the world of strangers and the world of friends, and the action takes place in a foreground of personal interest set against a background of public concern. In *Felix Holt* the background *is* the foreground. In all her novels George Eliot shows a special capacity to imagine these connections between private and public, between the momentary inclination and social institutions. In *Felix Holt* she diversifies the centers of private interest and so brings into relief the problems of negotiation between them.

This novel traces the "mutual influence of dissimilar destinies" (p. 51), attending mainly to parallels between individuals who scarcely know each other. For example, both Felix Holt and Harold Transome declare themselves to be politically "radical." One is a working man, the other heir to Transome Court, and they have little in common either as radicals or as sons and suitors. The novel's title suggests with subtle irony the impossibility of "radical" change in a world where complex circumstances condition every action. Careless of this context, Harold trusts "in his own skill to shape the success of his own morrows, ignorant of what many yesterdays had determined for him beforehand" (p. 189); and Felix, full of idealistic zeal, finds that his efforts have unpredictable consequences and that support can come from unlikely quarters. In their different ways both characters learn the hard way to respect the powerful web of circumstances; and through this network of circumstances "Felix Holt made a considerable difference in the life of Harold Transome, though nature and fortune seemed to have done what they could to keep the lots of the two men quite aloof from each other" (p. 52).

The plot in *Felix Holt* operates at two levels, each strangely separate from the other. On the one hand, there is the daily domestic contact between individuals, on the other, the tangle of legal entails bearing on these individuals, first secretly and then directly. The legal status of the characters almost seems like a repressed part of their lives, relegated by time and some strategic planning on the part of a few to a kind of shadow existence. This separation between the foreground and background of the plot emphasizes how remarkably far-reaching are the levels of disconnection in the society of Treby Magna. But the assorted clues to the past are bound by a single secret which, when it comes to light, brings with it a new, reordered social arrangement in which Esther Lyon and Harold Transome play rather different parts than those for which they had prepared themselves. Esther and Harold are not who they think they are, socially or legally, and the discovery of these ambiguities presses directly on their strength of character as individuals. Esther discovers that the man who she thought was her father is really an adoptive father and that the wealthy life she has only dreamed about is actually hers by inheritance. Poor Harold discovers a series of false bottoms in his past that utterly confuse his sense of who he is. He is a sort of fake Transome because his ancestors took over the name of another, degenerate family; worse, he is not even a fake Transome in actual parentage but secretly the son of Matthew Jermyn, the man he most hates.

The central parallel in the novel lies between Esther Lyon, the young woman with a future, and Mrs. Transome, the aging woman with a past. Mrs. Transome is a sort of historical alter ego for Esther, a possible version of herself, an embodiment of one alternative which Esther may choose if she decides to become mistress of Transome Court. As a girl Mrs. Transome trifled away her intelligence in being clever and in trying to "rule"; she loved elegance, gaiety, and, above all, the admiration of men—the very qualities in Esther that Felix rudely challenges. Like Mrs. Transome in her youth, Esther loves French romantic novels, has contempt for Wordsworth, imagines an imperial future in which she will move in a starring role through life, and loves chivalry in men. She likes to "rule" and, despite Felix's ridicule, thinks of power in terms of sexual politics, romantically conceived. For example, Esther "was fond of netting, because it showed to advantage both her hand and her foot; and across this image of Felix Holt's indifference and contempt there passed the vaguer image of a possible somebody who would admire her hands and feet, and delight in looking at their beauty, and long, yet not dare, to kiss them" (p. 177).

Harold Transome actually materializes, like an answer to a careless prayer, to fulfill this daydream. Chivalrous, condescending, polite, kind, he has arrived in England from a life in the Far East, where he had married a slave, and, the suggestion goes, kept her on in that capacity as a wife until her death. He treats his son with good intentions but as part of the baggage. He has not known Esther a week when "he had made up his mind to marry her; and it had never entered into that mind that the decision did not rest entirely with his inclination" (p. 388). Soon after Miss Lyon has occasion to exclaim of this paragon:

> "How chivalrous you are!" said Esther, as Harold, kneeling on one knee, held her silken netting-stirrup for her to put her foot through. She had often fancied pleasant scenes in which such homage was rendered to her, and the homage was not disagreeable now it was really come; but, strangely enough, a little darting sensation at that moment was accompanied by the vivid remembrance of someone who had never paid the least attention to her foot. (p. 390)

Harold elaborates. "A woman ought never to have any trouble. There should always be a man to guard her from it" (p. 391). This kind of protection, carelessly offered on an assumption of superior mastery, resembles the "protection" of the kind extortionists impose upon their victims. The ominousness of his remark is clearest in the context of his behavior to his mother and of her former lover's behavior to her. Mrs. Transome's history is a "parable" of violence, or an "underworld" with "thorn-bushes," and "thick-barked stems" that "have human histories hidden in them; the power of unuttered cries dwells in the passionless-seeming branches, and the red warm blood is darkly feeding the quivering nerves of a sleepless memory that watches through all dreams" (p. 10, Introduction). The contrast between Esther's fantasies and their realization in Mrs. Transome link the two characters and link the fantasy with its terrible consequences.

The politics of homage in domestic life resembles the politics of dominance and submission characteristic of the traditional political system that forms the context for *Felix Holt's* romantic plot. The traditional governance by hierarchies based on inherited rank conflicts with the emerging politics of consensus for which Felix Holt campaigns. This connection between private habits and public systems is one of this novel's most striking accomplishments.

In contrast to Esther's encounter with Harold in the scene just quoted, her conversation with Felix earlier in the novel establishes among other things the difference in tone and quality between the two relationships. I quote at length to catch the poise and mobility of this psychological exchange. Felix, according to his custom with Esther, begins chastizing her for spending time on "trifles," in particular, romantic novels. She responds with irony:

"You are kind enough to say so. But I am not aware that I have ever confided my reasons to you."

"Why, what worth calling a reason could make any mortal hang over this trash?—idiotic immorality dressed up to look fine, with a little bit of doctrine tacked to it, like a hare's foot.... Look here! 'Est-ce ma faute, si je trouve partout les bornes, si ce qui est fini n'a pour moi aucune valeur?' ['Is it my fault, if I find limits everywhere, if what is completed has no value for me?'] Yes, sir, distinctly your fault, because you're an ass. Your dunce who can't do his sums always has a taste for the infinite...."

"Oh, pray, Mr. Holt, don't go on reading with that dreadful accent; it sets one's teeth on edge." Esther, smarting helplessly under the previous lashes, was relieved by this diversion of criticism.

"There it is!" said Felix, throwing the book on the table, and getting up to walk about. "You are only happy when you can spy a tag or a tassel loose to turn the talk, and get rid of any judgment that must carry grave action after it.... I can't bear to see you going the way of the foolish women who spoil men's lives.... I'll never love, if I can help it; and if I love, I'll bear it, and never marry...."

"I ought to be very much obliged to you for giving me your confidence so freely."

"Ah! Now you are offended with me, and disgusted with me. I expected it would be so. A woman doesn't like a man who tells her the truth."

"I think you boast a little too much of your truth-telling, Mr. Holt," said Esther, flashing out at last. "That virtue is apt to be easy to people when they only wound others and not themselves. Telling the truth often means no more than taking a liberty."

"Yes, I suppose I should have been taking a liberty if I had tried to drag you back by the skirt when I saw you running into a pit."

"You should really found a sect. Preaching is your vocation. It is a pity you should ever have an audience of only one."

"I see; I have made a fool of myself. I thought you had a

more generous mind—that you might be kindled to a better ambition. But I've set your vanity aflame—nothing else. I'm going. Good-bye." (pp. 128, 129–30)

This skirmish could not differ more from the genteel flirtation between Esther and Harold. There each retains privately an agenda that conflicts with the other's (each intends to rule). There the opposition is unstated and so remains divisive. But here the differences acknowledged provide a basis for sympathetic understanding: not agreement, not compromise, but clear difference of the sort that escalates irritation into anger, that leads people to overstate what they mean, that eventually ends like Romola's argument with Savonarola, unsatisfactorily for both. Yet it is a difference that forms the basis for a relationship, literally an engagement to be married by the end. Felix is partly right and partly foolish ("I'll never love, if I can help it; and if I love, I'll bear it, and never marry"); Esther is partly foolish in her tastes and partly right in her fury at Felix's impertinence ("You should really found a sect"). Nobody here makes an absolute claim, so nobody forecloses the connection. Here the conflict of valid claims, partly thanks to the relatively trivial stakes, shows its creative possibility. Esther's running battle with Felix differs considerably from the cold oppositions between Mrs. Transome and her men. Opposition makes Mrs. Transome afraid; it stimulates Esther's intelligence and anger.

Beyond these comparisons this conversation also reveals something new, a fuller sense of tension *within* individuals, a sense of the gap between outward gesture and inner consciousness. There is nothing like it in *Adam Bede* or *Silas Marner* and little in *The Mill on the Floss* or *Romola*. In *Adam Bede*, for example, Dinah Morris and Adam experience their conflicts between inclination and duty in less-subtle and less-internal ways. Dinah seems to live comfortably enough without much private life, and then, after meeting Adam, she chooses to get happily married. Though the narrator tells us of her private turmoil, we are not made to feel the struggle. By comparison with Arthur Donnithorne's emotional journey, hers seems very deliberate and clear. Adam undergoes his dark night of the soul with similar deliberateness. Both Dinah and Adam seem to know where they are however problematic their situation may be. Dinah always speaks in the same calm voice, whether she is speaking to Seth, or Hetty, or a congregation, or herself. The sense of distinction between private and public life, the sense of faceted consciousness and inward tension simply do not blur Dinah's clarity. She knows how to choose. This, too, is a human possibility, one that George Eliot associates with a traditional social structure or with Evangelicalism's best influence. But these supports to psychic life are failing even in the first novel, *Adam Bede*, and unavailable in the last, and as they fade the importance of exchange between individuals increases. Clarity of self-definition depends upon contact with others; in Feuerbachian terms, the "I" depends upon exchange with "Thou." In the exchange between Felix and Esther, for example, there is more irony, as well as more self-consciousness, than there was between Dinah and Adam, between Maggie and Stephen.

The mutual influence of dissimilar destinies spreads wide in *Felix Holt*, beyond a group of families or a neighborhood to a national life on the brink of structural change. This historical moment, that of the Reform Bill, appears only in the margins, but acts to extend the sense of connection between widely separated lives. Echoing the activity of the narrator and of the artist, this introduction of a wider social life requires the reader to recognize distinctions and to make connections where the characters often do not. This activity is as central to sympathy as sympathy is to moral life and as both are to aesthetic activity. All three—sympathy, moral life, and aesthetic activity—depend upon that ability to make connections, which follows from the ability to perceive difference or separation.

NOTES

1. "Life and Opinions of Milton," in *Essays of George Eliot*, ed. Thomas Pinney (New York: Columbia Univ. Press, 1963), p. 156.

2. *The George Eliot Letters*, ed. Gordon S. Haight, 9 vols. (New Haven: Yale Univ. Press, 1954–78), VI, 98; hereafter cited as *Letters*.

3. Ludwig Feuerbach, *The Essence of Christianity*, trans. George Eliot, Torchbook ed. (New York: Harper and Row, 1957), pp. 122, 123, 158. Marian Evans' translation appeared in 1854; Feuerbach's work originally appeared in German in 1841.

4. Feuerbach, *The Essence of Christianity*, p. 159.

5. George Eliot quotes more than once this phrase from Comte: "Notre vraie destinée se compose de *resignation* et *d'activité*." See *Letters* II, 127, 134.

6. *Essays of George Eliot*, p. 432.

7. George Eliot to John Blackwood, 30 Jan. 1877, *Letters*, VI, 335–36.

8. *Romola*, ed. Andrew Sanders (Harmondsworth and New York: Penguin Books, 1980), p. 627; subsequent references are to this edition and are included parenthetically in the text.

9. Letters, III, 392 (19 Mar. 1861); and *Letters*, III, 360 (28 Nov. 1860).

10. *Silas Marner: The Weaver of Raveloe*, ed. Q. D. Leavis (Harmondsworth and Baltimore: Penguin Books, 1967), pp. 56, 92, 63; hereafter citations in my text are to this edition.

11. *Middlemarch*, ed. Gordon S. Haight, Riverside ed. (Boston: Houghton, 1956), p. 397.

12. *Daniel Deronda*, ed. Barbara Hardy (Harmondsworth and Baltimore: Penguin Books, 1967), p. 36.

13. *Felix Holt, The Radical*, introd. George Levine, Norton Library ed. (New York: Norton, 1970), p. 23; further citations in my text are to this edition.

HAROLD FISCH

Biblical Realism in Silas Marner

I

If the hero of *Silas Marner*, like the author of the book, has broken with evangelical Christianity, he has not rejected the Bible along with it.[1] For him, as for George Eliot, it remains to be re-interpreted and re-understood. When Dolly Winthrop hears of some of the strange practices of the Lantern Yard conventicle, she wonders whether theirs was the same Bible as the one to be found in the parish church of Raveloe. Silas assures her that it was:

> "And yourn's the same Bible, you're sure o' that Master Marner—the Bible as you brought wi' you from that country—it's the same as what they've got at church, and what Eppie's a-learning to read in?" "Yes," said Silas, "every bit the same." (chapter xvi)

The Bible then connects Silas's earlier faith with his life in the present and future. If Eppie signifies, as the epigraph from Wordsworth indicates, the promise of "forward-looking thoughts," then we are here reminded that she has been "a-learning to read" in the same Bible that Silas had known in his dark Puritan past. But, the Bible is more than a key to the characters and their thoughts; it is a key to the conception of the novel itself as a moral history exhibiting the specific kind of realism and economy which mark the Old Testament narratives.

From *Identity and Ethos: A Festschrift for Sol Liptzin on the Occasion of His 85th Birthday*, edited by Mark H. Gelber. © 1986 by Peter Lang Publishing, Inc.

Like the Genesis-stories or those relating to Samuel, Saul, and David, *Silas Marner* is a story of trial, retribution, and redemption.[2] The characters are morally tested, forced to acknowledge their trespasses. "There's dealings" says Silas, or, as Dolly Winthrop puts it in her more stumbling fashion, there's "Them above." Faults hidden in the past come to light. Silas, who has suffered from malice and injustice, lives to gain a blessing. The characters come to us weighted with their previous history; as Auerbach says of the heroes of the Genesis-narratives, they are "fraught with background."[3] Silas's personality is conditioned by what has happened to him in Lantern Yard and earlier. Similarly, Godfrey Cass's past, which he conceals from his wife, will eventually constrain him and there will be a reckoning. Providence works wonderfully and mysteriously, calling the past to remembrance, turning sin and suffering into a path of salvation.

There is throughout a sense of the momentousness of our moral choices, a momentousness too in the doings of simple people—seemingly trivial doings very often, but loaded with "the intensity of their personal history."[4] This is something that Eliot had learned not only from the Bible but, collaterally, from Wordsworth, whose "Michael" (from which she had drawn her motto) provides examples of the same phenomenon. In that poem, too, a simple act by an unlettered shepherd can take the moral weight of the universe. After Michael's only son Luke leaves him, we are told that the old shepherd returns to the sheepfold they had together begun to build:

> many and many a day he thither went,
> And never lifted up a single stone.

The detail becomes momentous, its power a function of its utter simplicity. But this is not strictly a separate influence: for it is clear that "Michael" too in its "high seriousness" recalls at every turn the Genesis narratives. Michael and his wife, with their only child born in their old age, with their simple loyalties and hopes, recall such patriarchal households as that of Abraham and Sarah. The sheepfold of which father and son lay the cornerstone is to be a covenant—"a covenant/'Twill be between us ..." When they are far from one another, the heap of stones, like that begun by Jacob at Bethel (Genesis, 28:18) in sign of God's promises and his own, or like that raised by Laban and Jacob at Gilead (*ibid.*, 31:51-2), will be a witness to their mutual exchange of vows. When Luke betrays his trust, it becomes the betrayal of a covenant with all the weight of tragic meaning which such a dereliction implies. George Eliot evidently sensed the Biblical element in Wordsworth's poem, and she fortified and enriched it with her own first-hand understanding of the imaginative possibilities of the Biblical mode of narration.

It may be worth pointing out some of the specific Biblical echo-structures in Eliot's novel. They are more numerous than critics have hitherto recognized; indeed, in their accumulated force they would seem to have had a shaping effect on the novel as a whole. The coming of the infant Eppie to Silas on New Year's eve bringing to him her gift of love has been termed a "Christ-event,"[5] and perhaps there is some such Christian typology at work here, but the Biblical episode, which is actually evoked in the text, is the rescue of Lot from the cities of the plain in Genesis 19:

> In old days there were angels who came and took men by the hand and led them away from the city of destruction. We see no white-winged angels now. But yet men are led away from threatening destruction: a hand is put into theirs, which leads them forth gently towards a calm and bright land, so that they look no more backward; and the hand may be a little child's. (chapter xiv)

Like the story of the rescue of Lot, Eliot's tale is one of retribution, redemption, and rescue. The angel has been domesticated into a child, but the sense of the wonder and the miracle remains. There is an echo here too of the beginning of Bunyan's *The Pilgrim's Progress*, where we are told that Christian fled from the City of Destruction and "looked not behind him." Critics have been right in emphasizing the importance of Bunyan's presence in the novel.[6] But here too, as in the example of Wordsworth's poem, we are not speaking strictly of a separate influence, because the same Biblical source stands behind Bunyan's text at this point. In the marginal gloss, Bunyan directs us to the story of Lot's escape in Genesis 19:17 as the Biblical analogy for Christian's flight from the City of Destruction.[7]

The Biblical underpinning can be even more unambiguous than this. In speaking to Dolly Winthrop in chapter xvi, Silas recalls the evil done to him by his friend William Dean in his Lantern Yard days, an iniquity which left him friendless and bitter for fifteen years. There was no longer a God of righteousness in whom he could believe. "That," he said, "was what fell on me like as if it had been red-hot iron." And he continues:

> "... because, you see, there was nobody as cared for me or clave to me above nor below. And him as I'd gone out and in wi' for ten year and more, since when we was lads and went halves—mine own familiar friend in whom I trusted, had lifted up his heel again' me, and worked to ruin me."

The Biblical language and parallelism ("nobody as cared for me or clave to me") give the passage its particular solemnity, but this is not just a matter of general colouring: there is also the literal echoing of Psalm 41 where the relevant verses read:

> All that hate me whisper together against me: against me do they devise my hurt. An evil disease, say they, cleaveth fast unto him: and now that he lieth he shall rise up no more. Yea, mine own familiar friend, in whom I trusted, which did eat of my bread, hath lifted up his heel again against me. (Psalm 41: 7-9)

Silas here formulates his trouble in terms of a Biblical verse. But, there is a paradox here: if his bitterness at the outcome of the casting of lots and the evil which he had met with from the members of the Lantern Yard community had led to the loss of his faith ("there is no just God that governs the earth righteously"), it had manifestly not led him to abandon the Biblical sources of that faith. Indeed, we may see Psalm 41 as a key to the understanding of Silas's crisis and its outcome. The crisis is defined by the three verses quoted above, and the outcome of the drama seems to be structured by the continuation of that same psalm. For after the victim's complaint at the evil done to him by those who had devised his hurt, God mercifully raises him up:

> And as for me, thou upholdest me in mine integrity, and settest me before thy face for ever. (*ibid.*, verse 12)

The force of these words had evidently not been lost on the author. She conceives Silas's existence as a moral pilgrimage in which there is both judgement and reward. Whatever her theoretical position on such questions, when Eliot came to construct her fictional plot, here and elsewhere, these categories remained meaningful. We are thus not speaking of some secularized "Religion of Humanity,"[8] but of a re-constituted Biblical faith, rather like that which Matthew Arnold was teaching in this same period. In keeping with that inspiration, she speaks in her novels not of blind fate, like Hardy, but of redemption and reward and of moral decisions taken with a kind of Biblical solemnity.

Critical from this point of view is the choice of Hephzibah as the name for the foundling who has come to Marner's door. Dolly doubts whether it is really "a christened name," but Silas retorts by saying that "it's a Bible name." Silas thus establishes the character of his new-found source of comfort by reviving the Puritan fashion of naming. The name, as David Carroll has pointed out, takes on special significance when the Biblical source in Isaiah 62 is considered:

> Thou shalt no more be termed Forsaken; neither shall thy land be any more termed Desolate: but thou shalt be called Hephzibah, and thy land Beulah: for the Lord delighteth in thee, and thy land shall be married. (Isaiah 62:4)

Carroll sees in the name Hephzibah and the verse that it recalls "a reassurance to Silas that his instinctive affection for Eppie will not be betrayed."[9] It is perhaps more to the point that she comes to bring to an end the years in which he has been *Desolate* and *Forsaken*. She represents the promise of joy and delight ("My Delight is in Her"). The giving of a new name—always a covenantal act in the Bible (see Genesis 17:5, 16;43:10-11, etc.)—confirms and establishes this promise. When Silas goes to church in the village for the very first time, it is for the christening of Eppie. We are told that he finds the Anglican forms entirely alien—"He was quite unable, by means of anything he heard or saw, to identify the Raveloe religion with his old faith." (chapter xiv) But, the Biblical name he has given the child, we may say, provides the link. Unwittingly, Silas has found a text which will bind his past and future symbolically together. Not only Eppie but the Biblical word, by which she is henceforward denominated, has the saving function of binding his days each to each by natural piety. Eppie will compensate him for past sorrows at the same time as she will afford him the joy of "forward-looking thoughts."

Eppie is indeed the focus of the covenantal pattern of the book; she visibly signifies the redemptive process. The high-point in this respect is chapter xix; there Eppie makes her momentous choice between Silas and Godfrey Cass, giving her loyalty firmly to the adoptive father who has cherished and reared her rather than to her natural father. It has not, to my knowledge, been noted by critics that the high drama of this chapter recalls, and is designed to recall, the story of Ruth and Naomi. In the book of Ruth also, the daughter-in-law chooses her adoptive mother, "cleaving" to her in preference to her natural kin—"Orpah kissed her mother-in-law; but Ruth clave unto her." (Ruth 1:14) Eppie's declaration of attachment to Silas and rejection of Godfrey echo that chapter of Ruth:

> Thank you, ma'am—thank you, sir, for your offers—they're very great, and far above my wish. For I should have no delight i' life any more if I was forced to go away from my father, and knew he was sitting at home, a'thinking of me and feeling lone. We've

been used to be happy together every day, and I can't think o' no happiness without him. And he says he'd nobody i'the world till I was sent to him, and he'd have nothing when I was gone. And he's took care of me and loved me from the first, and I'll cleave to him as long as he lives, and nobody shall ever come between him and me.

The last clause recalls the closing verse of Ruth's declaration to Naomi: "The Lord do so to me, and more also, of ought but death part thee and me." (Ruth 1:17) The effect of this echo is to bring into the novel the memory not merely of the two verses (14, 17) which are literally recalled but the entire context of the story of Ruth and Naomi. Naomi who went out full and has come home empty is the prototype of Silas, robbed of his wealth and bereft of happiness. If Ruth brings a blessing and forward-looking thought to the widowed and childless Naomi (see Ruth 4:15), so Eppie proves to be a blessing for barren Silas, holding to him more firmly than a natural child might have done, being better to him indeed than seven sons.

There are also wider reverberations. Eliot seems to wish to endow Eppie's decision in chapter xix with far-reaching historical significance. In her love and loyalty she represents the antitype to the evangelical pieties and superstitions of Lantern Yard, on the one hand, and to the purely "organic" or earth-bound religion of Raveloe, on the other.[10] No less than Hester Prynne and Pearl in Hawthorne's novel of the same period, her heroine is seen as "the angel and apostle of the coming revelation." Eppie's saving message is addressed to natural man, but it signifies the transcendence of the natural in the interests of a higher bond of loyalty. She also challenges a social structure based on class and inherited privilege in this hinting at a new conception of the relations between men. This, too, would seem to owe something to the story of Ruth who is the ancestress of David and whose story marks the beginning of a salvation history which will transform a nation.

If Eppie reminds us of Ruth, her father Godfrey Cass reminds us of another Biblical character, viz. Judah, the ancestor of Boaz. He, too, had secretly "come in unto" a strange woman by the wayside; she had then born him a child whom he had ultimately acknowledged as his own, but only after he had been brought to admit his fault. The Judah-Tamar story (Genesis 38) and the related narrative of Joseph and his brothers seem to lurk behind the whole history of Godfrey and his brother Dunstan. When Dunstan's body is found together with Silas's lost gold, the skeleton is identified by three items of accoutrement, as Godfrey tells Nancy:

There's his watch and seals, and there's my gold-handled
hunting-whip, with my name on. (chapter xviii)

It is the discovery of Dunstan's guilt, confirmed by these three identifying
pieces of personal property, which prompts Godfrey to confess his own
hidden guilt. The Bible-conscious reader is surely reminded here of Tamar's
producing the three identifying personal effects, which confirm Judah's
paternity in Genesis 38:

By the man, whose these are, am I with child: and she said,
Discern I pray thee, whose are these, the signet, and bracelets and
staff. (38:25)

The acknowledgment of guilt (and in this case the acknowledgment of
fatherhood) is, of course, the theme of the whole cluster of narratives relating
to Joseph and his brothers. Immediately following the Judah and Tamar
episode, we are told how the brothers of Joseph are tested by a series of
strange and bewildering mishaps, among them the seizing of Simeon by the
Egyptian ruler. This triggers a process of repentance, causing them to
remember their crime of many years previously:

And they said one to another, We are verily guilty concerning our
brother, in that we saw the anguish of his soul, when he besought
us, and we would not hear; therefore is this distress come upon
us. (Gen. 42:21)

There is no logical link between the two episodes that the brothers know of,
but chords of memory are struck by the sight of another brother bound and
helpless. Similarly there is no logical reason why the discovery of Dunstan's
body should have led Godfrey to reveal the matter of his fatherhood of
Eppie, but the laying bare of Dunstan's crime triggers off a moral process in
Godfrey and causes him to reveal his own guilty secret stemming from the
same period. His mood is like that of Joseph's brothers in the above-quoted
passage when he says to Nancy:

Everything comes to light, Nancy, sooner or later. When God
Almighty wills it, our secrets are found out. I've lived with a
secret on my mind, but I'll keep it from you no longer.

Lot led by an angel out of the city of destruction; Judah made to confess his paternity; Ruth declaring herself for her adoptive mother against the claims of mere nature—all have something in common. All are stories of redemption.[11] Lot and his daughters are saved for the future; Judah redeems Tamar from her widowed and childless state and a future is assured; finally, in the story of Ruth, redemption becomes the central theme. At the simplest level, a parcel of land belonging to Elimelech, the dead husband of Naomi, has to be redeemed. To Boaz (though not the first in line by kinship) belongs the "right of redemption." In performing his duty he also gains a wife and establishes a line which will culminate in the birth of David, the Messianic king. Naomi too, will be redeemed; her *go'el* is the newborn Obed (4:14), who will compensate her for her long years of exile and loss.

Eliot had, it seems, lost her faith in a personal God whom one could address in the forms established by the Church, but, paradoxically, she had not lost her sense of wonder at the mysterious workings of a providence that brings good out of misery in the long passage of years. It would seem that some such movement was for her both a religious and aesthetic necessity. And, the great moments are when the wonder enters into the consciousness of the characters themselves. In chapter xix Silas achieves his awareness of the wonderful as the stolen money is restored to him in time for it to serve as a dowry for Eppie—"It's wonderful—our life is wonderful." And Godfrey, for whom the past has come back with a sterner admonition, has a sense of the awfulness and mystery of those same "dealings":

> The eyes of the husband and wife met with awe in them, as at a crisis which suspended affection. (chapter xviii)

III

It should be emphasized, however, that the wonder and the awe that the characters feel do not transport them—or us—beyond the visible and material world. Coleridge, speaking of Wordsworth's achievement in the *Lyrical Ballads* remarks that the realism of everyday is enhanced and deepened by "a feeling analogous to the supernatural."[12] This feeling is just as powerful in George Eliot's story, but the realism is even greater, for she has chosen the medium of the novel to give expression to the "unassuming commonplaces" of village life. In the nature of things, the world of the novel is a prose world, one of material things, of small, contingent particulars rather than symbols. The leech-gatherer whose appearance and speech Wordsworth describes in "Resolution and Independence" was, we know, drawn from life,[13] but in the emphatic imagery of the poem he achieves a larger-than-life quality—he becomes a prodigy, a portent, his coming and going equally mysterious:

> As a huge stone is sometimes seen to lie
> Couched on the bald top of an eminence;
> Wonder to all who do the same espy,
> By what means it could thither come, or whence.

Characters in a novel necessarily have a more quotidian character than this; their sublimity, if they have it, is pitched nearer to that of our own lines. Eliot seems to have had a problem here, a problem of finding the exact mode of realism for her tale. She tells her publisher in a letter dated February 24, 1861 of the way the idea of *Silas Marner* came to her:

> It came to me first of all, quite suddenly, as a sort of legendary tale, suggested by my recollection of having once, in early childhood, seen a linen weaver with a bag on his back; but as my mind dwelt on the subject, I became inclined to a more realistic treatment.[14]

A "legendary tale" of Silas would have made him more like the leech-gatherer; indeed, Silas's catalepsy may have been suggested by another passage in that same poem of Wordsworth:

> Motionless as a cloud the old Man stood,
> That heareth not the loud winds when they call;
> And moveth all together, if it move at all—

But, she was anxious to bring Silas out of the legendary Words-worthian state into the orbit of ordinary everyday concerns—those of the villagers who sit and converse in the Rainbow where we are not likely to find Wordsworth's huntsmen and shepherds and certainly not his leech-gatherer.

The felt need to overcome the propensity to the fabulous in the tale as it had originally "come to her" thus becomes a central problem in the strategy of composition; more than that, it becomes in a sense the theme of the novel! We are told in the first chapter how the Raveloe folk had at first found Silas strange and portentous. The word "mysterious" occurs four times in the account of their first impressions of him:

> for the villagers near whom he had come to settle [his appearance] had mysterious peculiarities which corresponded with the exceptional nature of his occupation. (chapter i)

They see him as in league with the Devil, an impression strengthened by Jem Rodney's account of having met him in one of his cataleptic fits. But the effect of the narrative as it proceeds is to demystify Silas as he comes nearer to the people of the village and as they draw closer to him after the robbery. By chapter x, the village-folk, following the lead of Mr. Macey the parish-clerk, have decided that there is nothing portentous about him and that he is nothing more than a "poor mushed creatur." The transition from the legendary to the realistic is here a matter of the attitude of the villagers to Silas; they now begin to see him as one of them.[15] But, in the metapoetics of the narration this process of demystification signifies the determination to adapt and recast the high invention of the ballad of mystery or the "greater romantic lyric" so as to bring it within the confines of everyday reality. This was the task the author set herself and it was a remarkably difficult one.

I would wish to argue that the Biblical narratives—the parables of the New Testament but, more particularly, Ruth and the Genesis narratives—provided her with the key to that balance of the wonderful and the everyday, the fabulous and the realistic, that she was seeking. The story of Ruth has epic overtones; it situates itself at the crossroads of history "in the days when the judges ruled" and in the days before a king reigned in Israel. Mysteriously, the story of the choices made by Ruth and Boaz will mingle with this larger theme. Not merely will a broken line be restored, but a world will be made new. And yet attention focuses itself on the matters of everyday, on the gleaners in the field, on legal forms and modes of greeting in a rural society, on the passage of the seasons from the barley harvest to the wheat harvest. We seem to be in a real world of struggling men and women.

Bible stories also exhibit human weaknesses and confusions. Judah's embarrassment at the loss of his seal, his bracelets, and staff has the force of the actual; his history, like that of a character in a novel by Iris Murdoch, is not smoothed over or harmonized in the manner of a legend. So much, says Auerbach of the Genesis stories, is contradictory, so much is left in darkness.[16] This is precisely the comment of Dolly at the end of George Eliot's novel: "It's the will o' them above as many things should be dark to us." There are many loose ends, as in real life; many things are left unexplained. What became of the people Silas knew in Lantern Yard? Was the secret villainy of William Dean ever discovered? Silas will never know, nor shall we. Only those matters which need to be illuminated are illuminated. And, what is illuminated in the tangle of circumstances which makes up the lives of men and women is the strange twisting path of salvation itself, a path marked out by a very small number of obstinately significant details, such as Silas's catalepsy, or Eppie's golden hair, or Godfrey's hunting-whip. These details are illuminated because on them, strangely, the whole history of trial and suffering and redemption seems to hinge. Here the fabulous and the realistic combine. They are like the ram caught in the thicket in the story of the Binding of Isaac, or the coat which Joseph leaves in the hands of Potiphar's wife, strangely recalling the coat of many colours, which his brothers stripped off him earlier in the story, or like Absalom's long hair. With such few details, trivial and yet portentous, the Old Testament narratives concern themselves. They give these stories their special kind of realism. Eliot has struggled to capture the same kind of realism in the rigorous selection of details which make up her spare narrative and she has succeeded to a marvellous degree. It is what makes this novel not only unique in her writings, but practically unique in English literature. Joan Bennett asserted that it is "the most flawless of George Eliot's works,"[17] and Walter Allen went even further and claimed that "*Silas Marner* is as perfect a work of prose fiction as any in the language, a small miracle."[18]

IV

In the same letter to John Blackwood cited earlier, Eliot speaks not only of the need to arbitrate between a legendary and a realistic treatment, but of the opposing attractions of verse and prose as the medium for her tale:

> I have felt all through as if the story would have lent itself best to metrical rather than prose fiction, especially in all that relates to the psychology of Silas; except that under that treatment, there could not be an equal play of humour.[19]

The reason she gives here for her choice of prose is a bit lame, for the fact is that there is little humour in the treatment of her main characters. Humour is mainly confined to the villagers in the Rainbow tavern. In this, *Silas Marner* is strikingly different from *Brother Jacob*, another moral tale of trial, sin, and retribution from the same period,[20] where the jocular tone is very marked throughout. It would thus seem that her choice of prose in preference to metre in *Silas Marner* was determined by other considerations. What one would want to say is that the attempt to capture the "still small voice" of the narrative portions of the Hebrew Bible dictated an utter simplicity and directness of style and the avoidance of anything suggestive of artificiality. The archness, for instance, of Fielding's "comic epic poem in prose" would have been incompatible with George Eliot's purpose here. At the same time, she needed height, sublimity. She found the answer in the utterly simple prose of the Bible, the *sermo humilis*, which some of the Church Fathers upheld in opposition to the high rhetoric of the Ciceronian tradition. The lowliness of the *sermo humilis* enabled one to invest the trivial things of everyday with a certain sublimity.[21] It was prose reduced to its simplest elements, and yet it could be pregnant and lyrical in the manner of poetry.

While the *sermo humilis* of the Bible had been part of the tradition of the English novel from the time of Bunyan and Defoe, the fact is that it had never been totally assimilated. At some point the literary tradition of the West resists such a radical canon of simplicity. Even Eliot, who uses it as her standard in this novel, does not apply it consistently. Her narrative voice, for instance, is not that of the Biblical narrator. Moreover, if we analyse the different stylistic strands in the prose of the novel, we find that the Biblical combination of loftiness and simplicity is really specific to Eppie and Silas and the scenes in which they appear. It becomes, we may say, not so much a way of telling the story, as a "criticism of life." The style itself is foregrounded and is beheld in contrast to other styles. In the confrontation between Eppie and Silas, on the one hand, and Godfrey and Nancy, on the other, in chapter xix, we become aware that the feelings and expressions of the "upper class" pair are cruder and more vulgar than those of Eppie and Silas. Nancy and Godfrey belong to the class of what Matthew Arnold called the Barbarians—they were, he says, much given to field sports—and their language is to that extent differentiated from that of Eppie and Silas.

Let us see how the stylistic aspect of the confrontation is exhibited in chapter xix. Godfrey is voluble at first on the subject of the robbery and discusses the hardships of the weaver's life which he would like to do something to ease. The something, of course, is his plan to take Eppie from him, though he says nothing of this at first. Marner's responses are brief and awkward:

> Silas, always ill at ease when he was being spoken to by "betters" such as Mr. Cass—tall, powerful, florid men, seen chiefly on horseback—answered with some constraint—"Sir, I've a deal to thank you for a'ready. As for the robbery, I count it no loss to me. And if I did, you couldn't help it: you aren't answerable for it."

Godfrey then reveals the main object of his visit. Saying nothing at this stage about his fatherhood, he proposes simply that, being themselves childless, they take Eppie away to live with them and make a lady of her. Marner would be rewarded for the trouble of bringing her up. He concludes:

> she'd come and see you very often, and we should all be on the look-out to do everything we could towards making you comfortable.

The moral insentivity here is compounded by the easy clichés which Godfrey uses ("be on the look-out," "making you comfortable"). The narrator's comment draws attention to the clichés:

> A plain man like Godfrey Cass, speaking under some embarrassment, necessary blunders on words that are coarser than his intentions, and that are likely to fall gratingly on susceptible feelings.

In a reversal of the traditional division of styles as taught in the ancient schools of rhetoric and as practised in the theatre or in the literature of romance,[22] here the upper-class character is the "plain man" whose expressions are "coarser than his intentions," while Silas, the handweaver, has the "susceptible feelings" and the language that goes with them. The reader is now being prompted at every stage to observe the manner of speaking of the different characters. Eppie's first real speech in this meeting is marked by a Wordsworthian simplicity and a Biblical cadence; above all, it is free of cliché:

> "Thank you, ma'am—thank you, sir. But I can't leave my father, nor own anybody nearer than him. And I don't want to be a lady—thank you all the same ... I couldn't give up the folks I've been used to."

Godfrey, angered by their refusal to accept what he has persuaded himself is a generous offer, now declares the truth about his "natural claim" to Eppie. He is, he says, her real father. The simplicity and truth of Silas and Eppie have now forced Godfrey to reveal his truth, his manifest claim as well as his sin. But, Silas's is still the higher truth, as he angrily opposes to the claims of "nature"—claims long concealed—the power of those august signifiers by which human relations are fundamentally ordered and which are in a sense independent of the natural relations which they signify. In this case, the word "father" has its own peremptory rights of love and authority, drawn as much and perhaps more from the sphere of the sacred as from biology:

> "Your coming now and saying 'I'm her father' doesn't alter the feelings inside us. It's me she's been calling her father ever since she could say the word."

Nature must bow to the language of the heart—is what Silas seems to be saying. And again, the narrator's comment serves to foreground the stylistic aspect of this extraordinary confrontation:

"But I think you might look at the thing more reasonably, Marner," said Godfrey, unexpectedly awed by the weaver's direct truth-speaking.

He ends by denying that Eppie will really be separated from Marner, even though Godfrey will have taken over the word "father" as his natural right.

"She'll be very near you, and come to see you very often. She'll feel just the same towards you."

In the great speech which he now utters, Marner exposes the shallowness of Godfrey's sentiments—his upper-class complacency, as well as the idleness of his rhetoric:

"Just the same?" said Marner, more bitterly than ever. "How'll she feel just the same for me as she does now, when we eat o' the same bit, and drink o' the same cup, and think o' the same things from one day's end to another? Just the same? that's idle talk. You'd cut us i' two."

Again, it is to Silas's simple language with its Biblical cadences that our attention is drawn, a language to which Godfrey is unattuned:

Godfrey, unqualified by experience to discern the *pregnancy* of Marner's *simple* words, felt rather angry again. (emphasis added)

The express link with the Bible and its style is made clearer when we find the author commenting in precisely the same terms on the language of the Bible and the Collects, as she had heard them read one Sunday in the Little Portland Street Chapel. The letter—to Sarah Hennell—was written in July, 1861, just a few weeks after the publication of *Silas Marner*:

What an age of earnest faith, grasping a noble conception of life and determined to bring all things into harmony with it, has recorded itself in the *simple pregnant, rhythmical* English of these Collects and the Bible.[23] (emphasis added).

Eliot's moral and linguistic criticism in this chapter is very much bound up with the sociological aspect of the confrontation. The ultimate point of insensitivity in Godfrey's discourse is reached when he remarks that if Eppie fails to accept his offer, "she may marry some low working-man." It is this fate that the "high society" of Godfrey and Nancy's home, with its balls, its horse-riding, and its drinking, will preserve her from! In short Godfrey and Nancy stand not only for natural bonds, but for natural bonds linked to a system of class gradations which are likewise held to be natural. Opposed to this in the dramatic evolution of the dialogue, is the Biblical, covenantal system of relations which cuts across the rights of class and property. The kind of love and loyalty to which this system has reference is that implied in Ezekiel's parable of the foundling girl whom the passerby finds and adopts and finally takes for his wife (Ezekiel 16:5f)—it is his way of talking about the covenant between God and Israel. And this same higher loyalty finds expression in the story of Ruth and Naomi. It is, of course, the latter text which Eppie's reply immediately calls to mind in the passage already quoted. It merits citation once again:

> "And he says he'd nobody i' the world till I was sent him, and he'd have nothing when I was gone. And he's took care of me and loved me from the first, and I'll cleave to him as long as he lives, and nobody shall ever come between him and me."

While Nancy still attempts to counter this by an appeal to such terms as "nature," "duty," and "law," Godfrey has nothing more to say. He is silent. It is the victory of language and, specifically, the language of those lively oracles, which Silas had salvaged from the ruins of Lantern Yard and brought with him to furnish his onward pilgrimage.

NOTES

1. Cf. Q.D. Leavis, Introduction to George Eliot, *Silas Marner, the Weaver of Raveloe* (Harmondsworth: Penguin Books, 1967), p. 14.
2. Cf. Walter Allen, *The English Novel* (Harmondsworth: Penguin Books, 1958) p. 227.
3. Erich Auerbach, *Mimesis* (Trans., W. Trask), (New York: Doubleday, 1957), p. 10.
4. *Ibid.*, p. 15.
5. J. Wiesenfarth, "Demythologizing *Silas Marner*," ELH, XXXVII (1970), 242. The fact is, however, that the arrival of Eppie occurs not at Christmas, but, somewhat pointedly, a week later, on New Year's Eve (see chapter xii).
6. Cf. Q.D. Leavis, pp. 7, 13.

7. See John Bunyan, *The Pilgrim's Progress* (Ed., E. Venables), (Oxford: The Clarendon Press, 1900), p. 13.

8. Bernard J. Paris in "George Eliot's Religion of Humanity," ELH, XXIX (1962), 418-443, argues for a practical identity between Eliot's views on religion and those of the materialist philosopher Ludwig Feuerbach. There is textual evidence for this in her letters. See letter to Mrs. H.F. Ponsonby, dated December 10, 1874 in *The George Eliot Letters* (Ed., Gordon S. Haight), (New Haven: Yale University Press, 1955), Vol. VI, 98f. It does not seem to me, however, that the matter is nearly as simple as this and in any case, where poets and novelists are concerned, it is unwise to draw conclusions from their theoretical positions and apply them directly to their literary productions. In the case of Eliot, Paris himself recognizes that her being a theoretical determinist does not prevent her, as a novelist, from emphasizing the importance of virtue and free choice (440). He might have extended this insight to include her recognition of the action to divine providence in the lives of her characters.

9. David Carroll, "Reversing the Oracles of Religion," 1967, reprinted in *George Eliot: The Mill on the Floss and Silas Marner: A Casebook* (Ed. R.P. Draper), (London: Macmillan, 1977), p. 212.

10. John Holloway, *The Victorian Sage* (London: Anchor Books, 1962), p. 114: "The little village [of Raveloe], off the beaten track in its wooded hollow, is half submerged in the world of nature.... The passage of time and the rotation of the seasons affect humans and animals and plants all alike."

11. As a matter of fact all three stories, those of Judah and Tamar, Lot and his daughters, and Ruth and Naomi are part of a single family history, for Lot is the primitive ancestor of Ruth the Moabitess, while Judah is the direct ancestor of Boaz, the husband of Ruth. There are important structural parallels between the three stories. (See Harold Fisch, "Ruth and the Structure of Covenant History," *Vetus Testamentum*, 32 [1982], 425-437.) But, it would be fanciful to suggest that these links were present to George Eliot or that they communicate themselves to the reader of the novel. What the various echoes from different parts of Scripture have in common is the general theme of redemption.

12. S.T. Coleridge, *Biographia Literaria* (1817), chapter xiv.

13. See *Journals of Dorothy Wordsworth* (Ed., Mary Moorman), (London: Oxford University Press, 1971), p. 42 (for Friday, 3rd October, 1800).

14. *Letters*, III, 382 (to John Blackwood). For useful discussion, see Lilian Haddakin, "Silas Marner' in *Critical Essays on George Eliot* (Ed., Barbara Hardy), (London: Routledge and Kegan Paul, 1970), pp. 61-62.

15. Cf. Wiesenfarth, pp. 237-240.

16. *Mimesis*, pp. 7-9.

17. Joan Bennett, *George Eliot: Her Mind and Art* (Cambridge: Cambridge University Press, 1962), p. 138.

18. Walter Allen, *George Eliot* (New York: Collier Books, 1967), p. 118.

19. *Letters*, III, 382.

20. Written in 1860, published in the *Cornhill*, July 1864.

21. Cf. Erich Auerbach, *Literary Language and Its Public in Late Antiquity and in the Middle Ages* (Trans., R. Manheim), (New York: Pantheon Books, Bollingen Series, 1965), chapter I, *passim*.

22. *Ibid.*, p. 38.

23. *Letters*, III, 442.

ANGUS EASSON

Statesman, Dwarf and Weaver:
Wordsworth and Nineteenth-Century Narrative

On 24 February 1861, as *Silas Marner* neared completion, George Eliot wrote to John Blackwood, her publisher, about his response to what he had seen so far: 'I don't wonder at your finding my story ... rather sombre: indeed, I should not have believed that any one would have been interested in it but myself (since William Wordsworth is dead) if Mr. Lewes had not been so strongly arrested by it.' No doubt George Eliot had in mind the Wordsworth of *Lyrical Ballads* and of *The Excursion* (whether the story of Margaret or of the Solitary or of the various folk in Grasmere churchyard) and she emphasized the connection by her choice of an epigraph from 'Michael', which not only suggests the central role of the child but also, through Wordsworth's tragic pastoral, ways in which the story might be read. The presence of Wordsworth in nineteenth-century literature is a familiar enough idea, as is the vitality of that presence in the novel. Bayley has noted that it 'is arguable that the novelists rather than the poets of the nineteenth century are the real beneficiaries of the great Romantic endowment',[1] with no real sense that the argument would be contradicted, and George Eliot's *Adam Bede* makes the inheritance ironically explicit when Arthur Donnithorne (though enthusiastically endorsing the romance of 'The Ancient Mariner') dismisses most of *Lyrical Ballads* as 'twaddling stuff': Wordsworth's pathetic account in 'The Thorn' of the abandoned woman and

From *The Nineteenth-Century British Novel*, edited by Jeremy Hawthorn. © 1986 by Edward Arnold (Publishers) Ltd.

dead child proves to be the emblematic concentration of Arthur's seduction of Hetty. *Silas Marner's* epigraph ('A child, more than all other gifts/That earth can offer to declining man,/Brings hope with it, and forward looking thoughts')[2] stresses the Wordsworthian child of power, while the very nature of George Eliot's narrative, in which interior rather than exterior drama is crucial, has percolated from Wordsworth's generic and structural challenges to story-telling, whether in the sympathetic mockery of 'Simon Lee' ('and I'm afraid that you expect/Some tale will be related') and the comic frustrations of the poet/narrator in 'The Idiot Boy' or in the shape and possibility of 'Michael', where the physical objects of the landscape, if interpreted aright, yield up a history:

> a straggling heap of stones!
> And to that place a story appertains
> ...though it be ungarnish'd with events (ll. 17–19)

Wordsworth did not, of course, effect this change in the novel single-handed. Nonetheless, I want to suggest, by a closer examination of two novels, the kinds of shifts that were undoubtedly taking place between the eighteenth- and nineteenth-century traditions and in which Wordsworth played a crucial mediating role. The connection between *Silas Marner: The Weaver of Raveloe* and Wordsworth's 'Michael' (his hero a 'statesman', one of those Lake District men who owned his own small parcel of land by which he maintained his family)[3] was made by George Eliot herself; the connection between *Silas Marner* and Walter Scott's *The Black Dwarf*, apart from an (apparently casual) brevity of form, lies in similarities of character and situation, even while their differences, the more marked for these surface likenesses, serve to illustrate what had happened in the novel between Scott and George Eliot. This is not simply a matter of dates, of course, since Scott, who published *The Black Dwarf* in 1816, had 'Michael' and the other *Lyrical Ballads* available to him. Rather, Scott represents, as is generally agreed, the culmination and the end of an eighteenth-century tradition of fiction (by no means the exclusive tradition), while George Eliot, only beginning her career in fiction in the 1850s, had worked out an aesthetic that took full advantage of the shifts in ideas about fiction in the earlier part of the century, so that from the first she wrote without the hesitations or influences that were the seedbed for her coevals Dickens and Thackeray twenty years before.

The shifts, none of them absolute, which I think it is commonly accepted took place between Victorian fiction and its predecessors, and which I want to exemplify by *Silas Marner* and *The Black Dwarf*, and to try to account for by the practice of a poem like 'Michael', are from the dramatic to the lyric in tone and technique; from the romantic to the realistic in plot and situation; and (more marginally) from the upper and middle classes to the common people for central characters and milieu. With the first, there is progress from a dominant plot structure, strongly influenced by the stage and its particular conventions, as the controlling organization of the work, to a stress upon feeling and the psychology of character, where, in Wordsworth's words, 'the feeling therein developed gives importance to the action and situation and not the action and situation to the feeling' (Preface, *Lyrical Ballads*, p. 248). With the second, what is likely or possible is stressed through 'incidents and situations from common life', even while the writer employs 'a certain colouring of imagination, whereby ordinary things should be presented to the mind in an unusual aspect' (Preface, 1802, *Lyrical Ballads*, p. 244). Clearly, in fictive terms, these three areas are interrelated; equally clearly I should emphasize that I am not denigrating the dramatic or the romantic as imaginative modes: Shakespeare, opera, and Scott himself provide supreme examples of the integration of both. Related to these fictive shifts was a new emphasis upon concerns such as Time and Childhood. While many Victorian narratives are retrospective and to some degree gain their 'colouring of imagination' through a nostalgic sense of the past, the slow passage of time is crucial to the process of interior change in terms both of psychological likelihood and temporal extensiveness: the alternatives in Victorian fiction are the temporal intensity of illness or else supernatural machinery, such as Dickens used respectively in *Martin Chuzzlewit* and *A Christmas Carol*. The handling of time allows for situations and characters that outwardly seem static and undramatic to be tackled. Time is vital in our response to 'Michael' or to *Silas Marner*: Michael's 60 years of pastoral activity, Marner's 15 years of isolation at the loom, are more than mere lapses of days, they are part of the men themselves and establish contexts in a way difficult to believe of the Dwarf, whose few months' sojourn on Mucklestane Moor (from Autumn 1706 to Spring 1707) gives no importance to where or how he lives. By rejecting the stage's tendency to compress time, writers could move from an often illusory freedom of physical action to the freedom of mental, emotional and spiritual action: a man could be totally bound by his class or his occupation, his struggle outwardly 'mere inconsistency and formlessness', yet still, as the Prelude to *Middlemarch* underlines, be revealed as a 'passionate ideal nature'. The Victorian novelists no longer needed to be afraid of reshaping narrative conceptions, even if they did not quite commit themselves to the 'eccentricity' of Wordsworth's narrative structure in 'Simon Lee' or 'Michael'. The way was found by abandoning the symmetry of mere plot and moving towards an 'organic' form through character development.

Credit might be claimed for the Gothic novel in psychological development and a stress on feeling, yet little of importance was done here that Wordsworth or other Romantics were not to do better. Even the Gothic response to scenery, as in Ann Radcliffe, is to landscape as painting, and the conventions of Gothic were familiar to Scott, who mocked their excesses through Dousterswivel in *The Antiquary*, even while prepared in the same novel to utilise their frisson so admirably in the Countess of Glenallan's nocturnal funeral (ch. 25). If Scott shows his 'Gothic' sensibility in the lowering sunset at the opening of ch. 6 or in the fresh morning at the beginning of ch. 7, yet the suggestion that the Dwarf might seem the demon of the coming storm stands as little more than a fancy gesture, the figure in the landscape that would provide the picture's title. Wordsworth enforced a new kind of response to nature: Greenhead Ghyll in 'Michael' provides 'an utter solitude' (1. 13), with 'rocks and stones, and kites' (1. 11), and the heap of stones is only given significance, as the poem goes on to reveal the meaning of the sheepfold, by its informing human history. There is no such meaning, either proposed by characters within the work or implanted by the author himself, in the Dwarf's cottage, remarkable though it is as a building feat, and object of superstition by its mysteriously rapid construction though it may be. Silas Marner at Raveloe is alienated: 'Nothing could be more unlike his native town, set within sight of the wide-spread hillsides, than this low, wooded region, where he felt hidden even from the heavens... There was nothing here, when he rose in the deep morning quiet and looked out on the dewy brambles and rank tufted grass, that seemed to have any relation with that life centring in Lantern Yard' (p. 63). If Silas 'felt', the feeling is scarcely a response to landscape; rather it is a response to an effect which has its origin in himself. The hills near his native town may remind him and us of those to which 'I will lift up mine eyes from whence cometh my strength', even while the bramble, though dewy, and the grass in its rankness, unnoticed by Marner, placed in the account by the author, hint at difficulty and sterility. Though at this moment the landscape enforces Marner's individual sense of loss and desolation, this place is to become a haven, Lantern Yard is to prove a false 'altar-place of high dispensations'. Their metamorphosis, though, is not through Silas's appreciation of landscape, which may demand a certain cultivation, of the kind the Black Dwarf, educated and wealthy, might have, but through the cultivation and response of the reader who has been taught to read such detail by the *Lyrical Ballads*. This move to the lyric and inward was attended with the thought that Wordsworth saw as the essential adjunct of the truism that 'all good poetry is the spontaneous overflow of powerful feelings' (Preface, *Lyrical Ballads*, p. 246), and in his thinking Wordsworth developed the structure and symbol which George Eliot recognized explicitly as an inheritance.

The Black Dwarf, published in 1816, the first within the fictional frame of the *Tales of My Landlord*, is a work of considerable power—despite the various strictures upon it, including those of Scott himself and of the 'friendly critic' of Scott's 1830 Preface which determined Scott to huddle to a conclusion in half the story's projected length: the handling of the humorous but never foolish Hobbie Elliot; the linking of the Jacobite conspiracy to the personal violence of the border robber Westburnflat; Isabella Vere's appeal for aid to the Dwarf, are all finely done. As the title insists, the Dwarf himself is in some way crucial to the whole. In Scott's own Preface (to which I shall return) he is termed, stressing his active importance, an 'agent' in the story, and an 'ideal being' in the sense of a fictional creation based on a 'real' prototype. The Black Dwarf, otherwise Elshender the Recluse or Canny Elshie or the Wise Wight, proves in the event to be the landowner Sir Edmund Mauley, linked by his past to both Vere of Ellieslaw, father of Isabella, and to Earnscliff, Isabella's eventual husband. The Dwarf's initial and apparently central role in the tale is that of misanthrope. He appears, without apparent antecedents, on Mucklestane Moor and sets about building a house from the stones scattered there (being assisted in labour and in materials by Hobbie Elliot, Earnscliff, and others). Believed by the superstitious locals to have more than natural powers, he performs cures, but only, it seems, as a reinforcement of his misanthropy, since he claims these apparent acts of good are productive of greater evil: Westburnflat's restoration means the robber can destroy Hobbie Elliot's house and carry off not only property but also Grace Armstrong, Hobbie's bride-to-be. Yet if the Dwarf seems bent on mischief, his misanthropy is also curiously tempered: having been instrumental in Grace Armstrong's kidnapping, he voluntarily secures her safe release; gives Hobbie Elliot gold in compensation of his material losses; and prevents Isabella Vere from contracting a marriage against her will. Isabella's visit to the Dwarf to beg his help is a scene of great power, melodramatic yet highly effective in context, and part of Scott's typical cumulative dramatic force. There is a real sense of moral crisis here, since we know, though it is knowledge we may have scarcely digested, that Isabella is the daughter of the Dwarf's betrothed who married his supposedly true friend, Ellieslaw. All is explained: the Dwarf's mystery is tied to his betrayal by Ellieslaw and to his sense of guilt for an act of manslaughter (the victim being Earnscliff's father). At the end, by the power of money and the claims of the past, the Dwarf can intervene at the very altar to prevent Isabella's forced marriage before he retires from the world, his part in the action done, his whereabouts known only to the faithful steward Ratcliffe. In the chapel scene the stage sense of catastrophe and revelation, with all the characters gathered, is predominant, and the plot sense, with all ends tied up, however contrived and final, is paramount.

Scott was habituated to the dramatic in narrative: a novel like *Ivanhoe*, diffuse though its elements and temporal span may seem to make it, is essentially a three-act dramatic comedy, of The Tournament, The Siege, and The Rescue of Rebecca. In *The Black Dwarf* this dramatic aspect is superficially underlined by 10 epigraphs (out of 18) being from plays; more significant is the dramatic clue in the epigraph which heads the fourth chapter, in which the Dwarf's appearance, the building of his shelter, and his behaviour are detailed. It comes from Shakespeare's *Timon of Athens:*

I am Misanthropos, and hate mankind;
For thy part, I do wish thou wert a dog,
That I might love thee something. (ch. 4, p. 21)

Timon is the key to Elshie's character and behaviour, his outward deformity (not, of course, shared by Timon) apparently reflecting his inward deformity, though Scott is also at pains to make clear both self-loathing and something unbalanced in the Dwarf, who became, as Ratcliffe suggests, 'the most ingenious self-tormentor' (p. 112), mistaking the scoff and sneer and laughter (though of the rabble and the brutal vulgar and the common people) for the 'true sense which the world entertained of him' (p. 113)—evidence one might be forgiven for feeling had some force in it. Like Timon, he scorns the courtesies of the world. Hobbie suggests that at least thanks might be a return for his labour at building the Dwarf's cottage: '"Thanks!" exclaimed the Dwarf, with a motion expressive of the utmost contempt. "There, take them and fatten upon them! Take them, and may they thrive with you as they have done with me, as they have done with every mortal worm that ever heard the word spoken by his fellow reptile! Hence; either labour or begone!"' (p. 24) His retirement, his expressed contempt for men and the conventionally valued powers of mind and feeling, his concern to do the world good to produce more evil, are all in Timon's vein. Westburnflat is surely worked up from the hint of Shakespeare's three Bandits to whom Timon gives gold providing they punish mankind (unlike them, Westburnflat is not near persuaded, by Elshie's conduct, from his occupation), while Hubert Ratcliffe parallels Timon's faithful Steward, so that it is not only upon character and situation but also upon action that Scott models himself. And as with Timon's retreat, one notices how quickly Elshie's desolate place becomes a place of traffic, though at least Scott has, arguably, reason in the Dwarf's choice of place, since Mauley wishes to see the monument to his betrothed raised at his instigation in Ellieslaw's house, though it then becomes part of the plot's unlikeliness that Ellieslaw, despite

Elshie's notoriety in the neighbourhood, the open presence of Ratcliffe in his household, and the raising of the monument, has, until the chapel scene, assumed Mauley to be dead and indeed has no previous knowledge of the Black Dwarf, who dwelt so close at hand.

Scott's use of Shakespeare's Timon raises questions of identity. Scott might seem not to be accepting the logic of his own creation. Is Elshie the complete misanthropist? Or is he mad, driven insane by his own deformity and the world's mockery, compounded with society's injustice? As a Timon-figure, he should have no grace for anyone, though his soliloquies do suggest, even as they hint at his past and of the motives of his behaviour, that he inwardly struggles to subdue a nature both better and more truly himself. Ratcliffe insists that the Dwarf, though 'disordered', is not mad in his 'common state of mind', which is 'irregular, but not deranged', and claims that Elshie only with great ingenuity can reconcile 'to his abstract principles of misanthropy a conduct which flows from his natural generosity and kindness of feeling' (pp. 114–15). His misanthropy and madness spring, then, from an unnatural suppression of his true nature; his generous acts (the rose and promise given to Isabella that she redeems; the release of Grace Armstrong; the gold given to Hobbie) arise from that same nature's humanity and sanity. Yet if this explains the seeming inconsistencies in this misanthrope (whose misanthropy is better established in the early chapters than his conduct is explained in the late and compressed narrative of Ratcliffe), the issue stands of the Dwarf's role as agent. What need is there for the Dwarf? His centrality is stressed alike by the novel's title and by his prominence in the story. We might of course view the work in terms of Harry E. Shaw's classification of novels like *Quentin Durward* as 'disjunctive',[4] where, though the hero's action 'is the organising principle for the novel, it leads to but does not embody the novel's historical meaning and effect' (p. 155). *The Black Dwarf* shows, typically of Scott, turning-points: Hobbie, longing for adventure though essentially law-abiding, is the figure of the settled Whig future as against the reiver West-burnflat, the last of the Border raiders, and whom, indeed, Scott acknowledges in a note (p. 364) to be an anachronism by 40 or 50 years; while a shift in politics consolidated by the 1707 Act of Union, though minor compared to the out-turn of the Young Pretender's rebellion in *Waverley*, occurs when the very real possibility of a successful Jacobite uprising is let slip. The two elements of community and politics are interconnected, since Hobbie is the more strongly impelled to defeat the political rebellion because of Ellieslaw's involvement in the apparent free-booting attack on Hobbie's house, itself encouraged by Westburnflat's abettors because Hobbie, being a loyal Whig, was not prepared to give up his weapons and so constituted a threat to the Jacobite enterprise. These threads, in which the Dwarf has no concern, for he is neither part of this community nor involved with politics, are yet interwoven with the Dwarf's actions, whether the cure of Westburnfleet; the release of Grace Armstrong; or the defeat of the uprising as part of Isabella's rescue, from a marriage itself designed to secure Sir Frederick Langley's political commitment. Further, Scott's control of these threads and his intermingling of them, so that they become interdependent is masterly. (Does Hobbie help suppress the uprising because of personal grievance or because of attachment to the Dwarf or because of his Whig politics? The answer is, all three.) Yet the question must again be asked: why the Dwarf? He is, as Scott intended, an agent as the story goes, but is it necessary he be a dwarf? Or is he necessary to the story at all? The final crisis of the chapel scene lacking Elshie would not be so effective, with its contrast of the living dwarf and the dead woman's monument (its statue in turn reflected in the living beauty of Isabella), but clearly other catastrophes might have been devised. True, his past history means there is some suspense as to whether Elshie will indeed fulfil his promise of help. Again, the physical sense of the Dwarf emphasizes the stage and clearly only such a creature would feel as he does and would have chosen to dwell in this particular place. Yet to stress the Dwarf's motives raises the question of whether the main actions in his past, the act of manslaughter when defending his friend and the betrayal by his friend and betrothed when suffering the penalty of that defence, require him to be a dwarf. Scott's conception of the Dwarf in stage terms, of the external, the physical, the rhetorical, is enforced by Elshie's exit speech:

> 'I thought,' he said, 'that tears and I had done; but we shed them at our birth and their spring dries not until we are in our graves. But no melting of the heart shall dissolve my resolution. I part here, at once and for ever, with all of which the memory (looking at the tomb) or the presence (he pressed Isabella's hand) is dear to me. Speak not to me! attempt not to thwart my determination! it will avail nothing; you will hear of and see this lump of deformity no more. To you I shall be dead ere I am actually in my grave, and you will think of me as of a friend disencumbered from the toils and crimes of existence.' (p. 128)

Scott's dramatic mode insists that events control character: the Dwarf is agent and is removed, essentially unchanged except for the revelation of his true social status. There is a potential in the prototype, even in Scott's conception of the Dwarf, which is not seized upon, whereas George Eliot can make a not dissimilar character central to her narrative and make him someone whose development and growth is part and parcel of the seriousness of theme and aesthetic conception.

To read *Silas Marner* in close proximity to *The Black Dwarf* emphasizes obvious similarities. Silas is ugly, his physical appearance frightening the boys who peer through his cottage window; he is isolated, living away from the main settlement of Raveloe; and for a time he performs cures. There is like conformation too in the plots, the triangle and betrayed loyalties of Silas, William Dane, and Sarah matching, without the extremity of manslaughter or imprisonment, the love betrayed of the Dwarf, Ellieslaw, and the betrothed. These likenesses, though, are more apparent than real and by superficial comparison help to point up what has happened, over 40 years, to the possibility of the novel. Scott's 1830 Preface, with its account of David Ritchie, the Dwarf's prototype, the 'real' from which the 'ideal being' of Elshie was derived, highlights the differences between the two stories as well as the narrative problems Scott was not able to cope with or else not prepared to challenge.

The Preface tells of Ritchie, the Dwarf's original, the son of a slatequarry labourer, who was trained as a brushmaker. The physical likeness of Ritchie is reproduced in the Dwarf, along with details of character, he being of a 'jealous, misanthropical, and irritable temper' (p. xx), though in the Dwarf these are romanticized by his class and history. Scott also refers to Ritchie's interest in gardening, devotion to the beauties of nature, and his emotional response to the idea of a future state. Knowing what the nineteenth-century novel could do, we might well feel a sense of excitement at the potential of David Ritchie and of disappointment when we realize how Scott has virtually ignored it. There is a problem in handling passive characters and like Timon in the wilderness, Ritchie offers essentially a static figure. Yet narrative lies not just in physical action and George Eliot's depiction of Silas, also in many respects passive, proves how even with passivity there can be crisis, as in the drawing of lots in Lantern Yard, or event, as in the broken water pot. Scott's shift from Ritchie, the brushmaker, to Sir Edward Mauley, the deformed yet rich gentleman, is indicative of his need to transform his materials to a romantic level (in a largely pejorative sense: not here Wordsworth's 'a certain colouring of imagination') and his failure to realize the *donée's* potential. Partly the treatment stems from Scott's idea of what may constitute the central as opposed to a subordinate character, though it stems also from neither having a model of how to set about realizing that potential other than through conventions of the stage and earlier fiction nor the wish to break with those conventions. The brushmaker had not, for Scott, been realized as the central figure of a serious action: for

George Eliot the weaver had, through figures like Wordsworth's statesman Michael. Elshie is given the freedom of action and the power of a gentleman and yet this seems at odds with the vividly established misanthrope of the opening. From plot hints thrown out in Elshie's speeches, it is clear that Scott did not establish the Dwarf and then, having run into an impasse with a static character, tack on the plot. Still, the narrative seems huddled and overweighted by the later revelations, and even if the novel had run its full intended course, it is difficult to believe the effect would have been essentially different. Rather as with *Oliver Twist*, the power of Scott's tale does not lie in the unravelling of plot mysteries. Elshie's character and situation initially impress and their dark suggestiveness seems dissipated by the flummery of Sir Edward Mauley. Even at the plot level, Scott has not fully utilized the example of Shakespeare, as George Eliot may be thought to have done. Eliot early reveals Silas's origins and Godfrey's marriage, so that the reader, like the Shakespearean audience, watches process in the light of knowledge. In Scott everything is tied in, and yet there is no real explanation or exploration of the Dwarf. Although in *Silas Marner* we never learn what happened to William Dane and even Lantern Yard has disappeared,[5] that disappearance is not part of a mystery, however it may puzzle Marner, for by a force given in the narrative and in the commentary, this lost physical place is apprehended as belonging to a life that is no longer significant for Silas: Lantern Yard, while ceasing to be physical reality, yet remains a symbol.

Wordsworth knew that there may be found a 'tale in every thing'; including (indeed, especially) in a David Ritchie; even if the course of that narrative may not necessarily be as we expect it. Simon Lee is a grotesque, with his swollen ankles and little body half awry, but he is to be accepted as the tale itself, not as the prelude to some kind of gratuitous excitement. The anecdote of severing the root is seemingly trivial, yet in the complexity of outcome—the narrator's embarrassed recognition of Simon Lee's impotence, the sense of tears in the nature of things—thought can bring significance. 'Michael', we are assured, is a story 'ungarnish'd with events'. Its narrative structure might seem to turn upon and culminate in the sending of Luke to the city and his failure there. It is an event carefully prepared for: yet how briefly, even summarily, his career in the city is treated, so that we are turned back upon Michael and the meaning of that failure for Michael. In *Silas Marner*, the weaver's 'return to life' depends upon an interrelationship between his whole life and events and feeling. Objects, in a characteristically Wordsworthian way, become informed with human significance, from the nature of their use, as with the familiar example of Silas's earthenware pot (p. 69). When Scott finally admits us into the Dwarf's cottage (ch. 16), what significance do the objects in it have? 'Wooden shelves, which bore a few books, some bundles of dried herbs, and one or two wooden cups and platters, were on one side of the fire; on the other were placed some ordinary tools of field-labour, mingled with those used by mechanics' (p. 117). The details are realistic, but what tale do they tell? What books? What is the life lived here? Compare the significant detail of Michael's life as shepherd and of his household. The sheep, the storms, the household routine are part of a realism, but one which underpins the meaning of being a statesman in the Lakes and of the marginal yet close-knit existence that Michael's commitment to his land preserves and Luke's failure will destroy, a realism moving into symbol that finds its clearest and fully explicit meaning in the sheepfold. The same careful detailing of Silas's life also chronicles a process of change: 'Strangely Marner's face and figure shrank and bent themselves into a constant mechanical relation to the objects of his life, so that he produced the same sort of impression as a handle or a crooked tube, which has no meaning standing apart' (p. 68). Yet Eliot also makes clear, in the broken pot, that there can be a relationship with objects beyond their utility. In *The Black Dwarf*, the rose Elshie gives Isabella is a token, perhaps an allusion also to her beauty (and to her dead mother's), but as it functions in the plot, a button or a ring or a glove or a weed would have served as well. The rose has no significant necessity; even its perishable quality is irrelevant, since the Dwarf will respond to a single petal, however faded. For Michael and for Silas Marner, whether consciously (Michael rather than the narrator talks of covenants at the sheepfold) or unconsciously, things have qualities and are extensions of their personalities. Michael's land provides him with his livelihood, yet he is tied to the property beyond its cash value. He has put himself into it and holds it in trust. And that extension of self, which trust makes unegotistical, is confirmed by time, as with the statesmen Wordsworth describes in *The Guide to the Lakes*, who had 'a consciousness that the land, which they walked over and tilled, had for more than five hundred years been possessed by men of their name and blood' (p. 68). Michael too has that consciousness which is bound up with the poem's crisis and its meaning:

> if these fields of our
> Should pass into a Stranger's hands, I think
> That I could not lie quiet in my grave. (II. 240–2)

The significant narrative use of time can be highlighted by a conjectural calculation, which Wordsworth does not make explicit, of time spans in 'Michael'. Wordsworth as narrator heard the story 'while I was yet a boy' (l. 27); since Michael dies aged 91, his birth can be dated about 1670–80, and his parents would be born about 1630–40, his grandparents in the sixteenth century, each generation holding the land for the next. This span, underlying the poem, gives Michael his place in the natural scheme, like rocks or fields, as Marner is established in his 30 years at Raveloe, with his long withering and gradual return to life, and as the Dwarf in six months, merely the temporal span in which the action is played out, cannot be, whatever Sir Edward Mauley's past associations with the Veres. In narrative, this dedication of Michael and of Marner serves to enforce symbolic values; the sheepfold is a centre of Michael's land, its incompletion a witness of Michael's desolation. Even money, though no equivalent to the land for Michael or to Eppie for Marner, is treated significantly and significantly differently by Scott on the one hand and by Wordsworth and George Eliot on the other. For Scott, money is a plot manipulator, without raising issues of source or value: Grace Armstrong is freed by the Dwarf's gold; Hobbie is recompensed, with no sign of difficulty, by a bag of gold; Vere is defeated by the power of Elshie's gold, and its power is taken for granted. For Michael, the security called in provokes a crisis in which the sum has little importance except as it focuses on the value of land and of child. Either way, the decision is hard, though Michael prefers to risk Luke, since the son may redeem the land: the land, once gone, never could be redeemed. Yet Michael recognizes that his choice may mean, as it does, losing son and land both. With Marner, the money is a symptom of his withered humanity and also marks, very obviously, the transition from his old to new life, both in the community's response to him in his loss and famously when Marner, believing his gold has returned, 'stretched forth his hand; but instead of hard coin with the familiar resisting outline, his fingers encountered soft warm curls' (p. 167). The gold has gone and the child has come.

The child, evoked by the Romantics as a creature of power and transformed by the Victorians into a creature of emotions, was used by both as a test. The child's importance in Romanticism is rightly a commonplace, and George Eliot's epigraph enforces her inheritance. This commonplace may be given new force when we note Scott's unresponsiveness to its possibilities. Wordsworth's Michael is given, in old age, the child that offers new life and continuity; Silas is given Eppie; but Elshie's 'child' is Isabella, a young woman, and her influence on Elshie, though significant for the plot, hardly changes his life. *Silas Marner* has plot in the ordinary sense: Godfrey's marriage and Dunsey's theft; the eventual discovery of the thief and the claim on the child; all skilfully handled. Yet this action, instead of being the dominant interest, feeds into the novel's central emotional and moral courses of Marner's restoration, while the narrative crisis lies in Eppie's decision to stay with her true rather than go to her biological father, a decision that links back into all that Silas is. Eppie refuses to be a lady (p. 230), where Scott, one conjectures, would be inclined to see the recognition as Eppie's 'reward' and her elevation to quality as the correct fictional decision.

The crises in Marner's life, as in Michael's, are clearly marked and are tied in to character, time, property, and a child. What is the moral crisis for Scott? Chiefly, Elshie's decision to aid Isabella. Yet Scott has pre-empted much of the interest by the Dwarf's earlier promise to do so, come what may, while the motives for Elshie to renege on that promise are scarcely digested by the reader, from Ratcliffe's narration, before the interview takes place. Wordsworth's narrative pacing, the elaborated establishment of Michael's way of life, the detailed accounts of Luke's birth and childhood, the lengthy accounts of family and the stress on sheepfolds and covenants, may seem oddly proportioned, yet the crisis, centred not in Luke's loss but in Michael's response, has been prepared for:

> There is a comfort in the strength of love;
> 'Twill make a thing endurable, which else
> Would break the heart:–Old Michael found it so. (II. 457–9)

Scott's failure is partly a matter of narrative distribution, of the points at which information is given, but it is also a failure in analysis and in close detailing of process. Although the Dwarf's veiled references to the past show Scott well aware of the plot's structure from the beginning, Scott, like George Eliot, has chosen a potentially static character, whose isolation seems to preclude the activity of encounter and conflict. Eliot knows of ways to articulate this character, where Scott could only rely upon revelation, artificial connectedness, and extremes of romantic passion. Eliot finds (a common enough observation, but one to re-emphasize here) the inner growth of a humble character, infused with all her conviction of the spiritually organic, which itself feeds from the Romantic poetic of organic form. It is useful to ask why *The Black Dwarf* is so short. Scott says he intended it to be twice the length, its hasty termination being his response to the 'friendly critic' (p. xxiv) who found the idea of the Solitary too revolting and more likely to disgust than to interest the reader, allowing Scott to joke at the end of his Preface, with an abuse of metaphor that still surfaces in critical writings, that he has 'perhaps produced a narrative as much disproportioned and distorted as the Black Dwarf who is its subject' (p. xxiv). That 'friendly critic' and Scott himself responded with the expectations of an older sensibility. By the time the novel appeared, Scott's conventions in narrative, fictional character, and milieu had all been challenged and that challenge was absorbed by the Victorians. The challenge had come not exclusively but crucially in Wordsworth: in 'Simon Lee'; in 'The Idiot Boy'; in 'The Thorn'; and, most clearly for *Silas Marner*, in 'Michael'.

Let me try to pull together Wordsworth's part in the differences I have been tracing. Wordsworth made the ordinary a central and serious subject for fictional narrative. In the Preface to *Lyrical Ballads*, Wordsworth, as well as stressing common life, linked feelings and ideas, so that he might investigate 'the fluxes and refluxes of the mind when agitated by the great and simple affections of our nature' (p. 247). It is not that Scott *can't* handle ordinary people: famously, he can, as in Mucklebackit's response to Jonathan Oldbuck on the day of Steenie's burial (*The Antiquary*, ch. 34). But Wordsworth shifts the ordinary from the periphery, dignifies it without romanticizing, and establishes a new idea of heroism.

And together with this new milieu, Wordsworth shows a new way to conduct narrative. If the events, the outcome, the meaning of 'Michael' depend upon Luke's actions and Luke's fate, then what Luke does is summarily treated indeed. Five and a half lines dispose of the youth from the beginning of his dissipation to its end:

> Meantime Luke began
> To slacken in his duty, and at length
> He in the dissolute city gave himself
> To evil courses: ignominy and shame
> Fell on him, so that he was driven at last
> To seek a hiding-place beyond the seas. (II. 451–6)

Is this (and Luke's disappearance, so far as any direct mention goes) the culmination of 450 lines? Even preparation for Luke's departure has dealt rather with his parents' and above all with his father's feelings for the son and for the land. The tale is not of Luke's adventures, but of love of person and place. Luke is most important not as prodigal or failure, but as a child, the late born and long hoped for, seemingly God-given son (the parallels with Abraham and Isaac are clear). In the lines that George Eliot uses for her epigraph, we are reminded that:

> a child, more than all other gifts
> That earth can offer to declining man
> Brings hope with it, and forward-looking thoughts,

though her omission of the next two lines:

> And stirrings of inquietude, when they
> By tendency of nature needs must fail

serves to underline her transformation as well as her uses of Wordsworth. In Luke's upbringing. Wordsworth depicts a toughness, harshness even, as when the boy is reproved for failing in tasks beyond his powers, whereas George Eliot's account is softer, within the context of comedy. But the shape and proportion of Wordsworth's narrative; the stress upon feeling; the shift to realism in social realization, even while the detail (of the spinning wheels, the lamp, the sheepfold) is so much more than merely realistic, since it serves to establish a world of values covenants, connections in a landscape involved with feeling—these provide, not simply a tale to give cultivated persons the pleasurable sensations that might be derived from 'Rope-dancing, or Frontiniac or Sherry' (Preface, *Lyrical Ballads*, p. 257), but a serious presentation of a man and his passions integrated in place and time. These features help stress, juxtaposed with George Eliot's achievement in *Silas Marner*, the importance of Wordsworth not only in Romantic poetry, but also in nineteenth-century narrative. Without decrying Scott or saying George Eliot could not otherwise have been a great writer, I think it fair to claim that *Silas Marner* could not have been written, certainly not written as it is, without Wordsworth, nor indeed could so much else in Victorian fiction.

NOTES

Editions used and cited in the text by page or line number are:

William Wordsworth and S.T. Coleridge, *Lyrical Ballads*, ed. R.L. Brett and A.R. Jones (London, Methuen, 1963, rvsd 1965). This prints the first texts of the editions of 1798 and 1800, together with Wordsworth's Preface of 1800 and the additions to the Preface of 1802; 'Michael', the final poem in the second volume of the 1800 edition, was subsequently revised and the text known to George Eliot different in detail but not in substance from that of 1800.

William Wordsworth, *Guide to the Lakes*, ed. Ernest de Sélincourt (Oxford and London, Oxford University Press, 1977). A reprint of de Sélincourt's 1906 edition of the Fifth Edition (1835).

Walter Scott, *The Black Dwarf* (London, Adam and Charles Black, 1896), standard ed., vol. V. First published 1816.

George Eliot, *Silas Marner*, ed. Q.D. Leavis, Penguin English Library (Harmondsworth, Middx, Penguin, 1967). First published 1861.

Criticism. The presence of Wordsworth in the nineteenth century has been often discussed though not yet satisfactorily synthesized. A good recent exploration is in Donald D. Stone, *The Romantic Impulse in Victorian Fiction* (Cambridge, Mass., and London, Harvard University Press, 1980); in particular ch. 5, 'Elizabeth Gaskell, Wordsworth, and the Burden of Reality', and ch. 6, 'George Eliot: the Romantic Legacy': Stone's notes to both chapters give useful suggestions for further reading. Jerome Thale, *The Novels of George Eliot* (New York, Columbia University Press, 1959) and U.C. Knoepflmacher, *George Eliot's Early Novels* (Berkeley, University of California Press, 1968) both discuss the relationship between Wordsworth and George Eliot; and the latter also has 'The Post-Romantic Imagination: *Adam Bede*, Wordsworth and Milton', *ELH* 34 (1967), 518–40. Rather general but not unsuggestive is John Speirs in *Poetry towards Novel* (London, Faber & Faber, 1971).

1. John Bayley, *The Romantic Survival: a Study in Poetic Evolution* (London, Chatto and Windus, 1957), 1969 edition, p. 15.
2. 'Michael', *Lyrical Ballads*, p. 231; Eliot quotes Wordsworth's later revision, her second line not appearing in 1800.
3. Wordsworth, *Guide to the Lakes*, pp. 67–8.
4. Harry E. Shaw, *The Forms of Historical Fiction: Sir Walter Scott and His Successors* (Ithaca and London, Cornell University Press, 1983), ch. 4 and in particular pp. 155–9.
5. It is, presumably, only a coincidence, though an intriguing one, that it is from a brushmaker that Marner asks for Lantern Yard (p. 240).

KERRY McSWEENEY

Adam Bede *(1858) and* Silas Marner *(1861)*

What strikes me in *Adam Bede* is the attentive, meticulous, respectful, poetic and sympathetic portrayal of the humblest, most hard-working life ... And also the sense of the gravity of an evil intention, of a failure of the will whose dire repercussions are borne everywhere by the solidarity among human creatures, and the sense of the mysterious grandeur of human life and the life of nature, of the sublime mysteries of which we are part though as little conscious of it as the flower that grows (cf., *Silas Marner*) ... Extremely keen feeling for nature which animates rather than depicts it. Especially in its tranquillity ... Exact, picturesque, witty, eloquent way of making caricatural characters speak without caricature ... Feeling for how things and our hearts change over a lifetime. Return of Silas to [Lantern] Yard, etc. In places, proof of a good knowledge of philosophy.

Marcel Proust

In August 1859 Marian Evans noted that 'at present my mind works with the most freedom and the keenest sense of poetry in my remotest past'. Two examples of this predisposition of her creative mind during her first years as a novelist are the genesis of her first and third novels. The 'germ' of *Adam*

From *George Eliot (Marian Evans): A Literary Life.* © 1991 by Kerry McSweeney.

Bede, begun in October 1857, was an anecdote told her by her Methodist aunt one afternoon at Griff in 1839; while *Silas Marner*, on which work was begun in August 1860, 'unfolded itself from the merest millet-seed of thought': the 'recollection of having once, in early childhood, seen a linen-weaver with a bag on his back' and an 'expression of face' that led her to think 'he was an alien from his fellows' (*L*, iii, 128–9; ii, 502; iii, 371, 382, 427).

But unlike the *Scenes of Clerical Life*, which also sprang from early memories, *Adam Bede* and *Silas Marner* are set further back in time than the remote personal past of Marian Evans. Both offer richly detailed pictures of traditional rural life in the Midlands at the close of the eighteenth century, some two decades before their author was born. *Adam Bede*, 'a country story—full of the breath of cows and the scent of hay', is set in Hayslope, a village in a rich, undulating district of Loamshire; while *Silas Marner*, 'a story of old-fashioned village life' is set in Raveloe, a community nestled in a well-wooded hollow in an equally fertile part of the rich central plain of England (*L*, ii, 387; iii, 371).

One reason for Marian's interest in these pre-nineteenth-century village cultures was her concern, shared with Lewes, Spencer and other mid-century thinkers, with the decline of a sense of community in Victorian Britain. A key distinction in their thinking was that between two different types of social organisation—'community' and 'society'. The former term referred to organic agricultural units with stable hierarchical stratifications of rank that were 'modelled on the family and rooted in the traditional and the sacred'; the latter denoted heterogeneous urban aggregates, divided along shifting class lines and 'shaped by the rational pursuit of self-interest in a capitalistic and secular environment'.[1] Marian's concern with this subject had been stimulated by the *Naturgeschichte* of Wilhelm Heinrich von Riehl, two of whose studies of the German peasantry had been the subject of her long 1856 review essay, 'The Natural History of German Life'. The close connections between this essay and both *Adam Bede* and *Silas Marner* are clear from the following passage, in which Marian remarks that in order for her English readers to appreciate what Riehl is saying about the German peasantry,

> we must remember what tenant-farmers and small proprietors were in England half a century ago, when the master helped to milk his own cows, and the daughters got up at one o'clock in the morning to brew,—when the family dined in the kitchen with the servants, and sat with them round the kitchen fire in the evening. In those days, the quarried parlour was innocent of a carpet, and its only specimens of art were a framed sampler and the best

teaboard; the daughters even of substantial farmers had often no greater accomplishment in writing and spelling than they could procure at a dame-school; and, instead of carrying on sentimental correspondence, they were spinning their future table-linen, and looking after every saving in butter and eggs that might enable them to add to the little stock of plate and china which they were laying in against their marriage.

(Essays, 273)

The daughters in the second half of this passage prefigure Nancy and Priscilla Lammeter, the children of a gentleman farmer in *Silas Marner*; while the first half anticipates the picture in *Adam Bede* of the life of the Poyser family at the Hall Farm, though its farm yard, kitchen garden and dairy are described as well as its kitchen, and farm labourers as well as servants are shown eating with the family—meals that include cold veal, fresh lettuce and stuffed chine on one occasion, a plate of cold broad beans on another, and roast beef and fresh-drawn ale during the harvest supper.

It is just as telling that the defining characteristics of the traditional rural societies described by Riehl—rank, custom, the conservative spirit, and co-operation or community—are all abundantly illustrated in the two novels. Rank was one's inherited position in the organic structure of society, the psychological and historical roots of which went very deep. Squire Cass, for example, the principal personage among the petty gentry of Raveloe, 'had been used to parish homage all his life, used to the presupposition that his family, his tankards, and everything that was his, were the oldest and best; and as he never associated with any gentry higher than himself, his opinion was not disturbed by comparison' (ch. 9). And in *Adam Bede* it is the title character's attitude to rank—his deference to his betters and the 'large fund of reverence in his nature, which inclined him to admit all established claims'—that causes the narrator to remind the reader that Adam 'had the blood of the peasant in his veins, and that since he was in his prime half a century ago, you must expect some of his characteristics to be obsolete' (ch. 16).

For the peasant, custom (tradition and hereditary attachments) was more important than abstractions or individual feelings. In the two novels there are detailed descriptions of a number of customary occasions and activities which foster the sense of community, reaffirm the existing social order and give a sustaining sense of continuity in time. Secular examples in *Adam Bede* include the young squire's coming-of-age feast, to which five chapters are devoted, and the harvest supper described near the end of the novel, which is the climax of the annual cycle of communal agricultural activities that gives a pronounced seasonal rhythm to rural life. And in *Silas*

Marner there is a long and colourful account of the annual new year's dance at Squire Cass's: its climax comes when the dancing begins in the accustomed way: 'That was as it should be—that was what everybody had been used to— and the charter of Raveloe seemed to be renewed by the ceremony' (ch. 11). It is the customary element in religion that makes it such a powerful force in the community and in an individual's life. In *Silas Marner* it is through his appropriation of 'the forms and customs of belief which were the mould of Raveloe life' that the title's character's regeneration becomes complete. Silas is shown to benefit greatly through coming to share in 'the observances held sacred by his neighbours' (chs. 16, 14). And in chapter 18 of *Adam Bede*, participation in the Sunday service is shown to be for Adam, who is mourning his father's death, 'the best channel he could have found for his mingled regret, yearning, and resignation; its interchange of beseeching cries for help, with outbursts of faith and praise—its recurrent responses and the familiar rhythm of its collects, seemed to speak for him as no other form of worship could have done'.

As the above examples suggest, both novels contain predominantly positive representations of traditional rural life in the Midlands. Given that the aesthetic flags under which both novels sail is faithful-representing-of-commonplace-things-realism, and that the narrators of both make strong, if implicit, claims to be serious social historians, it would not be unreasonable to ask how accurate and inclusive the representations are. After all, Marian Evans could have had no first-hand experience of the turn-of-the-century communities she depicts. It has been pointed out that in neither novel is there any indication of 'the vast upheavals in rural life which typify the 1790s'[2]; and while Henry James found that the novels contained 'strong internal evidence of truthfulness', he also thought their 'atmosphere too redolent of peace and abundance', and wondered about the fact that there were no instances 'of gross misery of any kind not directly caused by the folly of the sufferer. There are no pictures of vice or poverty or squalor. There are no rags, no gin, no brutal passions'.[3] Indeed, such features seem deliberately excluded from the worlds of *Silas Marner* and *Adam Bede*. Molly Farren, the alcoholic, opium-addicted wife of Godfrey Cass, who cherishes 'no higher memories than those of a barmaid's paradise of pink ribbons and gentlemen's jokes' (ch. 12), dies in the snow in her dirty rags on the outskirts of Raveloe. And after her crime and disgrace, Hetty Sorrell disappears not only from the pages of *Adam Bede* but also from the thoughts of the characters (except for Adam).

On the other hand, it is worth remembering that when he first visited Warwickshire, Thomas Carlyle was struck by the natural fertility of the land, which seemed, in comparison with the harsh soil of his native Scotland, to have 'a touch of paradise'.[4] One might further note that there are similar contrasts *within* the two novels. North of Raveloe lies a great manufacturing town in a dismal corner of which, near a jail and past bad-smelling alleys and doorways from which sallow, begrimed faces look out, is found the place where the narrow religious sect to which Silas Marner had belonged once assembled. And not far from the lush fields of Loamshire lies Stonyshire, in which is located the grim and unsheltered town of Snowfield, with its cotton mill in which Dinah Morris is employed.

After a point, however, it would be just as tendentious to pursue such a line of argument as it would be to insist on the historical omissions in these two fictional texts. *Adam Bede* and *Silas Marner* are novels, and their socio-historical representations should not be considered apart from their other informing concerns. The epigraphs to both novels do not come from Riehl; they are taken from poems of Wordsworth and their subject is the potentially positive effect on the human sympathies of a fallen woman in one case and a small child in the other. The principal aesthetic concern in both novels is the extension of the reader's sympathies through the faithful representing of ordinary life—the very subject Marian had discussed at the opening of 'The Natural History of German Life'. Later in the essay she had remarked that 'a return to the habits of peasant life [would be] the best remedy for many moral as well as physical diseases induced by perverted civilization' (*Essays*, 280–1). If one could not do this literally (for example, by emigrating to the other side of the ocean), the next best thing would be to be imaginatively transported back to an earlier socio-cultural world by an author intent—as Marian described her purpose in writing *Silas Marner*—on setting 'in a strong light the remedial influences of pure, natural human relations' (*L*, iii, 382).

Like the five other George Eliot novels, *Adam Bede* and *Silas Marner* employ an intrusive omniscient narrator. This presence is the single most important technical feature that the seven novels have in common. It is what more than anything else holds together and modulates the various other elements of which each novel is composed. One of the most noticeable features of this narratorial mode is its intrusive commentary. Sometimes these interruptions are both felicitous and telling; for example, the end of chapter 14 of *Silas Marner*:

> In old days there were angels who came and took men by the hand and led them away from the city of destruction. We see no white-winged angels now. But yet men are led away from threatening destruction: a hand is put into theirs, which leads them forth gently towards a calm and bright land, so that they no more look backward; and the hand may be a little child's.

The tenor of this passage is Feuerbachian: the supersession of a putatively divine causation by human instrumentality. But its largely monosyllabic simplicity also recalls the blank verse of Wordsworth's 'Michael', which supplies the novel's epigraph. And like its simplicity, the proverbial ring of the passage is perfectly adapted to a story with legendary overtones about common people and pure, natural human relations.

At other times, however, intrusive commentary can be distinctly infelicitous. A small-scale example occurs in chapter 29 of *Adam Bede* when the narrator cannot resist an utterly redundant parenthetical sarcasm concerning a character's attempt to placate his conscience: 'Pity that consequences are determined not by excuses but by actions!' A more conspicuous example is the page-long encomium to 'Old Leisure' in chapter 52. This 'wretched piece', as Raymond Williams complained, offers 'a sleepy fantasy of the past' in the personified figure of a contemplative, rather stout old gentleman of excellent digestion, 'a class figure who can afford to saunter' and whose leisure is dependent upon 'the sweat of other men's work'.[5] This whimsical intrusion is not simply gratuitous; it is also undermining of the more realistic presentation of rural life in the body of the novel.

Intrusive narratorial commentary had been found in such distinguished antecedent novelists as Fielding, Scott and Thackeray. But since the time when Jamesian and Flaubertian canons of impersonal narration became influential, these intrusions have had a counterproductive effect on many readers of the George Eliot novels. For James, the principal objection to such interventions was that they destroyed the narrative illusion by reminding readers that what they had before them was a fictitious construct. James, however, did not distinguish between two different kinds of intrusive narrators—distancing narrators and engaging narrators—and as a result was ill-equipped to appreciate how some novelists used the latter in order to add to the sense of reality of their narratives. In *Adam Bede*, for example, intrusive commentary, including direct addresses to the reader, is used to establish a sympathetic bond between the reader and the characters, and to emphasise the similarities between the novel's world and the reader's.

Even the most extended narratorial intrusion in the novel, chapter 17, 'In Which the Story Pauses a Little', can be seen to serve this end. When the narrator mentions that the source of certain information she possesses is Adam Bede, to whom she spoke in his old age, the boundary between the novel's fictional world and the real world of the reader grows appreciably fainter. Implicitly, the reader is being asked to receive the opinions of the narrator in the same way that she has taken in Adam's observations about one of the clerical successors of Mr Irwine. So, too, when the narrator directly addresses the reader, not with a reminder, in the manner of Thackeray or Trollope, that the characters are subject to authorial whim, but to persuade him/her 'to be in perfect charity' towards Mr Irwine, 'far as he may be from satisfying your demands on the clerical character'. And elsewhere in the chapter, the reader is invited, so to speak, to cross the boundary between the two worlds and join forces with the narrator in the necessary human enterprise of tolerating, pitying, and loving one's fellow man.[6]

There is a particular kind of narratorial commentary that is a distinctive feature of the George Eliot novels and an essential constituent of them: the discursive moral and psychological generalisations—the sayings, sententiae, maxims and dicta—that are an essential tool of characterisation, are closely linked to the dramatic and narrative situation, and are another important stimulus (though a more reflective one) to the interaction of text and reader. One cluster of examples are the comments in *Adam Bede* concerning early love. They will be presently examined, but it is better first to consider the moral and psychological dicta in relation to the most crucial single feature in the George Eliot novels of the omniscient narratorial mode: the employment of psychological omniscience. This device allows for the provision of various kinds of inside information: a particular movement of consciousness or moment of choice can be detailed; a summary can be provided of a character's private history; character profiles can be provided, ranging from sketches to detailed portraits; hidden motives can be revealed; and judgements can be rendered. The quality and kind of attention that a character receives from the psychologically omniscient narrator is a crucial aspect of his/her characterisation and of the reader's sense of the character; and there can be important thematic implications as well. This is just as true of the rustic characters in *Adam Bede* and *Silas Marner* as it is of the more complex central characters of the later novels. In fact, the comparative simplicity of the characters and (in some cases) the comparative crudity of their characterisation make it easier to identify and exemplify most of the varieties of psychological omniscience employed by the narrators.

Let us take *Adam Bede* as an example. One of its four principal characters is the well-intentioned but irresolute Arthur Donnithorne. On his first appearance in chapter 5, the reader is given a generic, outside view ('If you want to know more particularly how he looked, call to your remembrance some tawny-whiskered, brown-locked, clear-complexioned young Englishman whom you have met with in a foreign town'). It is not until chapter 12 that the point of view moves inside; but here the narrator is largely content to report what Arthur thinks of himself (for example, 'he had an agreeable confidence that his faults were all of a generous kind') rather than to offer a more penetrating assessment, and to maintain the generic frame of reference. By the end of chapter 16, when Arthur has begun to feel the opposing pulls of right conduct and desire for Hetty, a deeper inside view is offered in which the narrator speculates on Arthur's motivation in a way that the subject himself could not. And in chapter 26, a deeper stratum of the young man's being is momentarily illuminated not through analysis or speculation but through acute psychological notation. During the dancing at his coming-of-age feast Arthur at one point looks at Hetty and is struck by her expression, which makes him realise that she loves him all too well. This recognition oppresses him 'with a dread which yet had something of a terrible unconfessed delight in it ... at that moment he felt he would have given up three years of his youth for the happiness of abandoning himself without remorse to his passion for Hetty'. The narrator attempts to explain this powerful reaction by means of a peculiar generalisation about certain faces that nature charges with a meaning and a pathos that do not belong to the individual but rather smack of the 'joys and sorrows of foregone generations'. But this is surely a mystification; what Arthur is experiencing, as psychological notation makes clear, is the destabilising intensity of raw sexual desire. (This is one of the comparatively few places in the George Eliot canon where the omniscient narrator's *telling* seems out of phase with her *showing*.) Finally, in chapter 29, by which time Arthur can no longer disguise from himself the seriousness of his having trifled with Hetty's affections, narratorial omniscience is employed to give a close and authoritative moral scrutiny; and moral dicta are provided concerning 'the terrible coercion in our deeds'.

Compared with Arthur's, the characterisation of Hetty Sorrell is so heavy-handed that it has long raised questions concerning the narrator's impartiality and even her good faith. The characterisation of the title character of *Adam Bede* differs from that of Arthur and Hetty in that Adam enjoys a privileged position *vis-à-vis* the narrator, who actually talked with him in his old age. He is furthermore a paradigmatic character: a model workman, not an average man, but one of those rare persons reared 'here and there in every generation of our peasant artisans' (ch. 19). Since Adam is also morally impeccable, there is no need for the narrator to supply the analysis and evaluation she does for Arthur; nor need she bring to the surface Adam's beliefs. He articulates them himself, and whenever he does, it is clear that he is a spokesman for the narrator's own views on such key subjects as the terrible consequences of our deeds; the value of religion residing in feeling and practical activity rather than in doctrines; the positive value of suffering and sad experience; and its close connection with the power of loving.

Dinah Morris is also a spokesperson for the last of these concerns. But before considering her character/characterisation, it is well to remind oneself of what is too often overlooked in connection with *Adam Bede:* that the novel is as much a study of first love as it is of the later love that is linked to sorrow. There is a predominantly sober colouring in the novel, but there is early freshness as well. When, near the end, Adam wonders at the strength and sweetness of his new love for Dinah, the narrator is prompted to wonder 'How is it that the poets have said so many fine things about our first love, so few about our later love?' (ch. 51). It is puzzling that the question would even be posed, for the narrator had already implicitly answered it earlier in the novel in three remarkable passages of generalisation.

The first is the most high-pitched and conventional in its tropes, and the one most out of place in the landlocked rural world of *Adam Bede*. In chapter 3 the love of Seth Bede for Dinah is said to be 'hardly distinguishable from religious feeling'. Like 'autumn sunsets, or pillared vistas, or calm majestic statues, or Beethoven symphonies', the emotions of first love bring with them 'the consciousness that they are mere waves and ripples in an unfathomable ocean of love and beauty'. The second passage, in chapter 12, which generalises on Arthur's burgeoning feelings for Hetty, is more down to earth; but it is still rather too conventional in its comparison of the 'wondering rapture' of early love to that of a bud first opening to the morning; too effusive in its image of 'two brooklets that ask for nothing but to entwine themselves and ripple with ever-interlacing curves in the leafiest hiding-places'; and even bizarre in its figure of 'young unfurrowed souls [rolling] to meet each other like two velvet peaches that touch softly and are at rest'.

But the third passage is superlative—the foremost example in *Adam Bede* of how ravishing the *sententiae* of the George Eliot narrator can be, particularly in the early novels. The scene is the garden of the Hall Farm where Adam has gone to meet Hetty and help her gather currants. As he watches her, his heart fills:

> It was to Adam the time that a man can least forget in after-life
> —the time when he believes that the first woman he has ever
> loved betrays by a slight something ... that she is at least
> beginning to love him in return. The sign is so slight ... yet it
> seems to have changed his whole being, to have merged an
> uneasy yearning into a delicious unconsciousness of everything
> but the present moment. So much of our early gladness vanishes
> utterly from our memory: we can never recall the joy with which
> we laid our heads on our mother's bosom or rode on our father's
> back in childhood; doubtless that joy is wrought up into our
> nature, as the sunlight of long-past mornings is wrought up in the

soft mellowness of the apricot; but it is gone for ever from our
imagination, and we can only *believe* in the joy of childhood. But
the first glad moment in our first love is a vision which returns to
us to the last, and brings with it a thrill of feeling intense and
special as the recurrent sensation of a sweet odour breathed in a
far-off hour of happiness.

(ch. 20)

One of the felicities of this passage is that its images are not conventional or
imported, but drawn from the very garden where Adam is standing; the
chosen fruit is not the more literary peach or apple but the unsung apricot;
and images drawn from the more intimate and involving senses of touch and
smell replace visual and auditory images. Another is its richness of
implication. The romantic intensities of childhood are acknowledged but are
said largely to vanish from memory with the result that the rememberable
gladness of first love comes to fill the space of that lost radiance. Yet the
passage does not gainsay, so much as subtly reformulate, the Wordsworthian
view that in later life the soul remembers *how* it felt (but not *what* it felt)
during intense childhood experiences and thus retains what in the second
book of the *Prelude* is called 'an obscure sense / Of possible sublimity' that is
the enabling condition of the later transporting experiences. No wonder,
then, that like Wordsworth himself Marian Evans also found during her early
creative years that her mind worked with 'the keenest sense of poetry' when
it was in touch with the 'remotest past'.

Adam's later love is for Dinah Morris, who is an even more idealised
character than he. In her 1856 review of *Rachel Gray* Marian had observed
that in her experience of piety among the uneducated she had found no
example of religious intensity 'which has no *brogue*'; and she had complained
that the 'essentially beautiful' feelings of the title character exhibited
themselves as abstract virtues and not 'as qualities belonging to an individual
character, of mixed moral nature and uncultured intellect' (*Leader*, 5 January
1856, 19). Exactly the same complaint can be made concerning Dinah. Not
only has she no *brogue*; her 'mellow treble tones' have 'a variety of
modulation like that of a fine instrument touched with the unconscious skill
of musical instinct' (ch. 2). The total absence of self-consciousness in Dinah's
demeanour is another outward and visible sign of the fact that she has no ego.
Dinah is wholly filled with the divine presence and the divine pity. The
implications of this for her characterisation are serious. Since she has no
centre of self there is nothing for the narrator's powers of psychological
omniscience to work on. The only indications in the text that Dinah has the
capacity for a sublunary emotional life are strictly outside ones: the
involuntary blushes that colour her faint cheek whenever she is near Adam.

The blood also rushes to Adam's face when his mother suggests that he ask Dinah to marry him, advice that ultimately leads to 'The Meeting on the Hill' in chapter 54 and the coming together of Adam and Dinah, never more to part. Henry James is not alone in having expressed dissatisfaction with this union. The story should have ended, he urged, 'with Hetty's execution, or even with her reprieve'; Adam should have been left to his grief; and Dinah 'to the enjoyment of that distinguished celibacy for which she was so well suited'. In any event, thought James, their possible future together was 'matter for a new story'.[7] It is difficult to agree with this line of thinking. *Adam Bede* would surely have been incomplete without an exemplification of later love—the love of which sorrow and sad experience are essential constituents—to balance the evocations of first love. Moreover, the exemplification is finely realised. One key to its power and convincingness lies precisely in its eschewal of psychological omniscience. When Adam tells Dinah in chapter 52 that 'I love you with my whole heart and soul. I love you next to God who made me', a strictly outside point of view is used to communicate her reaction: her lips become as pale as her cheeks, her hands cold as death and she trembles violently. Another key is that there are no fine things said about this love by the narrator, no generalisations, no imagery of natural fecundity, pillared vistas, immeasurable ocean or mingling brooklets. There is rather the bare hill outside the 'little grey, desolate looking hamlet' of Sloman's End, a place of 'assured loneliness' where, as the afternoon shadows lengthen and the lights grow softer, Adam chooses to wait for Dinah 'away from all eyes—no house, no cattle, not even a nibbling sheep near—no presence but the still lights and shadows, and the great embracing sky' (ch. 54). And when they are joined in marriage the following month, it is on a rimy morning in late November. There is much more in *Adam Bede* than characterisation and sententiae, and a wider lens is needed to bring into focus the aspect of the novel that is an unqualified success: its depiction of a world. Narratorial gaucheries, unsubtle characterisation and dogmatic insistence count for little next to the fullness and vividness of the picture of a rural community in the Midlands at the turn of the eighteenth century. The representation includes the descriptions of the natural world that Proust admired; such fully detailed pictures as Dinah preaching on the village green, Bartle Massey's night school, and parishioners conversing outside the Hayslope church before and after the Sunday service; and such characters as old Kester Bale, the farm worker whose forte was thatching and who would walk out of his way on a Sunday to admire his own work on the beehive ricks, and of course Mrs Poyser, whom Victorian and later readers have delighted in because of her sharp tongue, but whose utterance is never more memorable than in her comment on her aged father-in-law; 'Ah, I often think it's wi' th' old folks as it is wi' the babbies; they're satisfied wi' looking,

no matter what they're looking at. It's God A'mighty's way o' quietening 'em,
I reckon, afore they go to sleep' (ch. 18).

Silas Marner is a more slender and shapely work than *Adam Bede*, and a more
finely calculated one. The first point made by R.H. Hutton in his review was
that its 'conception is as fine as the execution is marvellous'. And if the more
limited scope did not permit it to approach the tragic power of parts of *Adam
Bede*, the shorter novel was a 'more perfect whole', with a 'more unique and
subtle' plot. Hutton went on to remark on another striking feature of the
work: 'the strong intellectual impress which the author contrives to give to a
story of which the main elements are altogether unintellectual, without the
smallest injury to the verisimilitude of the tale'. He gave as an example the
splendid scene in the Rainbow tavern, during which, as the village butcher,
farrier, tailor and parish clerk, wheelwright, and mole catcher converse in a
seemingly desultory way, 'a faint shadow of the intellectual phases of
"modern thought" ... begins to fall on the discussion' (*CH*, 175–7). And
Hutton could just as well have cited the scene between Silas and Dolly
Winthrop in chapter 16. While the conversation at the Rainbow touches on
epistemological questions concerning the difficulty of distinguishing
subjective and objective, the relation of substance to form and in which of the
two meaning could be said to reside, and the ability of the human mind to
apprehend apparitions, the subject of the conversation in chapter 16
concerns providential belief and the problem of evil. What Dolly tells Silas
in her homely idiom is both entirely in character and at the same time an
epitome of a common Victorian response to the affliction of religious doubt.
All that Dolly 'can be sure on', she says, is her trust in Providence:

> everything else is a big puzzle to me when I think on it. For there
> was the fever come and took off them as were full-growed, and
> left the helpless children; and there's the breaking o' limbs; and
> them as 'ud do right and be sober have to suffer by them as are
> contrairy—eh, there's trouble i' this world, and there's things as
> we can niver make out the rights on. And all as we've got to do is
> to trusten, Master Marner—to do the right thing as fur as we
> know, and to trusten ... I feel it i' my own inside as it must be so.

Hutton did not specify what was 'marvellous' about the execution of
Silas Marner, but he hardly needed to. The most impressive technical feature
of this comparatively brief work is the skill with which two different plots are
alternated, counterpointed and made mutually illuminating: the Silas Marner
plot, the story of how a common weaver, long estranged from his fellow men,

is recalled to life and to community through his love for a little child; and the Godfrey Cass plot, which has no trace of the legendary about it (as does the Marner plot), but rather studies the irresolute character of a member of the gentry who in several particulars resembles Arthur Donnithorne. The two plots are linked through several comparable features: Silas is betrayed by his closest friend and spiritual brother, William Dane, while Godfrey is deceived and manipulated by his brother Dunstan; the former is an epitome of what is narrow and perverted about the religious sect to which the young Silas belonged; while the wholly corrupt Dunstan epitomises what his older brother is in danger of becoming. In his hour of greatest need in Lantern Yard, Silas trusts in his God and looks to the drawing of lots to clear him. In his troubles, Godfrey is equally trusting in his deity, Chance, 'the god of all men who follow their own devices', to save him from unpleasant consequences (ch. 9). Both delusory beliefs are rooted in egotism rather than a wider, other-regarding vision of human life and as such are the obverse of Dolly Winthrop's belief in Providence. Finally, at the climax of the novel, Silas and Godfrey come face to face in the presence of Eppie as two contrasting versions of the 'natural' father.

If there is a serious flaw in the execution of *Silas Marner*, it occurs in chapter 18—the brief perfunctory scene in which Godfrey finally tells his wife Nancy what he has long failed to muster the courage to say: that he is the father of Eppie, the child whom sixteen years before Silas took for his own while he remained silent. Earlier in the novel the twistings of Godfrey's conscience and the pattern of his habitual indecision had been detailed; and the previous chapter had offered an extended inside view of Nancy that summarised her fifteen years of marriage, registered her perception that the lack of children was the one privation to which her husband could not be reconciled, and finely analysed the code of conduct and processes of thought that had led her to the view that adoption of children was against the will of Providence. But in chapter 18 no inside view is offered of either husband or wife. One learns nothing about the psychological circumstances that have led Godfrey to break his long silence, nor about any apprehensions he might have had concerning his wife's reaction. And Nancy's response to the news is registered solely through external notation. There is not a scintilla of information concerning her response to the revelation that her husband had been previously married and had fathered a child.

One suspects that the reason for the perfunctoriness of this chapter is a combination of authorial impatience to get to the climactic confrontation scene between the two fathers and the calculation that a fuller treatment of the Godfrey–Nancy interaction would have led to an imbalance in the plots. Whatever the reasons, chapter 19 is all that it should be and contains, *inter alia*, an acuity of psychological notation concerning Godfrey and Nancy that does much to compensate for its absence in the previous chapter. In this splendid scene Godfrey's nemesis—Eppie's refusal to change her station in life—is shown to be deserved not only because of his past irresolution and dependence on Chance but also because of a certain spot of commonness (to borrow a phrase from *Middlemarch*) linked to his privileged social position. In thinking that he has a right to Eppie, whose presence in his life would make his married happiness complete, Godfrey betrays a degree of unreflecting egotism not untypical of the way it is 'with all men and women who reach middle age without the clear perception that life never *can* be thoroughly joyous: under the vague dulness of the grey hours, dissatisfaction seeks a definite object, and finds it in the privation of an untried good' (ch. 17).

Husband and wife explain that they intend to make a lady of Eppie (it is what Hetty Sorrell hoped that Arthur Donnithorne would do for her). When Eppie replies that she can't leave her father and couldn't give up 'the folks I've been used to', Godfrey feels an irritation made inevitable by his inability 'to enter with lively appreciation into other people's feelings'; and his utterance is not unmixed with anger when he urges his 'natural claim ... that must stand before every other'. Even Nancy shows a similar spot of commonness connected with her 'plenteous circumstances and the privileges of "respectability"'. Despite the 'acute sensibility of her own affections', her sympathies are insufficiently extended to enable her to enter 'into the pleasures which early nurture and habit connect with all the little aims and efforts of the poor who are born poor'.

While the two plots of which *Silas Marner* is composed are roughly equal quantitatively, it is the Marner plot that is qualitatively superior. The key to the distinction of this half of the novel is found in extensive use of psychological omniscience on what would seem to be a most unpromising subject—an unlettered linen weaver of pinched background and narrow notions whose consciousness has been further shrivelled as a result of betrayal and subsequent estrangement from human or natural comforters. The decision to apply the fullness of narratorial omniscience to this subject was the key creative decision taken by Marian Evans. In her February 1861 letter to her publisher explaining her intention (setting 'in a strong light the remedial influences of pure, natural human relations'), she observed that 'since William Wordsworth is dead', she could imagine that few would be interested in such an endeavour. Presumably with Wordsworthian precedents in mind, she had felt that her subject—the linen weaver remembered from childhood that had come to her 'as a sort of legendary tale'—'would have lent itself best to metrical rather than prose fiction'. But as her mind dwelt upon the subject, she became 'inclined to a more realistic treatment' (*L*, iii, 382).

The treatment begins in chapter 1 with the flashback to Silas' youth and continues through the extended inside view in the following chapter, which details the growing desiccation of his consciousness after the move to Raveloe. In *Eugénie Grandet* Balzac's narrator observes that a miser's life is built on the rock of his egotism and manifested in feelings of vanity and self-interest. But Marner's growing obsession with his gold is rather shown to be the outer sign of an inward emptiness and aridity, and is said to be similar to the inner shrinking 'undergone by wiser men, when they have been cut off from faith and love'. By the present time of the narrative, Marner's life has become 'like a rivulet that has sunk far down from the grassy fringe of its old breadth into a little shivering thread, that cuts a groove for itself in the barren sand'.

The water begins to rise again through a seemingly providential dispensation: Silas' gold is stolen and its place taken by the golden-haired Eppie. But in a striking passage of precise notation at the end of chapter 12, the sudden beginnings of inner change in Silas are shown to be psychologically grounded in his past life. Eppie's little round form and shabby clothing remind him of his lost little sister, and under the double pressure of 'inexplicable surprise [finding Eppie on his hearth] and a hurrying influx of memories' Silas begins to experience sympathetic vibrations and intimations of a higher power:

> there was a vision of the old home and the old streets leading to Lantern Yard—and within that vision another, of the thoughts which had been present with him in those far-off scenes. The thoughts were strange to him now, like old friendships impossible to revive; and yet he had a dreamy feeling that this child was somehow a message come to him from that far-off life: it stirred fibres that had never been moved in Raveloe—old quiverings of tenderness—old impressions of awe at the presentiment of some Power presiding over his life; for his imagination had not yet extricated itself from the sense of mystery in the child's sudden presence, and had formed no conjectures of ordinary natural means by which the event could have been brought about.

At this moment Silas seems more than anything else a figure of the 'George Eliot' novelist with his millet seeds of early memories, his dreamy feeling and the sudden access of power. Certainly the trigger of the regeneration of Silas Marner is no more or less miraculous than was the conception of *Silas Marner*. And in both there is a subsequent inclining to more realistic treatment, as Silas' care for Eppie leads him out into the community, creating fresh links between his life and the life of others, sending him back to the natural world to look for the medicinal herbs that his mother had long ago taught him to use, and leading him to endorse the providential vision of Dolly Winthrop: 'There's good i' this world—I've a feeling o' that now; and it makes a man feel as there's a good more nor he can see … there's dealings with us—there's dealings' (ch. 16).

Like *Adam Bede*, *Silas Marner* ends with a wedding—another of those customary rituals that serve to foster the sense of community and of continuity in time. But there is no marriage at the end of *The Mill on the Floss*, the novel that came between these two recreations of past rural life. In her second novel, Marian Evans took as her social–historical subject not late eighteenth-century village life but the society of a nineteenth-century town from which the central character becomes alienated because of the uncontrollable intensities of her divided nature.

NOTES

1. Suzanne Graver, *George Eliot and Community: A Study in Social Theory and Fictional Form* (Berkeley: U of California P, 1984), 14.

2. John Goode, '*Adam bede*', in *Critical Essays on George Eliot*, ed. Barbara Hardy (London: Routledge & Kegan Paul, 1970), 19.

3. *Essay on Literature: American Writers, English Writers*, ed. Leon Edel (New York: Library of America, 1984), 914.

4. Fred Kaplan, *Thomas Carlyle: A Biography* (Ithaca, New Yrok: Cornell UP, 1983), 100.

5. 'The Knowable Community in George Eliot's Novels', *Novel: A Forum on fiction*, 2 (1969), 265–6.

6. I am indebted to Robyn R. Warhol, 'Toward a Theory of the Engaging Narrator: Earnest Interventions in Gaskell, Stowe, and Eliot', *PMLA*, 101 (1986), 811–8. Also see W.H. Harvey's 'The Ominiscient Author Convention', in his *The Art of George Eliot* (London: Chatto & Windus, 1961), 64–89.

7. *Essays on Literature*, 921.

PATRICK SWINDEN

Epilogue: Part 2 of Silas Marner

T he harsh truth about Part 2 of *Silas Marner* is that it is superfluous as far as the history of Eppie and Silas is concerned, but absolutely necessary to complete the history of Godfrey Cass. The end of chapter 14 sounds like the end of the whole novel in so far as it is about Silas: "In old days there were angels who came and took men by the hand and led them away from the city of destruction. We see no white-winged angels now. But yet men are led away from threatening destruction: a hand is put into theirs, which leads them forth gently towards a calm and bright land, so that they look no more backward; and the hand may be a little child's" (190–91). Nothing could sound more final than that. The fable of the hoard of gold that turned into the golden-haired child is over. From Silas's point of view, there is no need for the gold to be discovered, and since our interest in Eppie is wholly dependent on our interest in him, there is no need for Eppie's future history to be recorded either. The things we are told about Silas and Eppie are the things we already knew. "At first," he says to her, "I'd a sort o' feeling came across me now and then ... as if you might be changed into the gold again; for sometimes, turn my head which way I would, I seemed to see the gold; and I thought I should be glad if I could feel it, and find it was come back. But that didn't last long. After a bit, I should have thought it was a curse come again, if it had drove you from me, for I'd got to feel the need o' your

From Silas Marner: *Memory and Salvation*. © 1992 by Twayne Publishers.

looks and your voice and the touch o' your little fingers" (226).

The interview between Silas and Eppie and Godfrey and Nancy simply confirms, from the Marner side of the story, our sense of the reciprocal bond between father and adopted daughter. The condensed account of their life together provided in chapter 14 makes it unthinkable that it should be other than reciprocal. Any other outcome would have had to occupy much more space than the three or four chapters given over to it in the novel.

For Godfrey and Nancy it is different. Here there is much more that we want to know. It is right, then, that the paragraph just quoted from the end of chapter 14 should not be the last chapter of Part 1, but should be followed by a short chapter about Godfrey's engagement to Nancy, his looking forward to having children of his own whom he can acknowledge and care for, and his recognition of the father's duty he must accept with regard to Eppie. With Godfrey as the center of attention, there is a great deal that can happen and that can engage the reader's attention and, possibly, sympathy. The trouble is that it is likely to involve Eppie, and if it involves Eppie it is bound to involve Silas, too. In Part 1, the knitting together of the fortunes of the cottage and the Red House is the main source of the strength of the novel. But that is because it is either invisible or unacknowledged by the characters who live in those places. Now, whatever happens is likely to happen as a result of one or both of two things taking place: the discovery of Dunstan's remains and the disclosure of Eppie's identity. The one need not bring the other in its train, but it is likely to do so, and in the even it does. It does, not because of any logical connection between the two facts, but because the exposure of Dunsey's skeleton, as a result of Godfrey's own actions in arranging for the Stone-pit to be drained, brings so vividly before his mind the idea that "everything comes to light … sooner or later" (223). If this, why not his fathering of Eppie? And remember, his own whip—with his own name engraved on the handle—is the principal means of identification of the corpse. It is a hidden part of himself, the rejected self of 16 years seclusion that was the indirect cause of Dunsey's drowning, that is uncovered along with Dunsey's remains in the pit. The suggestive horror of the event far outweighs in his mind its actually fairly small implications for his future with Nancy. In fact the logical gap, or causal vacuum, between the discovery of the skeleton and the confession to Nancy reveals a great deal about Godfrey's inner life during his 16 years of marriage. These have been 16 years of childlessness that Godfrey has obscurely understood to have been caused by his rejection of that other child whose identity, he feels, must now be brought to light.

Godfrey cast only a single glance at the face of his dead first wife when he went with Dolly and Mr. Kimble to the cottage on the night of the New

Year's dance. But he remembers her last look so well "that at the end of sixteen years every line in the worn face was present to him when he told the full story of this night" (175). We were told this back in chapter 13. That is to say, we were alerted to Godfrey's buried remorse long before it was disinterred along with his brother's corpse. The dramatic event that forces him to tell the full story is therefore of great interest to us. Indeed, it is of such great interest that George Eliot doesn't have to dwell on it. It happens offstage, sandwiched between a casual reference to the draining of the pit and the lengthy confrontation between Godfrey and Nancy that follows. Godfrey's announcement of what has happened has the directness and simplicity of a ballad: "'The Stone-pit has gone dry suddenly—from the draining, I suppose: and there he lies—has lain for sixteen years, wedged between two great stones. There's his watch and seals and there's my gold-handled hunting-whip, with my name on: he took it away, without my knowing, the day he went hunting on Wildfire, the last time he was seen'" (222).

Nothing more needs to be said, apart from the conclusion, equally bluntly spoken by Godfrey, that "Dunstan was the man that robbed Silas Marner" (222). George Eliot reminds us that Nancy had been "bred up to regard even a distant kinship with crime as a dishonour" (223), and we feel the full force of that fact all the more emphatically as a result of the characterization of Nancy that has preceded this scene in chapter 17. There, the impression we received of her at the Red House all those years ago is subtly and painfully reinforced. She betrays the same "mingled pride and ignorance of the world's evil" (219) as she did then, equally moderated by "the spirit of rectitude and the sense of responsibility for the effect of her conduct on others" that was present before her marriage and before the loss of her first child. It is perfectly understandable that Godfrey is shocked by what he has found out about Dunsey and the money, because he knows how difficult it will be for Nancy to come to terms with the taintedness she must feel at being associated with the crime. The existence of Godfrey's child must come as an even greater and less welcome surprise to her. She had attributed her childlessness to an act of Providence. She had accepted that to have children was something that for her "was not meant to be" (217). Ironically it was this way of looking at things, bred in her out of her attachment to principles based on a very unsatisfactory but deeply excavated theological foundation, which persuaded her not to agree to Godfrey's earlier proposal that they should adopt Eppie as their own child. "How could she," then, "have any mercy for faults that must seem so black to her, with her simple, severe notions?" (224). No wonder "Godfrey felt all the bitterness of an error that was not simply futile, but had defeated its own end."

By the time we arrive with Godfrey and Nancy at the cottage we understand very well what a fraught interview will follow. Opportunities for the display of divided loyalties, embarrassed self-regard and self-justification, conflicting moral judgments, and compromised authority are legion. There is a great deal George Eliot can do with Godfrey and Nancy in this scene. But there is next to nothing she can do with Silas and Eppie. Theirs is obviously going to be a united front of loving parent and dutiful child. And this in turn means that the reader's attention is likely to be very unevenly distributed between the two parties, throughout the confrontation.

And so it proves. Silas's and Eppie's behavior is as expected. Everything they do is exemplary of their very simple characters. Silas's complex attitude toward his reputation, his gold, his religion, and his standing in the community has been simplified with the coming of Eppie, and Eppie is the symbol of his salvation. The fairy tale has ended with the exchange of the gold for the child. In naturalistic terms, the return of the gold could only perplex and complicate the relationship between Silas and Eppie and the village. It is not allowed to do so because the ending of the Silas/Eppie story is simply a long drawn-out way of saying that they lived happily ever after. But Godfrey and Nancy are quite another matter. For each of them the coming to light of what happened 16 years ago is a real test of character that is subtly imperfect. Godfrey's sense of shame and guilt is awkwardly compromised by the "exalted consciousness" (235) of doing the right thing with which he sets out for Silas's cottage. He was "possessed with all-important feelings" about what is due to him, as well as what is due from him to those he has sinned against. In this respect Nancy's sense of what is and is not right doesn't help him to follow a proper course of action. Like him, she fails to understand the claims of filial piety that belong to the adoptive father:

> Even Nancy, with all the acute sensibility of her own affections, shared her husband's view, that Marner was not justifiable in his wish to retain Eppie, after her real father had avowed himself. She felt that it was a very hard trial for the poor weaver, but her code allowed no question that a father by blood must have a claim above that of any foster-father. Besides Nancy, used all her life to plenteous circumstances and the privileges of "respectability," could not enter into the pleasures which early nurture and habit connect with all the little aims and efforts of the poor who are born poor: to her mind, Eppie, in being restored to her birthright, was entering on a too long withheld but unquestionable good. (232–33)

It is exactly the same with Godfrey, who "was not prepared to enter with lively appreciation into other people's feelings counteracting his virtuous resolves" (230). In both cases a narrowness of feeling, an inability to press beyond the limitations imposed on their way of looking at the world by their upbringing and their restricted range of experiences, makes it impossible for them to understand the quality of Silas's love for Eppie and therefore to acknowledge the right to her that this love confers upon him. Instead, they interpret Eppie's decision to remain with her foster father and to marry Aaron as a judgment on themselves. Silas has already pointed out, without malice, that "repentance doesn't alter what's been going on for sixteen years" (231), and Godfrey transforms this statement of fact into an accusation against him. When he says that "there's debts we can't pay like money debts, by paying extra for the years that have slipped by" (236), he is merely repeating what Silas has said. But he goes further when he interprets his loss of Eppie as an act of destiny, weighing guilt and punishment in an equal scale: "I wanted to pass for childless once, Nancy—I shall pass for childless now against my wish" (231). To his claim that "it's part of my punishment," Nancy can reply only in accordance with a "spirit of rectitude" that "would not let her try to soften this edge of what she felt to be a just compunction" (237).

Godfrey is severe on himself, and Nancy is severe on Godfrey, but no more so than George Eliot. She, too, felt that there was an almost divine logic in the doctrine of consequences, an "orderly sequence by which the seed brings forth a crop after its kind" (127). She had found deep down in Godfrey's consciousness, "half-smothered by passionate desire and dread," a sense that "he ought to accept the consequences of his deeds" (174), and this was *before* he even saw Molly's dead face on the pillow. This doctrine of consequences is what remained of her own religious experience in her evangelical and Methodist youth. It has something in common with the dour and unpitying doctrine of the Calvinists at Lantern Yard. In the novels the "orderly sequence" is capable of manifesting itself in the remorseless logic of Godfrey's collapse into compromise with his own best principles and the mediocrity of spirit that follows. Or it shows itself in the chapter of accidents that results in Silas Marner's initially "impressible self-doubting nature" (57) being further undermined and then reconstructed on the basis of a more secure understanding of what that nature really is.

In other works George Eliot calls this orderly sequence "Nemesis": "Consequences are unpitying. Our deeds carry their terrible consequences …—consequences that are hardly ever confined to ourselves."[1] So it is for Godfrey. Although he cannot understand why Eppie wishes to remain with

Silas rather than go back to the Red House with him and Nancy, his renunciation of her in the light of Silas's higher claim is very proper and utterly in keeping with George Eliot's stern view of the remedial power of renunciation. According to her, there is a kind of heroism in renunciation that is the secular equivalent of the sufferings of the martyrs. In a review article for the *Westminster* six years earlier, she had written about the beauty and heroism of renunciation. This is the unsentimental moralist in George Eliot speaking, but in the secular-mystical tones of her beloved Goethe, especially in acts 4 and 5 of the second part of *Faust*. She differs from Lantern Yard in her view that although consequences are unpitying, we should not be. Indeed the remorseless juggernaut of cause and consequence forces on us a duty of sympathy with those—all our fellow human beings—who experience its terrible progress over their lives. Let us, she writes in *Adam Bede*, "love that ... beauty ... which lies ... in the secret of deep human sympathy" (*Bede*, 224). Even, presumably, when it is called forth by people like Godfrey and Nancy who are incapable of feeling it themselves, who "had not had ... the power, of entering intimately into all that was exceptional in the weaver's experience" (218).

This is another Wordsworthian idea, akin to the "tranquil sympathies" that "steal upon the meditative mind, / And grow with thought" in the first book of *The Excursion*.[2] Godfrey is right to consider himself justly punished. Nancy's spirit of rectitude rightly makes it impossible for her to pretend things are otherwise than they are. Nevertheless, her power of sympathy, at this crisis in their relationship, is as relevant to the circumstances as is her sense of justice. She, too, advises resignation in the face of adversity, and she includes herself in this advice, since she will not take advantage of her knowledge of Godfrey's past misdeeds to reject him now that the truth has come to light.

There is a connection between this perception of the remorselessness of consequences and the attendant duty of human sympathy, and the kind of writing George Eliot recommends in her essays and produces in her own novels. What we have discovered in *Silas Marner* is the alternation of fable or romance (which she does not recommend), and documentary realism or novel (which she does). In *Silas Marner* neither supplants the other. In some places the element of fable or fairy tale is more pronounced, in other places the element of prosaic verisimilitude. But the strategy is dictated by George Eliot's intentions, which are basically of the second, prosaic kind. She uses the fairy-tale material not so much to suggest the irreducible and therefore inexpressible mysteries of the human condition, as to sketch out a preliminary scenario that is later to be rendered both morally and psychologically plausible through a process of realistic blurring, softening, and substitution.

There are two kinds of fairy-tale writing here. One is the dramatic, even melodramatic, handling of fantasy material (the theft of the gold by Dunstan, the appearance of the child on the hearth of Silas's cottage). The other is the almost imperceptible and continuous hum and murmur of a subterranean fabular theme (the allusions to the story of King Midas or of *The Winter's Tale*) beneath the surface outlines of a mainly realistic story. The fact is, though, that these outlines are not merely superficial. They help us to penetrate to the core of the novel's thematic content—the dense network of psychological conditions and moral judgments and invitation to sympathetic understanding that constitute the bulk of all George Eliot's writing. True, the detail of that network is more evident in the Godfrey/Nancy part of the story and rather less so in the Silas Marner part. This is unusual for George Eliot. Normally all of her principal characters are explained as thoroughly as Godfrey and Nancy. But we have seen that within the fairy-tale ambience of the Silas Marner story there is a good deal of local psychological drama. There is also some naturalistic description (after Silas's entry at the Rainbow) and character analysis (in the comparison between Silas and William Dane in chapter 1). This does a great deal to make Silas's character and predicament credible, even if it lacks something of the incomprehensible mystery that adds a surprising depth to some of the characters of, say, American romance.

George Eliot is most explicit about her intentions in an early chapter (chapter 3) of *The Mill on the Floss*. Here Mr. Tulliver has asked his friend Mr. Riley, the auctioneer, to give him an opinion about a teacher for his son Tom. Mr. Riley suggests that Mr. Stelling is the man, but Tulliver is unsure about Riley's motives. Without good reason, though. George Eliot explains:

> And he had really given himself the trouble of recommending Mr. Stelling to his friend Tulliver without any positive expectation of a solid, definite advantage resulting to himself, notwithstanding the subtle indications to the contrary which might have misled a too sagacious observer. For there is nothing more widely misleading than sagacity if it happens to get on a wrong scent; and sagacity persuaded that men usually act and speak from distinct motives, with a consciously proposed end in view, is certain to waste its energies on imaginary game. Plotting covetousness and deliberate contrivance, in order to compass a selfish end, are nowhere abundant but in the world of the dramatist. They demand too intense a mental action for many of our fellow-parishioners to be guilty of them. It is easy enough to spoil the lives of our neighbours without taking so much trouble: we can do it by lazy acquiescence and lazy omission, by trivial

falsities for which we hardly know a reason, by small frauds
neutralized by small extravagancies, by maladroit flatteries, and
clumsily improvised insinuation. We live from hand to mouth,
most of us, with a small family of immediate desires; we do little
else than snatch a morsel to satisfy the hungry brood, rarely
thinking of seed-corn or the next year's crop.[3]

In *Silas Marner*, as in *The Mill in the Floss*, George Eliot is enough of a
Victorian novelist to be unable to construct her story without a great deal
more melodramatic contrivance than she suggests is necessary here. But she
is more honest in her use of it. The fabular elements do not pretend to be
anything else, on the whole, and therefore convince on their own terms more
than the fabular elements in her more soberly realistic narratives do. Even so,
much that is best in *Silas Marner* has more to do with lazy omissions and
trivial falsities than with plotting covetousness and deliberate contrivance.
Even Dunstan's theft of the gold has more in it of self-deception and wishful
thinking than it has of deeply meditated intrigue or conspiracy. And
Godfrey's misfortunes arise entirely out of "small frauds neutralised [or not]
by small extravagancies." Probably the most melodramatic character in the
novel is William Dane. He disappears after the first chapter, and even there
his lies about Silas are explained by the corruption of his Calvinist faith and
his envy of Silas's engagement to Sarah.

The fairy-tale outlines of the melodramatic plot have to be softened
and obscured so as to bring into focus the basically explicable motives and
attitudes of the characters. In *Middlemarch*, Dorothea's perception of the
passionate egotism of her husband, Casaubon, becomes so sharp as to banish
all thoughts not only of melodrama but of tragedy. Everything about him
except his egotism was "below the level of tragedy" (*Middlemarch*, 460).
Awareness of tragedy involves not just pity, but, Aristotle wrote, terror also.
We need to be as much aware of the general condition, in which we ourselves
are included, as of the particular instance, which stands free of any merely
selfish regard. George Eliot's is an art of the particular instance: of Silas,
Godfrey, and Nancy, rather than the miser, the rake, and the saintly young
girl. Therefore her art is depressed "below the level of tragedy" in the higher
interest of pure compassion. Compassion transcends justice—which must
also be done, and, where possible, be seen to be done. Compassion is more
inward, more secretive, felt even when it is not seen. In her compassion for
Casaubon, Dorothea "was travelling into the remoteness of pure pity"
(*Middlemarch*, 402). It is what George Eliot want us to feel for Silas, and later
for Godfrey. It is what Nancy can almost bring herself to feel for Godfrey. In
the end it is what Godfrey is brought to feel for himself, along with at least

a residue of the justice Nancy and his own conscience have persuaded him is not to be ignored: "Well, perhaps it isn't too late to mend a bit there. Though it *is* too late to mend some things, say what they will" (237).

NOTES

1. *Adam Bede* (Harmondsworth: Penguin, 1980), 217; hereafter cited as *Bede*.
2. William Wordsworth, *The Excursion*, in Merchant, 663–94.
3. *The Mill on the Floss* (Harmondsworth: Penguin, 1979), 74–75.

TERENCE DAWSON

'Light Enough to Trusten By': Structure and Experience in Silas Marner

S*ilas Marner* (1861), always a favourite with readers, was until recently considered too obvious and too lightweight to merit serious critical discussion. In 1949, F. R. Leavis echoed the views of many when he described it as 'that charming minor masterpiece', an evident 'moral fable'.[1] In only one respect was the work seen as unusual: it appeared to have no direct bearing on its author's life.[2] Ever since the mid-1950s, however, it has gradually gathered advocates who have shown that it is not only as rich in ideas but also as firmly rooted in George Eliot's personal concerns as any of her other works and, somewhat surprisingly, these two issues have been increasingly seen as one.[3] In 1975, Ruby Redinger explored the theme of hoarding and concluded that 'the transformation of gold into Eppie justified George Eliot seeking and accepting money for her writing'.[4] Lawrence Jay Dessner looked at a wide range of parallels between the events of the novel and the author's circumstances at the time of writing, and noted that 'fear of being abandoned, fear of having one's secret revealed, antagonism towards a brother, love for a lost sister, concern for moral reputation [are all] common to the fact and the fiction'.[5] It was not until 1985, however, when Sandra Gilbert argued that Eppie is the central character and that the novel's principal theme is the riddle of daughterhood, that anyone specifically explored the implications for a woman of the relationship between Eppie and

From *The Modern Language Review* 88, part 1 (January 1993). © 1993 by The Modern Humanities Research Association.

Silas. Through Silas, she affirms, George Eliot was able to examine 'the dispossession that she herself had experienced as part of the empty pack of daughterhood'.[6] The common element in these otherwise different readings is that they are all, and almost exclusively, concerned with themes. They have established that many of the motifs at the heart of the text are pertinent to the situation in which Eliot found herself in 1860, but they have not explained the novel's structure as a whole. In the following pages, I re-examine the narrative structures in order to illustrate that this novel occupies a much more significant place in its author's literary development than has been recognized.

On the surface, the main plot would seem to be about the regeneration of a middle-aged weaver through love and his reintegration into the community in which he lives. Interlinked with this 'story' is another, generally described as the story of Godfrey Cass, the local squire's eldest son, who turns over something of a new leaf in the course of the events described. Faced by a novel in which there are two distinct plots, the critic's first task is to discover the connexion between them. The most frequent definition of the relation between the two stories in *Silas Marner* is that they are parallel, but move in opposite directions.[7] Not only is this view too vague to be helpful, it is also misleading, for there is no similarity whatsoever between Silas's situation at the beginning and Godfrey's at the end, or vice versa. Nevertheless, the two plots are unquestionably related: indeed, I shall argue that they show many more similarities than have been identified to date.

In purely narrative terms, the main events of the novel would seem to trace the parallel stories of the weaver and Godfrey Cass: I do not wish to argue otherwise. But in psychological terms, because the novel was written by a woman, one would expect it to reflect and describe a woman's experience. Such a view assumes that the events of a novel are shaped by the nature of a dilemma uppermost in its author's mind at the time of writing. In 1860 Eliot, having completed her preliminary studies for *Romola*, a novel about the Florence of Savonarola, had fallen into one of her periodic fits of depression. Just how much of this novel's action she had sketched when the idea for *Silas Marner* 'thrust' itself upon her so insistently that she shelved her historical novel in order to write her tale about the weaver of Raveloe we shall never know.[8] All that is certain is that Savonarola occupied a major place in her thoughts immediately prior to the vision (the word is not too strong) of 'a linen weaver with a bag on his back' (p. 382) which provided the initial seed from which *Silas Marner* quickly grew. If we can assume that a connexion exists between George Eliot's preoccupation with Savonarola, who may be described as a 'dark' father-figure who influences Romola for as long as she is attracted to the worthless Tito, and her own depression, then one can read this vision of a benevolent father-figure as a 'compensatory' urge which emerged, spontaneously, from her unconscious in order to shake her out of her increasingly gloomy thoughts. A primary aim of these pages is to argue that embedded in the surface narrative of *Silas Marner* are numerous thematic concerns which suggest that the events it describes are shaped by a psychological dilemma pertinent to Eliot at the time of writing. My intention is to show that the very structures of the text invite the reader to read this novel as an expression of a woman's psychological concerns.

My first objective is to demonstrate that the events of *Silas Marner*, not only those of the main plot but all the major events, including such scenes as the wonderfully comic conversation in the Rainbow Inn, can be shown to be directly related to a female character who functions as the 'carrier' of the author's unconscious personality. This character, I shall show, is Nancy Lammeter, an apparently minor figure hitherto almost completely ignored by critics.[9]

Surely one of the most striking features of this novel is the way in which it shifts from an almost exclusive emphasis on male characters, especially in the first nine chapters, to an emphasis on female characters, especially in the much shorter Part 2. It is worth comparing what each of the main characters achieves between the outset of the events and their conclusion. The theme of a novel can often be discovered by comparing the situations with which it opens and closes. *Silas Marner* begins in late November or early December of about 1803, with a description of Silas as a recluse and a miser, and it ends in May or early June of about 1819, with an account of Eppie's marriage to Aaron.[10] The most obvious transformation effected is Silas's integration into the community, but he is not, as Joseph Wiesenfarth maintains, the only character to change significantly in the course of the novel.[11] There are three other principal characters, Eppie, Godfrey, and Nancy, whose situations are also radically altered between these dates. At the outset, Eppie is an infant whose mother, Molly Cass (née Farren) is not in a condition to take proper care of her, and the novel ends with an account of Eppie's marriage. But she is an infant during the major scenes, and even in Part 2 she is never truly individuated, and for these reasons it would be difficult to relate the other events (such as the Lantern Yard episode or the scene in the Rainbow) directly to her change of circumstances. Godfrey and Nancy both undergo a significant change. At the outset, the engagement which they both had hoped for has all but fallen through; at the end, they reaffirm their love for one another. Because there is more emphasis on Godfrey in the early chapters, critics have been tempted to ask how the weaver's story relates to his. Nancy, however, plays a much more emphatic role in Part 2 than does her husband. Although she is no less directly transformed by the events than Silas, Eppie, and Godfrey, her function in the novel has never been adequately explained.

Nancy's role in Part I is not immediately evident. She is first mentioned in Chapter 3, where the narrator describes the villagers' collective supposition that 'if Mr Godfrey didn't turn over a new leaf, he might say "Good-bye" to Miss Nancy Lammeter'.[12] A few moments later it is revealed that Godfrey is already married. In other words, Nancy has not only been jilted, she is being cheated. It is not, however, until Chapter II, almost halfway through the text, that she makes her first appearance at Squire Cass's New Year party, but from this moment her importance increases. Part I closes with a reference to her marriage with Godfrey, and at the beginning of Part 2, the narrator all but tells the reader to pay special attention to her. This is how she is reintroduced:

> Perhaps the pretty woman, not much younger than [Godfrey], who is leaning on his arm, is more changed than her husband [...] to all those who love human faces best for what they tell of human experience, Nancy's beauty has a heightened interest [...]. The firm yet placid mouth, the clear veracious glance of the brown eyes, speak now of a nature that has been tested and has kept its highest qualities. (p. 195)

Given this signalling, it is astonishing how few critics have found anything substantial to say about her. She is central to every chapter in Part 2. Even Eppie's wedding, with which the novel ends, coincides with Nancy and Godfrey consolidating their own marriage. In the following pages I shall argue that the events in which Godfrey is involved should be read not as his, but as *Nancy's* 'story',[13] by which I mean that, in spite of her being a less prominent character, the events that make up this part of the novel can all be shown to be directly related to *her* concerns.[14]

The basis for this claim is derived from the analysis of the major episodes of the novel, all of which reveal thematic parallels with the dilemma of confronting Nancy. Even when she does not actually feature in the episodes in question, or plays only a minor role in them, the insistence with which their theme is related to her amounts to evidence that the entire narrative constitutes a symbolic representation of the dilemma facing her. My aim, then, is to demonstrate that not only is the so-called sub-plot principally about a process affecting Nancy, but so too is the entire novel: in other words, to reveal that the interconnected plots of the novel tell *one* story on two distinct 'levels' of fictional representation and to argue that, in psychological terms, both pertain to Nancy. In the first section, I look at the parallels between the two 'plots' to show that the events in which Godfrey features can indeed be said to be told from Nancy's perspective. In the next, I identify the nature of the dilemma confronting her by reference to some of Jung's key concepts.[15] I then examine the relation between the Silas plot and the way in which Nancy achieves a tentative resolution to this problem and, lastly, as my reading tacitly implies that the experience at issue was highly relevant to the author, I briefly relate the conclusions to George Eliot's situation in 1860–61.

First, let us remind ourselves of the main stages of Silas's story. At the outset of the novel, he is living in complete isolation, nursing the hurt of a wrong done to him some fifteen years previously by William Dane and the arbitrary result of the drawing of lots by the Lantern Yard brethren. On the day of Mrs Osgood's birthday party, his gold is stolen. A month later, he sees lying on his hearth a baby girl, the sight of which awakens 'old quiverings of tenderness' in him (p. 168). Sixteen years later, contrary to his fear that she might abandon him, Eppie chooses to stay with him, and the novel ends with her marrying Aaron. This pattern is remarkably similar to that of Nancy's story. At the time the novel opens, Nancy is privately nursing the hurt of a wrong done her by Godfrey. On the night of Mrs Osgood's birthday party, Dunstan falls to his death in the stone-pits, and some four weeks later, Molly dies while on her way to claim recognition, thus making it possible for Nancy to marry the man whom she loves. Fifteen years later, Godfrey, afraid that she might want to leave him, reveals his past to her. To his surprise, she forgives him and they consolidate their relationship.

These similarities are striking. Each plot begins with a contrast between two men, one of whom is well-intentioned but weak (Silas, Godfrey); the other, more dynamic but morally reprehensible (William Dane, Dunstan). The men are either brothers or the very best of friends (Silas and Dane are called 'David and Jonathan' by the Lantern Yard brethren (p. 57)). In the 'present', Godfrey's only remaining possession is his horse, appropriately called Wildfire. Even this he is prepared to sacrifice rather than admit to his marriage with a barmaid, Molly Farren, because he knows that his father would disinherit him for such a folly. In the 'past', when William Dane falsely accuses Silas, the latter is literally cast out by the community to which he belongs. Both stories are thus instigated by a similar combination of factors. In each case, a more vital, 'daring and cunning' brother is endeavouring to steal the birthright of a better but weaker brother (p. 87).

There is, however, a very considerable difference between the two situations. Godfrey does not want his 'degrading marriage' with Molly Farren brought to light; he is guilty of deceiving not only his wife but also

Nancy, whom he has continued to court. Silas, on the other hand, does *not* commit the crime he is accused of. If there is a parallel between the events in the 'present' and those in the 'past', it is between Silas and Nancy, who are equally blameless.

One notes that Godfrey's conduct is constantly being excused. We are asked to believe that he really is 'a fine open-faced good-natured young man' (p. 73). The facts do not bear this out: he is secretive and has behaved abominably towards both Molly and Nancy. He deserves to be disgraced. Why, then, should he not be exposed? Who stands to gain by his behaviour's not being revealed? Most obviously, of course, himself. One remembers that Nancy is proud and could not stand knowing that Godfrey has been deceiving her. At the end, he reminds her why he did not tell her about his marriage with Molly Farren: 'With your pride and your father's, you'd have hated having anything to do with me after the talk there'd have been' (p. 224). He is, of course, making excuses, but he is also probably right. Everything we learn about Nancy in Part I would corroborate his assertion. If she reacts differently in Chapter 18, it is because she has 'changed' by the time he reveals his past to her. In other words, it is essential that Nancy does not learn of his affair with Molly until she is ready to assimilate such information. Nancy would like Godfrey to be exonerated from as much censure as possible, for he can be the man that *she* wants him to be only if *his* shoddy behaviour is not a reflection of his own personality but has been provoked by another character. Thus Dunstan's function is ambiguous. At one level of reading, he seeks to inculpate Godfrey, whom he 'traps' into marrying a barmaid of whom he is ashamed because he wants his older brother 'turned out of house and home' by their father (pp. 74, 80). But at another, Dunstan, by his very existence, serves to extenuate Godfrey's guilt, and in this latter capacity, no matter how paradoxical this may seem, Dunstan serves Nancy's interests.

I shall look more closely at the similarities between Dunstan and William Dane in a moment. Meanwhile, it is worth noting those between Molly and Sarah, each of whom is associated with the stronger but morally reprehensible man: Molly becomes involved with Godfrey through Dunstan, and Sarah marries William Dane. The most striking feature that they have in common is their weakness. Sarah slips into marriage with William Dane and is never mentioned again, and Molly is kept away from Raveloe, in a neighbouring village called Batherley, where she slides into laudanum addiction until she finally succumbs to a longing for oblivion (pp. 164–65). There is a clear parallel with Nancy's situation. When Godfrey fails to propose to her, Nancy determines not to marry him and withdraws to her own home. Molly's isolation corresponds to Nancy's isolation, and Sarah's preference for William Dane corresponds to Nancy's continuing interest in Godfrey after his behaviour has become as hypocritical as that of William Dane. In thematic terms, then, the fifteen years of Silas's self-imposed isolation correspond to the period of about three years of Nancy's bitter doubts.

In corroboration of this, one notes the parallels between the ways in which Silas and Nancy react to the various wrongs done to them. They both ward off despair by devoting themselves to work. When the lots pronounce against him, Silas ceases to trust in a 'God of lies' (p. 61). To forget his pain, he abandons his home town, settles in as isolated a community as possible, and devotes himself to his work. Weaving, one of the dominant images of the novel, symbolizes the slow growth of a pattern through the patient interconnexion of opposites. Similarly, when Godfrey fails to propose to her, Nancy abandons all hope of marrying him. To forget her pain, she buries herself in domestic duties: her hands 'bore the traces of butter-making, cheese-crushing, and even still coarser work' (p. 147). Like linen, butter and cheese are the products of patient toil. Thus, at the outset of the events, both Silas and Nancy have been wronged, and have reacted in a similar fashion. They are both leading isolated and restricted lives, immersing themselves in transformative work in order to forget their hurt.

Nancy is equally central to the crucial events which take place on the evening of Mrs Osgood's birthday party and Squire Cass's New Year party. Mrs Osgood is Nancy's aunt: Godfrey's relations play virtually no part in the story. The night of her birthday party, we learn that Godfrey is very pleased to see Nancy. The same evening, Silas's gold, which stands in lieu of a 'purpose' in his life and is the visible symbol of his 'hard isolation' (p. 65), is stolen, causing him for the first time since his self-imposed exile to become aware of a 'lack' in his life. A few moments later, the thief, Dunstan, disappears from view (we subsequently learn that he has fallen to his death). This not only frees Godfrey from the negative influence upon him which Dunstan represents, but thereby opens the way for him to make things up with Nancy. We know that Nancy is still deeply attached to Godfrey: it is surely legitimate to infer that his pleasure in seeing her causes Nancy to become conscious of the distance that has grown between them—that is, of a 'lack' in *her* life. The theft of Silas's gold thus coincides with Nancy's becoming dimly aware of how she too has 'undergone a bewildering separation from a supremely loved object' (p. 166).

The parallelism between the two plots is even more apparent on the night of Squire Cass's New Year party. In the course of the festivities at the Red House, Ben Winthrop comments to Mr Macey: 'Well, I think Miss Nancy's a-coming round again' (p. 160). This remark not only tells the reader that Nancy's determination not to marry Godfrey is not as firm as she would like people to believe (p. 143), but also, at least in the eyes of one villager, lays the blame for the delayed engagement not with Godfrey, but with Nancy. This is so contrary to one's assumptions about the situation that it requires attention. Only Dunstan knows about Godfrey's secret marriage. No one else suspects Godfrey of anything other than coming under Dunstan's influence (p. 73). Ben's comment tells us that Nancy appears to have resolved to end her self-imposed isolation by responding to Godfrey's devotion. The dance in the Red House coincides with two crucial events, one occurring just outside the weaver's cottage and the other inside. Molly dies of laudanum intoxication and Silas discovers Eppie on the hearth and begins to feel 'old quiverings of tenderness' for the first time in several years (p. 168), thereby discovering a 'purpose' in life. Nancy's change of heart thus coincides not only with the death of a woman who is an obstacle to her ambition to marry Godfrey but also with the beginning of Silas's redemption through love. Moreover, the phrases used to describe Silas's emotions are equally applicable to Nancy: she also feels 'old quiverings of tenderness' towards Godfrey and thereby discovers a new 'purpose' in *her* life. Thus, just as Nancy's intimation of Godfrey's continuing affection for her, on the night of Mrs Osgood's birthday party, coincides with Silas becoming conscious of a lack, so her 'a-coming round again' in her attitude towards Godfrey, noticed by Ben on New Year's Eve, coincides with the awakening of Silas's love for another human being.

The ending of the novel reveals further parallels. When the stone-pits are drained, Dunstan's body is found and Godfrey confesses to Nancy that Eppie is his daughter. There is no obvious reason why the salving of Godfrey's conscience is either a satisfactory resolution to the events or in any way relevant to the Silas–Eppie–Aaron story. The ending is much more significant if it is seen as the resolution of a conflict that has faced the two female characters. Nancy forgives Godfrey his deception. The thought of leaving him does not enter her head; indeed, the suggestion is that their union is strengthened by the confession. Eppie also forgives her father for his behaviour, even though she cannot consider leaving Silas, the only father whom she has known. Her decision prepares the way for her marriage with Aaron. The ending of both stories thus involves a similar combination of factors: it puts the commitment and loyalty of the two female characters to the test. But the two characters who gain by this situation are Nancy and Silas, for nothing further can now threaten their happiness.

There are, therefore, remarkable parallels between the two plots. Nancy's story moves in the same direction as Silas's. In the first stage, confused by her own commitment to Godfrey, Nancy has isolated herself and is working tirelessly at her domestic duties; in the second, she responds again to Godfrey's evident (even if questionable) devotion; in the third, when a situation arises which threatens to leave her once again alone, she chooses to stay with him. In the first stage of Silas's story, he is living in isolation, working tirelessly at his weaving; in the second, he feels 'old quiverings of tenderness' for another human being; in the third, when a situation arises which threatens to leave him once again alone, his fears are quickly dispelled by Eppie's decision. That such extraordinary parallels should exist between these two very different plots implies that Nancy is very much more central to the novel than has been recognized.

I have indicated a pattern; this pattern demands interpretation. If the first part of my argument is derived from structuralism, then the second stems from Jung's theory of unconscious processes, for to ask what a novel signifies when considered as an expression of a dilemma confronting its author is to read it as if it were a product of its author's creative imagination. The meaning of a dream, according to Jung, lies in the symbolic value that its characters and situations have for the dreamer at that particular moment in his or her life. My aim in offering a reading of *Silas Marner* in the light of some of Jung's major ideas is thus twofold. In the first place, it is to uncover the possible origin of the dilemma which gave rise to the novel. Secondly, it is to reveal that the combination of structuralism and Jungian theory provides a useful means of unmasking a novel's structural coherence. In the following pages I argue that the dilemma from which this novel stems is a painful, self-destructive tendency that, although strictly speaking pertinent only to George Eliot at the time of writing, can also be ascribed to Nancy Lammeter.

I have looked at some parallels between Silas's story and Nancy's story. There is however one all-important difference. Silas is acted upon. Things happen to him. He is expelled from the Lantern Yard brethren. His money is stolen and he later discovers Eppie on his hearth. He is not abandoned at the end. When he acts (for example, when he decides to leave the Lantern Yard community, or to look after Eppie) it is compulsively. Silas is never an agent. In contrast, each of the main stages in Nancy's story is characterized by a decision which *she* makes. Her isolation corresponds to *her* determination not to marry Godfrey. Her resolve then wavers; she warms to him once again; at exactly the same time (although she knows nothing of this), she is liberated to marry him. At the end, when provided with a reason which, earlier, would have been sufficient for her to abandon him, she chooses to stay with him. The main events in Nancy's story correspond to her various attitudes and decisions. She *is* an agent. In this section, I want to show, by means of an analysis of the relation between Nancy and the other characters, that all the events are directly related to her: the opening situation offers a symbolic representation of a challenge facing her, and the course of events described in the novel reflects how she reacts to it.

The surprising number of attributes that Nancy and Godfrey have in common provides the most striking indication of the nature of their relation one to the other. Priscilla chides Nancy for 'sitting on an addled egg for ever, as if there was never a fresh un in the world' (p. 150). Godfrey is defined by his similar vacillation and moral cowardice (p. 77). His father describes him as a 'shilly-shally fellow' and adds: 'You take after your mother. She never had a will of her own' (p. 125). Nancy's mother died when she was a small child, and so too did Godfrey's. Although Nancy is reluctant to admit she loves him, she does not want to marry anyone else (pp. 224, 151), and Godfrey constantly puts off declaring that he loves her, while conceding that there is no other woman whom he wants to marry (p. 125). One way of looking at the characteristics they have in common is to maintain that they are drawn to one another because of their similar backgrounds. Such an explanation is insufficient. The parallels suggest rather that they 'mirror' one another: in other words, that their relationship is conditioned by psychological factors. Because the Nancy–Godfrey plot tells *her* story, one must conclude that Nancy is drawn to Godfrey largely because he 'personifies' or 'mirrors' aspects of her own weakness. This, in turn, implies that Godfrey is not so much an autonomous male character as a type or, more specifically, an 'image of a man' to which she is instinctively drawn.

According to Jung, just as every man has an inherent, albeit unconscious, mental image of the feminine that reflects his relationship with women, so every woman has a similar image of the masculine that mirrors her relationship with men. The image of a man encountered by a woman in her dreams and waking fantasies, personifying her inner or unconscious attitudes towards men, he called the *animus*.[16] That Godfrey's attributes so clearly mirror Nancy's suggests that he may be defined as an animus-figure.[17] In short, not only do the events in which Godfrey features tell Nancy's story, but this story may be defined as essentially psychological. It is not so much about two individuals as about the relation between a young woman and her own inherent image of masculinity: her animus. Clearly, regarding the relation between Nancy and Godfrey in this light invites one to read the novel not as a succession of episodes that represent a real situation, but as a reflection of a psychological process in which Nancy serves as the carrier of the author's unconscious personality.

Read in this way, the elements that compose the initial situation symbolize the impasse in which Nancy finds herself. At the time the novel opens, both Nancy and Godfrey live in houses dominated by a father-figure

(The Warrens by Mr Lammeter, The Red House by Squire Cass), Nancy's sister, Priscilla, is entirely contained in her relationship with her father, she is proud that she 'features' his family and spurns all other men:

> 'The pretty-uns do for fly-catchers—they keep the men off us. I've no opinion of men, Miss Gunn—I don't know what you have. And as for fretting and stewing about what *they'll* think of you from morning till night, and making your life uneasy about what they're doing when they're out o' your sight—as I tell Nancy, it's a folly no woman need be guilty of, if she's got a good father and a good home. [...] As I say, Mr Have-your-own-way is the best husband, and the only one I'd ever promise to obey.' (pp. 148–49)

This is not the speech of a liberated woman; it is an expression of Priscilla's over-attachment to her father and a corresponding confusion of 'father' and 'home' that prevent her from even contemplating a relation with a male 'other'. Priscilla does not change: at the end of the novel, she is as attached to her father as she was sixteen years before. She thinks of him as unique and is correspondingly scornful of other men: 'But joyful be it spoken, our father was never that sort o' man' (p. 213). She never distances herself from him.[18]

At the outset, in spite of her continuing love for him, Nancy has turned her back on Godfrey and is living at home with her sister and father: in other words, she has adopted her sister's maxim. This implies that Priscilla personifies an attitude which Nancy has adopted in spite of its being detrimental to her happiness. Jung used the term *shadow* to describe alter-ego figures of the same sex as the dreamer which he or she encounters in dreams and waking fantasies. The shadow personifies 'the "negative" side of the personality, the sum of all those unpleasant qualities we like to hide' (*CW*, VII, 103 n. 5). More specifically, it illustrates the way in which an individual *actually is behaving*, even when he or she is utterly unconscious of acting in such a manner. Nancy would like to marry Godfrey; instead, she is sitting at home pretending she has forgotten him. If Priscilla personifies an aspect of Nancy's character of which she is unaware, then her opinion about men in general tells the reader what Nancy is unconsciously afraid of: Nancy is worried at what Godfrey might be doing when he is out of her sight. Given that Nancy has no inkling of Molly's existence, her fears must represent tendencies in her own character.

The corresponding events in the Silas plot not only corroborate this claim, but also constitute a direct comment on what she is doing. One remembers that it is on becoming engaged to Silas that Sarah's manner towards him 'began to exhibit a strange fluctuation between an effort at an increased manifestation of regard and involuntary signs of shrinking and dislike' (p. 58). That is, as soon as Sarah becomes engaged to him, she begins to have negative feelings towards him. She is afraid of his epilepsy, and epilepsy may be defined as an 'absence' from oneself. Silas's 'absences' are equivalent to Nancy's feelings of emptiness when Godfrey goes away for 'days and days together' (p. 73). We are told that everyone in Raveloe thinks they would make 'a handsome couple' (pp. 73, 159–60), but Nancy turns her back on him in much the same way as Sarah abandons Silas. Imagining that Godfrey is unreliable, she retires to her own home. Yet, although she pretends she does not want to marry him, she continues to treasure some dried flowers for his sake (p. 151). She cannot bring herself to forget him; later, she asserts that there is no other man that she would ever have contemplated marrying (p. 224). In other words, she has surrendered herself to Godfrey, but only in her imagination. In reality, she is shunning him. *Silas Marner* offers a vivid representation of how and why such opposite tendencies arise.

The key to an individual's conflicting tendencies is the nature of his or her shadow-personality. I have defined Priscilla as Nancy's shadow, but an individual's shadow is often multiple. Priscilla represents Nancy's 'personal' shadow; Molly Farren can be defined as an archetypal aspect of her shadow. The events surrounding Molly are implausible in realistic terms, for it is equally improbable that a young village barmaid should have had access to laudanum and that Godfrey's relation with her could have been kept secret for so long in such small and tightly-knit communities as Raveloe and Batherley. The reason Godfrey's interest in her must remain secret is that Nancy could not bear its being disclosed. As Dunstan says to Godfrey, 'Miss Nancy wouldn't mind being a second, if she didn't know it' (p. 76). Even at the end, when Godfrey tells her about his first marriage, she asks him not to tell either her father or Priscilla about his affair with Molly (p. 236). None of the villagers learns of it. In other words, she does not want to face the fact of Molly's existence and, in psychological terms, whatever aspect of our personality we seek to repress belongs to our 'shadow'. Molly can therefore be defined as another, deeper or more archetypal aspect of Nancy's shadow. If Molly's concealed existence corresponds to Nancy's self-imposed isolation, then her addiction to laudanum symbolizes the narcotic quality of Nancy's fantasy surrender to Godfrey. She personifies a deeply unconscious aspect of Nancy, whose unnatural isolation and exaggerated fantasies about the man whom she loves are psychologically destroying her.

Not surprisingly, it is Priscilla who provides an explanation of why Nancy is doing this. Priscilla clings to the image she has of her father; Nancy does the same. For, although we are told little about Nancy's relationship with her father, there is much we can deduce about it. The narrator, describing Nancy's attitude, tells us that her father 'was the soberest and best man in the countryside, only a little hot and hasty now and then, if things were not done to the minute' (p. 144). One remembers that Squire Cass also thinks of his family as being the best in the neighbourhood, and he, too, easily loses his temper (pp. 121, 123). Godfrey lives in constant fear of being censured and perhaps disinherited by his father. If he is an animus-figure, it follows that *his* weakness (lack of confidence in himself) can be ascribed to *Nancy*'s lack of confidence in herself owing to her equal fear of being reproved by her father or of separating herself from him. The doubts she entertains about Godfrey are therefore directly related to her over-attachment to her father. Thus, for Nancy to 'imagine' Godfrey married to a woman who would degrade him signals not so much a petty jealousy as a lack of confidence in her own worth: compare her 'perpetually recurring thought': '"I can do so little—have I done it all well?"' (pp. 214–15). Nancy, while isolating herself from Godfrey, *unconsciously* thinks of herself as an unsuitable partner for such an eligible young man as Godfrey.

On the surface, everything pertaining to Nancy is 'of delicate purity and nattiness' (p. 147), but the other elements which compose the initial situation leave room to doubt whether this is the whole picture. They suggest that she is unconsciously projecting her doubts and suspicions onto those around her, and even weaving plots in order to disguise her fear of committing herself to Godfrey. Indeed, so unconscious is she of this tendency that she ascribes it not to any female character (any aspect of her female identity) but to male characters: not only to Godfrey but also to Dunstan and William Dane (aspects of her *animus*).

The connexion between Dunstan and William Dane needs little insistence. Dunstan 'traps' Godfrey into a degrading marriage and William Dane has 'woven a plot' in order to have Silas expelled from the Lantern Yard brethren (pp. 80, 61). Just as Godfrey falls easy prey to Dunstan's blackmail because he does not have the courage to stand up to his father, so Silas falls easy prey to William Dane because he does not have the courage to stand up the arbitrary decision of the Lantern Yard brethren. Indirectly, however, this trait reflects something happening to Nancy, for Dunstan can be defined as a destructive aspect of her animus that has undermined Godfrey's worth (that is, the worth of the true animus). He is, so to speak, the 'shadow' of the animus. In the same way as Nancy has adopted Priscilla's views, so Godfrey has come under Dunstan's negative influence. Thus, the quarrel between the two brothers can be seen as a conflict between two components of a woman's animus. The question, then, becomes: 'What reason does the text offer to explain why Nancy should imagine men as behaving in this way?'

Surprisingly, the answer is provided by the two scenes which feature groups of men, for they, too, can be shown to be related to Nancy. The Lantern Yard brethren are defined by their manner of arbitrarily judging a man by drawing lots. Although they are called 'brethren', they act towards Silas more like father-figures. According to Jung, the animus may well be experienced as 'rather like an assembly of fathers or dignitaries of some kind who lay down incontestable, "rational," *ex cathedra* judgments' (*CW*, VII, 332). He observed that a woman whose animus behaves in this way is prone to act upon just such arbitrary opinions as she unconsciously ascribes to all father-figures. One notes that Mr Lammeter is described as a 'grave and orderly senior' (p. 153), a phrase which could equally apply to the Lantern Yard brethren who fill Silas with awe, and that Nancy is described as having an opinion about everything: her opinions 'were always principles to be unwaveringly acted on. They were firm not because of their basis, but because she held them with a tenacity inseparable from her mental action' (p. 216; see p. 148).

Astonishingly, although the conversation at the Rainbow has occasioned a great deal of critical interest, no one has ever offered a reason why it should be entirely about Nancy's father. It consists almost exclusively of groundless and tenaciously defended opinions. The butcher, the farrier, Mr Macey, Mr Tookey, and Mr Winthrop all argue fiercely, each convinced that he alone knows what is right (p. 97), and its most significant feature is that it is *entirely* about Mr Lammeter: first, about his cows, then about his father's arrival in Raveloe, then about his unusual 'Janiwary' marriage, and finally about the previous owner of his home. One need scarcely add that this is not because he is a close friend of any of them: Mr Lammeter lives a retired existence. A literal reading of the events leads to observations about either social life in an isolated community or typically masculine attitudes. But given the tendency I have noted in Nancy, who is 'as constant in her affection towards a baseless opinion as towards an erring lover' (p. 148), we can infer that the villagers constitute yet another aspect of her animus. Thus, both groups of men described in the novel are associated with arbitrary opinionatedness. The Lantern Yard brethren offer an archetypal representation of the consequences of such a tendency. The villagers tell us that it stems from Nancy's father.

The culminating tale in the extraordinary conversation at the Rainbow is about the previous owner of the Warrens, and it provides the only lengthy description we are given of Nancy's home. Nancy is described as 'slightly proud and exacting' (p. 148). She is interested only in 'the young man of quite the highest consequence in the parish' and dreams of one day becoming '"Madam Cass," the Squire's wife' (p. 151). Her pride seems to come from her father. Mr Lammeter, like Godfrey, 'always *would* have a good horse' (p. 213). Appearances matter to them. It is fitting, therefore, that the previous owner of Nancy's home was a jumped-up tailor with an exaggerated concern with appearances. Determined to impress his neighbours at no matter what cost, Mr Cliff (or Cliff, as he is usually called) built and ran an enormous stable. He so bullied his son into acting like a gentleman that the boy died and, mentally unbalanced, he himself died soon after. The Warrens, where Nancy lives, is still haunted by the sound of stamping horses and cracking whips, which the terrified locals call 'Cliff's holiday' (pp. 102–03). Nancy has a similar determination to have her own way; Priscilla remarks how Nancy behaved as a child: 'If you wanted to go to the field's length, the field's length you'd go; and there was no whipping you, for you looked as prim and innicent as a daisy all the while' (p. 150). The reference to 'whipping' is perhaps not entirely fortuitous. The tale of Cliff's holiday, with the stamping of horses and the cracking of a whip, symbolizes Nancy's periodic fits of irrational, headstrong determination, a tendency that has emotionally isolated her.

That the Lantern Yard brethren function as father-figures for Silas, and the conversation in the Rainbow is entirely about Mr Lammeter, suggest that Nancy's problem with Godfrey stems from her relation with her father. This corresponds exactly to Jung's views on the animus. He held that a woman who has little understanding about the nature of her own animus will very often develop a tendency to express forceful and arbitrary opinions that 'have the character of solid convictions that are not lightly shaken, or of principles whose validity is seemingly unassailable' (*CW*, VII, 331). Not surprisingly, such a tendency usually stems from an exaggerated attachment to her father in her childhood (*CW*, XIV, 232). Thus, Mr Cliff's relationship with his son may be read as a symbolic representation of the psychological effect that Mr Lammeter has had, unwittingly, upon Nancy. The son who dies is 'equivalent' to the Godfrey on whom Nancy has turned her back. Cliff's holiday is a symbolic description of the irrational aggression which can take possession of a woman and its origins in the foibles of a doting father. The Lantern Yard's arbitrary judgement of Silas symbolizes the manner in which a woman whose animus demonstrates wildly conflicting tendencies might arrive at a decision of significance to her. His expulsion is therefore an archetypal representation of Nancy's need to distance herself from the 'assembly of fathers' that make up such a large part of her animus.

The surface narrative and the deeper structures implied by the text thus produce radically different readings of the events. On the surface, it appears that the reason for Nancy's self-imposed isolation is that her fiancé has jilted her, that the Lantern Yard brethren are just a narrow-minded sect, and that the villagers represent the conversation of rustics. A literal reading of the events can lead only to the conclusion that we should not look too closely at the novel's coherence. A psychological analysis of both structures and themes allows one to admire its coherence. It suggests that Godfrey's irregular attentions correspond to Nancy's fears and that the two groups of men described in the novel symbolize the reason for these fears: she is still so attached to her father that she is reluctant to trust any other man.

Jung defined the condition in which a woman falls prey to her own fantasies about her animus as animus-possession. By this term, he meant to indicate that opinion-atedness that can be shown to be conditioned by her animus does not reflect a woman's essential personality: it merely signals a maladjustment in her notions about men (*CW*, VII, 331; IX, ii, 29). The situation at the outset of the novel, in which Nancy in living in self-imposed isolation, in a home which is haunted by the sound of stamping horses and cracking whips, thus symbolizes a 'loss' of her true female identity. She has withdrawn into herself to the point of being almost invisible, and Eppie (the other important female character) is suffering from inadequate attention. In a novel written by a woman, their situation is not only significant but also disturbing.

The novel thus springs from the impasse in which Nancy finds herself as a result of an over-attachment to her father. Her anamnesis is easily deduced. She has grown up, like Priscilla, in an isolated home without a mother, with a tendency to overvalue her father and a corresponding tendency to undervalue other men, which has led to a fear of committing herself to another man. Her fear that Godfrey might not be the kind of man her father would be proud of (p. 153) and a related suspicion of what he might be doing when out of her sight signal a fundamental lack of confidence in her own worth. *Silas Marner* opens with a symbolic expression of the terrible emotional isolation into which a woman who is over-attached to her father can be plunged, causing her to become unconsciously reluctant to marry, and to weave fantasies that risk causing her increasing hurt.

It is time to look again at the way in which the two plots are connected and to examine further the part played by Silas, the weaver of Raveloe, in the events. Existing definitions of the relation between the two plots are unsatisfactory. It has always been assumed that the events concerning Silas form the main plot, and that those concerning Godfrey form the sub-plot.[19] It is also generally held that the Godfrey plot is the more 'realistic' and that the Silas plot is 'fairy-tale-like', 'mythic', or even 'archetypal'.[20] When considered separately, there is nothing surprising about either of these claims; considered together there is. For if one defines the main plot as archetypal and the sub-plot as realistic, then one is, in effect, claiming that the 'realistic' story serves to elucidate the 'archetypal' events. But a woman does not (at least not in the usual sense of the words) live within an 'archetypal' situation, from which she withdraws at night to dream of 'reality'. By definition, archetypal interactions are a symbolic representation of a 'real' dilemma: a woman living in 'reality' might very well dream of archetypal interactions. Thus, the usual definitions attributed to the two plots, in psychological terms, are problematic. For in psychological terms, the main plot is the one which can be shown to give shape to all the other events described, and it is doubtful whether the Silas plot can explain any of the events in what I have redefined as the Nancy plot. Moreover, in psychological terms, the main plot will inevitably be the one whose interactions are the most realistic. Thus, if the Nancy plot is indeed the more realistic, then one would expect the archetypal events to be a symbolic portrayal of its central concern. In this section, paradoxical though it may appear, I want to demonstrate that the more realistic events of the Nancy plot, in psychological terms, may be defined as the main plot and that the archetypal events of the Silas plot are a symbolic representation of the dilemma facing Nancy. Indeed, given the relation between the two plots, I want to propose that it is Nancy's gradually changing attitude that gives shape not only to the events in which she is, both directly and indirectly, involved, but also to the weaver's story.

This is a bold claim and needs some clarification. Such a relation as I am suggesting might exist between the two plots clearly cannot, *in sensu strictu*, be ascribed to any character (for example, Nancy): ultimately, any such relation must stem from the nature of the dilemma confronting the author. However, if the thematic content of the events in the archetypal narrative can be shown to correspond at all times and in all important features with the concerns of the more realistic narrative, then one can assert that the more realistic events shape the course of the archetypal events. Because Nancy is the central figure of the realistic events, one can relate the events of the Silas plot to her changing attitude, even if these are, ultimately, but a reflection of the author's unconscious transformation. My first task, then is to demonstrate in what ways the Nancy plot can be said to give shape to the course of Silas's story. At the outset, Silas is a miser. It is generally conceded that one cannot separate his money from Eppie; in other words, if his affection for Eppie represents a positive quality, then the hoarding of his golden guineas represents a misplaced sense of value.[21] The parallel with Nancy's situation is evident. His purposeless counting of his money symbolizes Nancy's equally purposeless sense of satisfaction during her self-imposed isolation.

Such a parallel suggests that Silas also personifies an aspect of a woman's personality. One notes that he is defined solely by feminine attitudes. Weaving is a craft traditionally associated with women, a point made explicit by one of the villagers: 'You're partly as handy as a woman, for weaving comes next to spinning' (p. 189).[22] His only social dealings are with the women of Raveloe (p. 55). His rich knowledge of herbs comes from his mother (p. 57). The instance given that his 'sap of affection was not all gone' is his love of an earthenware pot, an evidently feminine symbol (p. 69). He becomes not only a father but also a mother to Eppie (p. 180). Like Nancy, he comes from the North. Silas is described as 'one of those impressible self-doubting natures' (p. 57). Nancy is similarly impressible (shown by Priscilla's influence) and equally given to self-doubt (pp. 214–15). The 'unpropitious deity' from which Silas flees is equivalent to the Godfrey whom Nancy shuns. Silas's sense of benumbed pain is identical to Nancy's, and just as Silas does not want to believe in 'a god of lies', neither does she. The 'clinging life' he leads during his period of hard isolation corresponds to her comparable isolation, during which she 'clings' to her domestic duties. These parallels suggest that Silas, paradoxical though it may seem, personifies a significant aspect of Nancy's personality.

When the lots declare Silas guilty, he shows himself willing to carry the burden of his friend's guilt. He tells William Dane '*You* stole the money, and you have woven a plot to lay the sin at my door. But you may prosper for all that' (p. 61). This parallels Nancy's desire to exonerate Godfrey from the very guilt which she unconsciously attributes to him. This is perhaps the cornerstone of the novel. For although Nancy feels deeply hurt and imagines the worst about Godfrey, she keeps sufficient hold on herself not to spoil all chance of reconciliation by openly accusing him. The mechanism at work here is delicate. On the one hand, I claim that Nancy is projecting guilt onto Godfrey; on the other, I am saying she never accuses him. There is no contradiction here. What one imagines is not under one's conscious control. Nancy is unconscious of the fears that lead to her imagining Godfrey as married to Molly.[23] It is how she reacts to her situation that is important. It would have been easy for her to become vindictive of this animus/man whose irregular attentions she cannot decipher. That Silas seeks no revenge on William Dane suggests that Nancy nurtures no ill-feeling towards Godfrey. Later, we learn that even when he settles in Raveloe, nothing that the villagers say can 'stir Silas's benumbed faith to a sense of pain' (p. 64). That is, he remains (deliberately?) unconscious of the injury done to him, just as Nancy seems determined to believe the best of Godfrey. Instead of challenging Godfrey (which would probably have led to their permanent separation), she buries herself in cheese-making. Silas's faith in the outcome of his patient toil symbolizes Nancy's unconscious belief that her patient toil will reveal a solution to her problem.

One cannot change the past, Nancy realizes at the end (p. 236). At the outset of the events, Eppie is a neglected child, symbolizing Nancy's neglect of her own feminine worth. Eppie is Molly's child, and Molly personifies Nancy's unconscious doubts. And the child must be cared for, even if Nancy is not ready to take responsibility for the 'fantasies' she has spun. Just as Mr Lammeter has unwittingly had a detrimental effect on his daughter's emotional development, so Godfrey abandons Eppie. Another father-figure is therefore needed to right the balance. Jung made this point in a phrase both succinct and extraordinarily appropriate to *Silas Marner:* 'For "what has been spoiled by the father" can only be made good by a father' (*CW*, XIV, 232). Silas is a potential father-figure willing to carry the burden of responsibility for Nancy's shadow-personality (represented by William Dane's guilt and Molly Farren's child) and nurture Eppie until Nancy is strong enough to resign herself to the 'lot that has been given [her and Godfrey]' (p. 237). This is the sense of the 'mysterious burden' carried by weavers in 'that far-off time' (p. 51). At critical moments and in times of emotional stress, we all need an 'other': that is, an archetypal figure in whom to 'trust', who will carry the burden of our suffering until we are strong enough to assume the responsibility for ourselves.[24] Silas fulfils this role. In other words, he belongs to a deeper level of imaginal experience than Nancy: he is an archetypal image of a father willing to care for Eppie until Nancy is ready to accept fully the specific conditions of her lot. As Sandra Gilbert has pointed out, the daughter–father relationship is the key to the novel, but Eppie is not the only daughter-figure. Nancy, who spans the entire novel, is of far greater significance to the overall structuring of narrative events.

The two key events occur in the midst of festivities. Dunstan robs Silas while Nancy is dancing with Godfrey at Mrs Osgood's (p. 75), and Eppie finds her way to the weaver's door while Nancy and Godfrey are dancing at Squire Cass's New Year party. Festivities symbolize a ritual *ekstasis* (a suspension of ego-consciousness). The harmony of the villagers at this event signals that Nancy's tendency to act upon arbitrary opinions is temporarily inoperant. It is often upon the slightest decisions that everything hinges. It is this crucial change of attitude that allows Nancy to accept Godfrey's invitation to dance with him, which symbolizes their imminent union.

Silas's discovery of Eppie on his hearth, and the unexpected birth of his love for an abandoned creature, represent the renewal of Nancy's love for Godfrey. In other words, Eppie personifies an aspect of her nature that Nancy had been denying (or, in psychoanalytic terminology, repressing). Thus, if the rehumanization of Silas corresponds to Nancy's warming again to Godfrey, then Eppie personifies Nancy's burgeoning love. This is why Eppie has and requires no depth of character: she is an archetypal image of a daughter-figure in an older woman's imagination. It is because Nancy's difficulties stem directly from her over-attachment to her father that Eppie's education is entirely entrusted to a symbolic foster-father. Silas's growing devotion to Eppie signals a process deep in Nancy's unconscious, working towards the correction of her self-doubts.

Had Godfrey acknowledged Eppie at his father's New Year party, Nancy would have withdrawn still further from society and become another Priscilla: competent, no doubt, but never having had the experience of a relationship. In other words, he would have taken Eppie into the Red House, and she would have been left with only the dried leaves that she treasures for his sake, longing to marry him and have his child. The novel traces the 'process' she has to go through before she is ready to overcome her tendency to long for 'what was not given' (p. 215). Her dilemma determines not only the course of its two separate stories but also the nature of the interconnexions between them. Silas's redemption through love is a symbolic representation of the way in which Nancy gradually overcomes instinctive tendencies in her personality which might have become detrimental to both her aims and her happiness.

Within a year of Nancy's 'a-coming round again', she and Godfrey marry. Her continuing desire to do everything 'well' is represented in the archetypal story by the untiring assistance which Eppie's god-mother lends Silas. Dolly Winthrop personifies an unconscious level-headed matronly devotion to duty that allows Nancy to retain her self-respect throughout both her period of isolation and her childless marriage. Dolly thus functions as a 'positive' aspect of Nancy's shadow. It is wholly appropriate that it should be an aspect of Nancy's feminine personality (a woman's shadow is an image of a woman) that should chide Silas (a 'positive' figure, no doubt, but none the less an aspect of her animus) for not having more trust. It is Dolly who tells Silas he must learn to 'trust i' Them as knows better nor we do' (p. 137). He is partly but not entirely convinced.

Fifteen years after their marriage, Godfrey confesses to Nancy the truth about Eppie. By forgiving him (or, more accurately, by not using his confession as a reason for destroying their present relationship) Nancy reveals that in spite of her still being guided by 'rigid principles', she will no longer cling to them if given evidence that they do not apply. She has accepted that she and Godfrey are not going to have any further children: 'When you saw a thing was not meant to be, said Nancy, it was a bounden duty to leave off so much as wishing for it' (p. 217). Even so, she is willing to support Godfrey in his determination to claim Eppie and bring her back to live at The Red House. Eppie's decision to stay with Silas prevents this; it signals an intuition that the worlds to which she and her father belong are separate. Godfrey's willingness to allow Eppie to stay with Silas thus reflects Nancy's final acceptance of the lot given to her and her husband. Just as she did not become 'the Squire's wife' as she once wanted (she is plain Mrs Cass, childless but content (p. 196), so she has resisted the temptation of thinking she can change the past by adopting a child. Instead, she recommits herself to Godfrey, a gesture symbolized by Eppie's marriage to Aaron.

The purely symbolic nature of the latter union is indicated by its being between a motherless woman and a gardener (Eve and Adam).[25] Equally significant is that Aaron is Dolly's son: the fruit of the simple creed, unadulterated by intellectual preconceptions, held by this positive aspect of Nancy's shadow which has always been at hand to assist Silas with Eppie. But in effect, their marriage is only one half of the ending. The novel ends not just with their wedding but with an archetypal quaternity (Silas, Dolly, Eppie, Aaron): an age-old symbol, according to Jung, of psychic wholeness.[26] This quaternity symbolizes the successful outcome of the process in which Nancy has been unwittingly involved at the realistic level of the narrative: her immeasurably strengthened union with Godfrey. It implies that, like Silas, Nancy has at last consciously discovered 'light enough to trusten by' (p. 241).

This reading of the relation between the two plots of *Silas Marner* not only provides a frame for the examination of the many intricate features of this particular novel but also raises a great many issues relevant to the analysis of women's writing in general. If one is to understand the psychological implications of a text for its author, one must first establish the identity of the character to whom the narrative events are most directly related. This character is not always one of the protagonists of the surface structures. Nancy is a very minor character in Part I of the novel but, as I have shown, the events of Part I are all directly related to her and to the dilemma confronting her.

In psychological terms, the novel is not composed of two 'plots' of equal value. It tells one story on two different levels of fictional representation. It is about Nancy's relationship with Godfrey, which has been made difficult as a result of an over-attachment to her father and a corresponding tendency to suspect the worth of any other man. It tells how Nancy gradually overcomes a self-destructive tendency to indulge in unconscious fears, fantasies, and arbitrary decisions detrimental to the happiness she desires. By working at her relationship with Godfrey, she gradually overcomes those deeply-ingrained tendencies in her character which could so easily have led her into increasing emotional isolation and prevented her from making her peace with Godfrey, as she so evidently wants to do. The novel traces the process Nancy unconsciously goes through before she finally, albeit only tentatively, comes to terms with her situation: she is (and in all likelihood will remain) childless, but she now knows that the 'partner' in her own imagination fully accepts their situation.

Although I have endeavoured to show that one can deduce Nancy's central function in the novel only from textual evidence, the basis of my argument supposes that the dilemma facing Nancy must also be relevant to George Eliot. There are, however, few obvious parallels between Nancy and Marian Evans. The fictional character is clearly not the carrier of the author's conscious personality, but the carrier of an aspect of her unconscious personality. A good description of the distinction between these two concepts is supplied by Edward Whitmont's definition of the difference between the ego and the dream-ego:

> In any normal person's dream the 'I' as identity-carrier may appear altered and dissociated. It may seem to have lost the conscious ego's values and action capacities and to have taken on strange new ones; the dream-ego frequently feels and acts in a way which is uncharacteristic of the waking ego, or it cannot act at all, as in the dream of wanting to run away but instead standing paralyzed on the spot.[27]

There is no reason why the pivotal character in a novel should resemble the author. But, just as the dream-ego's *behaviour* will always reveal an important aspect of the ego's unconscious personality, so too, in a novel, will the pivotal character's reactions to the dilemma facing him/her reveal an important aspect of its author. Nancy's reactions have much in common with those of George Eliot.

Silas is about forty years old at the beginning of the novel, and Nancy is about forty years old at the end—Eliot's age at the time of writing. We know that the novelist's early life was considerably affected by her relation with her father.[28] When Nancy separates herself sufficiently from her father to set her hopes on Godfrey she is about the same age as Marian Evans was in 1842, when her refusal to go to church led to a violent quarrel with her father. In spite of this, however, he continued to influence her greatly, even after his death. Marian met G. H. Lewes in October 1851: he was still married, even though he was no longer attached to his wife. She knew the indignity of having to keep her affair with him secret—the parallel with Molly is obvious; Nancy, one notes, suffered no less for her 'secret' love for Godfrey. Her instinct to withdraw into herself and to cross-question herself mercilessly was shared by her creator, who was unusually depressed throughout 1860, occasioned at least in part by society's continued refusal to accept her relation with Lewes. In spite of all the love by which she was surrounded, and for all her literary success, she continued to be prey to an astonishing lack of confidence in herself. Dessner and others have drawn attention to a great many parallels between the life and the fiction.[29] There is ample evidence to suggest that the dilemma I have identified as confronting Nancy is comparable to that which faced Eliot in 1860. Its ending represents a tentative resolution to an enormously painful personal experience that 'thrust' itself upon Eliot in 1860.

Perhaps the most significant feature of this reading, however, is that it provides a substantial link between her previous and her subsequent novels. Maggie Tulliver loses her chance of true happiness when she rejects Stephen Guest and Romola is attracted to an opportunist who conceals both his character and Tessa from her: the parallel with Nancy's situation is self-evident. The vulnerability of both Maggie and Romola stems from their relationships with their respective fathers, relationships which prevent them from discovering their own independent worth until they have forfeited any possibility of the happiness they sought. All three works are centrally concerned with a father's unwittingly negative influence on a female character: the same, one might add, could also be held for *Middlemarch*. Thus, whilst in many ways surprising, this reading of *Silas Marner* in effect re-places the novel in its context. As to why it assumed the form it has, which seems to centre on two male characters, one can only speculate: for my part, as I maintained at the outset, I believe that the figure of Savonarola so weighed upon Eliot's spirits that her creative imagination spontaneously produced a 'compensatory' image whose purpose was to give her 'light enough to trusten by'.[30] If this was indeed so, *Silas Marner* is no less therapeutic than her other novels.

This conclusion raises one further question, and one must touch on it even though it cannot be satisfactorily resolved. To what extent was Eliot conscious of the nature of the dilemma I have outlined? We can never know, but that Nancy never fully realizes the debt that she, no less than Godfrey, owes to Silas signals that the ending represents but a tentative solution to the problem with which the novel is concerned. Nancy may never again give way to such fears as occasioned her initial withdrawal from life, but her author might. Indeed, one notes that a considerable part of *Felix Holt* is a development of the theme explored in *Silas Marner*, which would suggest that Eliot only very partially integrated the lesson learned by Nancy at the end of her tale about the weaver of Raveloe. One remembers Mrs Transome's bitter remark: 'A woman's love is always freezing into fear. She wants everything, she is secure in nothing [...] God was cruel when he made woman.'[31] *Silas Marner* illustrates how a woman who is uncertain of her feminine worth risks falling victim to negative fantasies of her own devising and illustrates the psychological origin of Eliot's own deep-rooted insecurity, succinctly expressed by Nancy's 'longing for what was not given'. It tells how a woman whose love had frozen into fear unconsciously discovered a 'light enough to trusten by' that allowed her to achieve at least a partial escape from her own self-doubts and a partial fulfilment of her desires.

Notes

1. F. R. Leavis, *The Great Tradition* (Harmondsworth: Pelican, 1970), p. 60.
2. W. J. Harvey, *Victorian Fictions: A Guide to Research*, ed. by Lionel Stevenson (Cambridge, MA: Harvard University Press, 1964), p. 296. See also R. T. Jones, *George Eliot* (Cambridge: Cambridge University Press, 1970), p. 31, and William E. Buckler, 'Memory, Morality, and the Tragic Vision in the Early Novels of George Eliot', in *The English Novel in the Nineteenth Century: Essays on the Literary Mediation of Human Values*, ed. by George Goodin (Urbana: University of Illinois Press, 1972), p. 159.
3. The most important of these early re-evaluations of *Silas Marner* are: Jerome Thale, 'George Eliot's Fable: *Silas Marner*', in *The Novels of George Eliot* (New York: Columbia University Press, 1959); Fred C. Thomson, 'The Theme of Alienation in *Silas Marner*', *Nineteenth-Century Fiction*, 20 (1965), 69–84; Ian Milner, 'Structure and Quality in *Silas Marner*', *Studies in English Literature*, 6 (1966), 717–29; David R. Carroll, '*Silas Marner*: Reversing the Oracles of Religion', in *Literary Monographs* I, ed. by Eric Rothstein and T. K. Dunseath (Madison: University of Wisconsin Press, 1967), pp. 167–200, 312–14.
4. Ruby Redinger, *George Eliot: The Emergent Self* (London: Bodley Head, 1976), p. 438.
5. Lawrence Jay Dessner, 'The Autobiographical Matrix of *Silas Marner*', *Studies in the Novel*, II (1979), 251–82. Redinger's and Dessner's findings have been questioned by Alexander Welsh in *George Eliot and Blackmail* (Cambridge, MA: Harvard University Press, 1985), p. 167.
6. Sandra M. Gilbert, 'Life's Empty Pack: Notes Towards a Literary Daughteronomy', *Critical Inquiry*, II (1985), 355–84 (p. 360).
7. John Preston, 'The Community of the Novel: *Silas Marner*', *Comparative Criticism*, 2 (1980), 121; also Susan R. Cohen, '"A History and a Metamorphosis": Continuity and Discontinuity in *Silas Marner*', *Texas Studies in Literature and Language*, 25 (1983), 414.
8. See George Eliot's Journal entry for 28 November 1860: 'I am engaged now in writing a story, the idea of which came to me after our arrival in this house, and which has thrust itself between me and the other book *[Romola]* I was meditating' (*The George Eliot Letters*, ed. by Gordon S. Haight, 7 vols (London: Oxford University Press, 1954–56), III, 360).

9. A striking exception is Lilian Haddakin, who writes that Nancy is 'vitally important in the rendering of "feeling and form" on the realistic level'. She thereupon drops the point: see '*Silas Marner*', in *Critical Essays on George Eliot*, ed. by Barbara Hardy (London: Routledge, 1970), p. 74.

10. The earliest events described at any length are those which take place in Lantern Yard, but they belong to an already 'remote' past. They are not the first stage of the plot. See Bruce K. Martin, 'Similarity Within Dissimilarity: The Dual Structure of *Silas Marner*', Texas Studies in *Literature and Language*, 14 (1972), 479–89 (p. 481).

11. 'Demythologizing *Silas Marner*', ELH, 37 (1970), 226–44 (p. 228).

12. George Eliot, *Silas Marner: The Weaver of Raveloe*, ed. by Q. D. Leavis (Harmondsworth: Penguin, 1967), p. 73. All page references are to this edition.

13. By 'story' I mean the complete series of episodes in which any individual character either features or is implicitly involved. The term is designed to signal the specifically *fictional* nature of such a sequence of events.

14. This claim will surprise some readers, as Nancy is very obviously a figure of some amusement to George Eliot. A moment's reflection, however, should remind us that this, in itself, is no obstacle to her being a central character as far as the shaping of the events in *Silas Marner* is concerned. Maggie Tulliver did not escape her gentle irony; nor do Nancy and Eppie.

15. Interest in Jung has concentrated too much on his ideas about archetypal images (the 'object' of experience), and not enough on the need to identify the 'subject'—the perceiving consciousness—of the experience in question. Clearly, how one interprets a dream depends on the identity of the subject whose dream it is. The same, I believe, is true of a novel.

16. C. G. Jung, *The Collected Works*, 20 vols (London: Routledge, 1953–76), IX, ii, paras 29–33; hereafter cited as *CW* followed by volume and paragraph number.

17. The need to define him as such is self-evident. If one is reading the novel in psychological terms, then one should be wary of assuming a one-to-one relation between any character and a possible real-life original. Godfrey certainly shares at least one major attribute of G. H. Lewes: devotion. But it would be mistaken to infer from this that Godfrey=G. H. Lewes. The alternative is to view Godfrey as an image of masculinity spontaneously produced by the author's imagination, towards which Nancy Lammeter is instinctively, almost irrationally, drawn.

18. One notes that at the end of the novel she is treating her father almost as if he were a substitute child: see pp. 211–12.

19. For example, Jerome Thale, *The Novels of George Eliot* (New York: Columbia University Press, 1959), p. 66, and Martin, p. 487.

20. For example, Thale, p. 59; Brian Swann, 'Silas Marner and the New Mythus, Criticism, 18 (1976), 101–21; Preston, p. 112.

21. See James McLaverty, 'Comtean Fetishism in Silas Marner', Nineteenth-Century Fiction, 36 (1981), 318–36.

22. Weaving is a motif frequently found in creation myths: see G. S. Kirk and others, The Presocratic Philosophers: A Critical History with a Selection of Texts, 2nd edn (Cambridge: Cambridge University Press, 1983), pp. 60–66; also Marie-Louise von Franz, Patterns of Creativity Mirrored in Creation Myths (Zürich: Spring Publications, 1972), pp. 88–89. This would suggest that Silas's patient interconnexion of opposites is a 'creation myth' pertinent to Nancy.

23. In the course of a seminar given in 1934, Jung described a woman analysand who was unconscious of her shadow personality in terms which might have come directly from Silas Marner: 'The feminine mind is not as a rule fully occupied, and so—like Penelope when [Odysseus] was travelling around the Mediterranean—women spin webs, they weave plots, which are apt to be [...] of a very immoral kind from the standpoint of respectability. [...] Usually women are very innocent and know nothing about these plots, but they arè there; and in analysis one trains people to become aware of them' (C. G. Jung, The Visions Seminars, 2 vols (Zürich: Spring Publications, 1976), II, 509). The somewhat irritating sexism of these lines need not be taken seriously. Most of those attending the seminar were women: the remark was just gratuitously provocative.

24. Silas's readiness to assume the burden of Nancy's shadow personality has obvious parallels with one of Christ's defining attributes, which is further evidence that Silas is an essentially archetypal figure.

25. See Wiesenfarth, pp. 243–44.

26. See CW, VII, 186; IX, i, 278, 425; IX, ii, 245.

27. Edward C. Whitmont, The Symbolic Quest (Princeton, NJ: Princeton University Press, 1978), p. 234.

28. See Gordon S. Haight, George Eliot: A Biography (Oxford: Clarendon Press, 1968), esp. Chapters 2 and 10; or Jennifer Uglow, George Eliot (London: Virago Press, 1987).

29. Lawrence Jay Dessner, 'The Autobiographical Matrix of Silas Marner', Studies in the Novel, 11 (1979), 251–82; see also Ruby Redinger, George Eliot: The Emergent Self (London: Bodley Head, 1976).

30. One of Jung's major theories was, of course, that the unconscious 'compensates' the one-sidedness of the individual's conscious attitude(s): for example, 'The unconscious processes that compensate the conscious ego contain all those elements that are necessary for the self-regulation of the psyche as a whole' (CW, VII, 279; also 282–83; VI, 574–75).

31. George Eliot, *Felix Holt*, ed. by Peter Coveney (Harmondsworth: Penguin, 1972), p. 488. For a discussion of parallels between *Romola*, *Silas Marner*, and *Felix Holt*, see Elizabeth Deeds Ermarth, 'George Eliot's Conception of Sympathy', *Nineteenth-Century Fiction*, 40 (1985), 23–42.

ALAN W. BELLRINGER

George Eliot's Shorter Fiction, including Silas Marner

Of George Eliot's six shorter prose-tales only *Silas Marner* is developed into a full novella with a double plot. The others conform to Henry James's notion of the short story as anecdote, where a single situation is carefully elaborated.[1] They all contain interesting narrative effects, like the two dialogue scenes run into the one chapter (Ch. 3) in 'Amos Barton', the rendering of Dempster's consciousness in a state of delirium tremens in 'Janet's Repentance' (Ch. 23) or the large time gaps in *Silas Marner*. In none of these tales do the chapters have titles or mottoes in aid of contemplation. If narrative haste is scarcely a quality to be associated with George Eliot, since she gives over so much space to narratorial comment, yet she can also use unexpected deaths and brief, suspenseful chapter-endings like Dunsey Cass's exit, 'So he stepped forward into the darkness' (*Silas Marner*, Ch. 4), to cut the content, though not the substance, of her stories. But what distinguishes each one of her shorter works is the impression given of a strong theme delicately handled. Behind the presentational cover of sympathy for commonplace people experiencing unromantic incidents in average communities set in ordinary landscapes, where there is 'nothing to break the flowerless monotony of grass and hedgerow but an occasional oak or elm, and a few cows sprinkled here and there' ('Janet's Repentance', Ch. 26), there is a nudging towards implicit radical analyses of complex and

From *George Eliot*. © 1993 by Alan W. Bellringer.

sensitive issues. The humorous and emotional side-effects cannot obscure the seriousness of the implications. Admittedly, 'The Lifted Veil' is exceptional in respect of several of these points made about George Eliot's shorter fiction, yet it too bears a very distinct mark, its fantasy content.

George Eliot's first published story, 'The Sad Fortunes of the Reverend Amos Barton' (1857), is a good example of a disturbing text, with a problem beneath its innocuously mild exterior. The effect is less surprising perhaps when we read that the subject came to the author when she was lying in bed one summer morning in a dreamy doze.[2] But what is the subject of 'Amos Barton'? Ostensibly it is the only one of the three *Scenes of Clerical Life* (1858) that lives up to the collective title. Here the clerical portrait is prominent. The awkward clergyman is followed in his avocations, visiting his parishioners, preaching to the poor, meeting with fellow parsons, consulting the squire. In these contacts Barton makes a poor showing, reflecting on them as disagreeable duties. The tone is satirical in a way that suggests Trollope,[3] with Martin Cleves, 'the true parish priest, the pastor beloved, consulted, relied on by his flock', set against the Reverend Archibald Duke, who thought 'the immense sale of the "Pickwick Papers", recently completed, one of the strongest proofs of original sin'; and the clergy's talk about their bishop left unspecified, 'lest we should happen to overhear remarks unsuited to the lay understanding, and perhaps dangerous to our repose of mind' (Ch. 6). The narrator's lay understanding is less inhibited near the end when we learn of 'some bitter feeling' aroused by the vicar's use of a pretext to remove Barton from his curacy so that the vicar might ultimately give it 'to his own brother-in-law' (Ch. 9). But the questioning of the ecclesiastical system is by now felt as a background concern in the tale.

The main misfortune of Amos Barton has already occurred at this juncture, the loss of his wife Milly after childbirth. Weakened by domestic labour and worries, she has had six children and is considered to be delicate: 'she won't stand havin' many more children' (Ch. 5). The narrator explicitly addresses the problems of the Barton household in economic terms: 'By what process of division can the sum of eighty pounds per annum be made to yield a quotient which will cover that man's weekly expenses?' But implicitly the problem is left as personal. In his pressing situation the only consolation for Barton must be sexual pleasure with his wife. Milly, it is emphasized, is a lovely woman who blushes tremulously and 'makes sunshine and a soft pillow' for Amos. 'The flowing lines of her tall figure made the limpest dress look graceful, and her old frayed black silk seemed to repose on her bust and limbs with a placid elegance' (Ch. 2). Her physical attractiveness to the ungainly but energetic Barton in his 'tight pantaloons' is unmistakable.[4]

To support this reading, the narrator associates the irregular, picturesque world of Shepperton with a careless fertility, with his own 'nurse', the 'school-children's gallery', 'the penetralia of private life' (this in a cancelled passage),[5] the 'pleasant rhythm' of the milk falling from 'the udders of the large sleek beasts', Barton in his sermons floundering about 'like a sheep as has cast itself' (Ch. 1), not to mention the workhouse rebel, Miss Fodge, who 'had contributed to the perpetration of the Fodge characteristics in the person of a small boy' (Ch. 2). Even a negative joke, like the reference to the unsympathetic cook to whom Mr Bridmain's man-servant 'did *not* make love' (Ch. 3), keeps up the atmosphere. The scandal surrounding the visit of the Countess Czerlaski, a former governess and widow of a dancing-teaching, is therefore predictable. When her brother decides to marry her maid, the Countess leaves in indignation and takes up residence with the Bartons, so that in the neighbourhood 'new surmises of a very evil kind were added to the old rumours' (Ch. 5). It is believed that Amos has taken her as a mistress during his wife's last months of pregnancy. The doctor surmises that Barton 'may have attractions we don't know of', and the Rector suggests that he may have 'some philtre or other to make himself charming' (Ch. 6). Such ribaldry, however unfair to Barton, is only a distortion of the truth, that he is a demandingly passionate husband, affectionate 'in his way' (Ch. 2). Milly's deathbed words, if the rash of dashes is cleared from them, 'You-have-made-me-very-happy' (Ch. 8), are not likely to refer to intellectual companionship! Indeed on his last visit to Milly's grave Amos confesses, 'I wasn't tender enough to thee—I think of it all now' (Ch. 10). The implication, that sexual problems do not disappear in marriage, but can have tragic consequences, comes subtly across to us. It is obvious that Barton had no knowledge of contraception; he who had gone through the 'Eleusinian mysteries of a university education' without being able to master English spelling and syntax (Ch. 2) was hardly the man to acquire advanced opinions or unprejudiced information on a taboo topic. But the sharp irony has its effect. If 'Amos Barton' succeeds in its purpose of stirring sympathy with 'commonplace troubles ... in very ordinary decent apparel' (Ch. 7) it does so because it deals not only with the details of a tiring life, Milly's 'assiduous unrest' of mending and so on (Ch. 2), but also most understandingly with 'unspoken sorrows' (Ch. 5), which its characters are not able to articulate. It is notable, as Dianne F. Sadoff has pointed out,[6] that as a widower Barton still needs a woman to make 'the evening sunshine of his life'; it is the elder daughter Patty, who, aged about thirty with 'some premature lines round the mouth and eyes', fills that surrogate role at his side (Conclusion). The pathos, then, has a hard core.

'Mr. Gilfil's Love-Story' (1857) is altogether more candid, which it can afford to be since its theme of fostering and snobbery is less controversial.

Set just before the French Revolution in Cheverel Manor, a castellated house which would have made a charming picture had 'some English Watteau' existed to paint it (Ch. 2), it has something of the trappings of a historical romance. The clerical element adheres mainly to the frame of the tale. The frame concerns the Reverend Maynard Gilfil's later life as a hunting and farming parson, preaching undoctrinal sermons and sipping gin and water in solitude, apart from the 'mutual understanding' he enjoys with his old brown setter. Gilfil has carried widowhood into the introspection of old age, keeping his long-dead wife's chamber intact with its 'blinds and thick curtains' drawn. Even in the 'antecedent romance' of his courtship of Lady Cheverel's musical protégée Tina, Gilfil cuts an everyday figure, giving earnest advice: 'Time and absence, and trying to do what is right, are the only cures' (Ch. 9), he tells Tina, who is passionately and hopelessly in love with the heir to the estate, Captain Wybrow. Though the worthy Gilfil at one point feels painfully that he has 'lost the being who was bound up with his power of loving' (Ch. 19), he wins her hand after all, once Wybrow has died unexpectedly, only to lose her again finally in her 'struggle to put forth a blossom' (Ch. 21). Gilfil has enough solidity to function effectively as the character who is on the receiving end of the incidents in the plot, but the principal interest is elsewhere.[7]

In 'Mr. Gilfil's Love-Story' George Eliot develops a tense situation between the Italian-born Tina and the English aristocratic set in which she is bred. Some of the dialogue has the touch of Jane Austen at her most serious, as when Miss Asher, the thin-lipped beauty to whom Captain Wybrow is betrothed, tells him, 'An honourable man will not be placed in circumstances which he cannot explain to the woman he seeks to make his wife' (Ch. 9). The narrator's explanation of this lady's gracious condescension to Tina as 'the malicious anger that assumes the tone of compassion' (Ch. 13) is psychologically acute, as is the ironic account of Wybrow's own divided feelings; he 'always did the thing easiest and most agreeable to him from a sense of duty' (Ch. 5). The interplay of dangerous personal relations in the great house is managed with wit, suspense and economy in twenty brief chapters. Sir Christopher's architectural passion, his dislike of 'insipid' Palladianism (Ch. 4) and his quarrel with his sister, both adequately sketched, play a part in tangling the circumstances surrounding Tina in her equivocal position. The decor is appropriately delicate, featuring pretty flowers, tender operatic arias, ornamental pictures, the gardener's turf and gravel, the willow-fringed pool 'laughing with sparkles' (Ch. 17), but the stately Lady Cheverel finds that her world is too complacent. Her idea of grafting 'as much English fruit as possible on the Italian stem' (Ch. 3), without properly adopting Tina, is superficial and predictably fails. The talented girl, torn between gratitude, resentment and guilt over the secret affair with the weak Wybrow, eventually contemplates murder. Rushing noiselessly and looking 'like the incarnation of a fierce purpose' (Ch. 13), she clenches a dagger, believing she will plunge it into her false lover's heart. Though the rather dull Gilfil exculpates the heroine by arguing that she could not *in fact* have brought herself to do what she admittedly meant to do, when she was prevented by Wybrow's death, which came as a result of a heart attack, yet we are forced to reflect that Tina was very lucky not to be put to the test. The narrator's ironic technique has made violence seem perfectly plausible.

A large contribution is made by the animal imagery. Tina's single parent, her father, who is Lady Cheverel's music-copyist in Milan, already refers to her as 'the marmoset' when he leaves her at his landlady's 'on the floor with her legs in a heap of peas' (Ch. 3). The narrator next compares her humorously with a kitten. Later in the narrative Tina's father dies, and she is taken, still in infancy, to England to be brought up as a useful companion to the childless Lady Cheverel; the idea that she is different from the family is constantly reinforced by the link with animals. Sir Christopher is always calling her familiarly his 'little monkey', 'the black-eyed monkey', 'you silly monkey', even when she is seventeen or eighteen years old. The diminutive and attractive Tina would seem naturally to suggest various small animals to characters and narrator alike. They bring in, apart from monkeys, a humming bird, a frog, a puppy, a linnet, a duck, a leveret, a grasshopper, a mouse, a waterfowl and even, when she is on her mission of hatred, a tigress, thus neatly combining condescension with a certain Darwinian apprehension of an instinctively fighting tenaciousness in Tina, the object of so much jealousy, affection and pity.

But the allusions to the animals and human–animal relationships do not function reductively. George Eliot assumes both an emotional value and a need for responsibility in humanity's dealings with animals. Much, for example, in the introductory chapter of 'Mr. Gilfil's Love-Story', is made of the clergyman's concern for Dame Tripp, whose attitude to her pet pig involves a comic assumption of equality. She will not have the pig slaughtered for bacon, because she appreciates its company: 'I do not mind doin' wi'out to gi' him summat. A bit o' company's meat an' drink too, an' he follers me about, an' grunts when I spake to 'un, just like a Christian.' Gilfil is sufficiently moved to make Dame Tripp a gift from his own store of bacon, even though she hardly ever attends his church (she is a leech-gatherer by profession, though not gravely Wordsworthian). Her need for company curiously prefigures Lady Cheverel's for Tina's, and is actually more understanding. At various points in the tale the narrator emphasises the gap between human and animal intelligence ('Animals are such agreeable friends—they ask no questions, they pass no criticisms', Ch. 7). No such gap exists, of course between Tina and the aristocratic circle in which she finds herself; the barrier set up by patronage, however benevolent it may be, frustrates her sexual passion and nearly causes a catastrophe. Tina recovers, however, at Foxholm Parsonage amid the 'unsentimental cheeriness of pullets, sheepdogs and carthorses' (Ch. 20), for long enough to give Gilfil a few months of happiness. In an impressive passage the narrator describes life as a 'mighty torrent, rushing from one awful unknown to another', mentioning the stars, the tides, human invention, commerce and politics, compared with all of which Tina's trouble is lighter 'than the smallest centre of quivering life in the water-drop' or the anguish of a bird that has found its 'nest torn and empty' (Ch. 5). But 'Mr. Gilfil's Love-Story' is carefully worded throughout to make the scale of high and low, large and small, in life seem only relative, leaving us with a sense of 'nature's social union', such as informs Burns's poem 'To a Mouse'.[8]

'Janet's Repentance' (1857) is the most ambitious of the *Clerical Scenes*. Longer by a third than its predecessor, it returns to the period which George Eliot could recollect from childhood. There is a gallery of local townsfolk, involved in sectarian disputes. In the climactic set-piece, an Evangelical clergyman, Mr Tryan, has to run the gauntlet of mockery from the High-and-Dry Church party. Here a crudely satirical play-bill, representing the 'keenest edge of Milby wit' (Ch. 9), is quoted in full.[9] This religious strife forms an unpleasant back-drop to the main centre of interest, Janet Dempster's alcoholism, her sufferings as a battered wife and her recovery under the guidance of the despised Tryan. The story has a single main thrust, Janet's demoralisation, her escape from marriage and her regaining of self-command. Her husband's reckless self-destruction and the consumptive clergyman's fatal self-sacrifice are contributory elements only. 'Janet's Repentance' has an underlying optimism, a trust in corrective nature, a belief in the dignity of woman and a respect for the purposive individual.

The theme of drink is handled tactfully, with humour and sympathy, as might be expected, but also with due regard for the grimmer aspects, the causes, danger-points, consequences. The narrator indicates that it is a problem which has not gone away; the prosperous Milby of the Victorian present, where ladies who take too much upon themselves 'are never known to take too much in any other way', is ironically contrasted with the dull Milby of more than a generation back, where 'many of the middle-aged inhabitants, male and female, often found it impossible to keep up their spirits without a very abundant supply of stimulants' (Ch. 2). Such passages, while offering a reason for apparent changes in behaviour, also question the extent of the changes.[10] Drink, directly or indirectly, affects all the characters in Janet's Repentance', from the dissenting Reverend Horner, 'given to tippling and quarrelling' (Ch. 2), to the doctor who puts his feet up in the Red Lion, having already 'been in the sunshine' while on his rounds (Ch. 1). Dempster the lawyer is proud of his ability to hold his drink, but it proves a habit which loses him his money, his wife and his life. Janet has her fear of his violent temper to excuse her own weakness; 'it's enough to make her drink something to blunt her feelings', as the understanding Mrs Pettifer remarks, 'and no children either, to keep her from it' (Ch. 3). But by loosening restraints on emotions drink makes the situation worse for all concerned. Dempster's chronic aggressiveness towards man and beast is only compounded by drink; Janet's retorts and gestures of despair, emboldened by drink also, whet his hatred. He is castigated by the narrator as 'an unloving, tyrannous, brutal man', moved by love of power and 'lust of torture', who 'needs no motive to prompt his cruelty; he needs only the perpetual presence of a woman he can call his own' (Ch. 13). The complex psychological and social factors seem to be producing an atmosphere of hopelessness. The influence of alcoholism is intelligently contextualised. The nadir is reached when Janet, driven from her home at night, but taken in by Mrs Pettifer, feels utterly helpless, her over-excited brain shaping the future in misery as 'a dreary vacant flat, where there was nothing to strive after, nothing to long for' (Ch. 16). She quite lacks the courage to attempt to live independently. There is, however, a structure of negatives and positives built into this tale. Nature is said to provide love over and above human justice, giving us 'fruit from no planting of ours' (Ch. 5). Milby is not only a dingy town, but one where in spring the roofs and chimneys can be clothed by rainbows 'in a strange transfiguring beauty'. It contains different mixtures, of 'purity, gentleness, and unselfishness' as well as 'griping worldliness, vanity, ostrich-feathers and the fumes of brandy' (Ch. 2). The biblical vocabulary intruded into such vivid accounts suggests a humanised Christian ethic rather than the pietism to be found in temperance tracts. And Mr Tryan's ministry to Janet, which is crucial to her cure, depends not on other-worldly doctrine, but on fellow-feeling. He confides to her that he too has something on his conscience: the suicide of a young girl, Lucy, who had left her father's home for him at College and then gone off 'with a gentleman' while he himself was on vacation (Ch. 18).[11] He has managed to live with his guilt by working to rescue others of life's failures, of whom Janet is clearly one. The narrator stresses the importance of personal contact in the steadying of Janet's character: when ideas are 'clothed in a living human soul with all its conflicts ... and shake us like a passion ... we are drawn after them with gentle compulsion, as flame is drawn to flame' (Ch. 19). The fire imagery, used again after Janet overcomes the temptation to relapse, when Tryan's prayer sustains her, 'as the broad tongue of flame carries upwards in its vigorous leap the little flickering fire that could hardly keep alight by itself' (Ch. 25), connotes here human warmth and supportiveness, which are accorded in this story a kind of mysterious energy. If the tone of 'Janet's Repentance' seems sometimes too earnest, it is no doubt because of the sensitivity of the subject and the difficulties of identifying the appropriate therapy.

In a brisker narrative Janet might have married her rescuer, but, as it is, with both Tryan and Dempster dead, she has to cope on her own, consolidating her self-conquest by adopting one of her husband's relatives as her daughter, who eventually brings her grandchildren, so filling the 'fatal blank' which childlessness had made in Janet's life. These particulars of her case are recorded in the tale rather as the 'large store' of neighbours' personal details are noted down by old Mr Jerome, the wealthy non-polemical Dissenter. Jerome, the possessor of a paradisiacal garden, carefully targets his charity on the actual needs of individuals, such as a horse or a mangle, and this helps them to stand on their own feet, without becoming dependent on parish welfare. Jerome's view of poor relief is that 'the parish shillins turn it sour'; and his to Janet, we are told, are 'truthful lips' (Ch. 26). It is precisely the sight of Jerome with his granddaughter that turns Janet's own thoughts to adoption, so there can be little doubt that his social role as operator of an informed benevolence is presented as exemplary, its principles even being applied by the heroine herself.

'The Lifted Veil' (published anonymously in 1859) is framed, on the other hand, as a warning. It presents a terrifying situation, in which there is no trust at all to fill up 'the margin of ignorance which surrounds all our knowledge' ('Janet's Repentance', Ch. 22). Instead there is unnatural mistrust; there are thought-readings, second sight, visions of the future and revivification of the dead by blood-transfusion, all revealing horrible truths, all pessimistic prophecies of the self-fulfilling kind. George Eliot herself called it 'a slight story of an outré kind—not a *jeu d'esprit*, but a *jeu de melancholie*'.[12] Written in the first person, it maintains throughout its two chapters the confessional note. The narrator, Latimer, is of a sensitive, unpractical nature, educated yet neither a scientist nor a poet; he has 'the poet's sensibility without his voice' (Ch. 1). We might feel that his supernatural insight into the future and into other people's minds aligns him more with the novelist than the poet, but, with a physique formed for passive suffering, he lacks the energy to write anything down, except for his last-minute apologia, which is the tale.

To add to his misfortune, Latimer falls in love with an even harder egoist than himself, Bertha, his brother's fiancée. Conscious of her negative nature, he foresees that she would prove a malevolent wife, but still marries her. He completely lacks religion, hope or sympathy, being conscious that other people's spoken words are 'like leaflets covering a fermenting heap' of frivolities, puerilities, meanness, caprices and 'indolent makeshift thoughts' (Ch. 1). Eventually he loses his telepathic gift, living instead 'continually in my own solitary failure' and fearful of the presence of 'something unknown and pitiless' (Ch. 2). That this intimation refers to his wife's intention to poison him has to be supplied by the reader, for the experiment of the talking corpse which leads to Bertha's exposure would have been unnecessary had Latimer foreseen it. The morbidity of 'The Lifted Veil' may have been a necessary release in which George Eliot could briefly explore a world where her usual moral aspirations are denied, but it also affords evidence of her willingness to evoke horrified curiosity over possibilities on the frontiers of science, and is not without entertainment value. She did not acknowledge it as her own until 1877 when it appeared in the Cabinet edition of her works.

'Brother Jacob' (written in 1860, published in 1864) is overtly comical in a sardonic way. Henry James called its central character, David Faux 'an admirable picture of unromantic malfeasance'.[13] This rogue, who prospers for some time under another identity after stealing his mother's money, takes on a particularly ludicrous persona in becoming a confectioner, skilled in fleecing his customers. He is, in fact, so unscrupulous and disloyal as to earn the narrator's contempt for his poor spelling, sallow complexion and self-congratulatory 'active mind' (Ch. 1). Nemesis for David takes the unexpected form of his idiot brother Jacob, a genuine 'innocent', representing that incalculable element in human relations which schemers and cheats are liable to ignore. Jacob helps to expose David's real background just when he is about to marry into respectable Grimworth society. Since he has violated the sanctities of family life by robbing his mother, manipulating his handicapped brother and disappearing abroad without sending them a word until he has a chance to claim a legacy, he can hardly make excuses; 'he smiled a ghastly smile' (Ch. 3). The contradictions in David Faux's other role as a genteel suitor give rise to some of George Eliot's most comical writing: 'His views on marriage were not entirely sentimental but were as duly mingled with considerations of what would be advantageous to a man in his position as if he had had a very large amount of money spent on his education'. The piquancy extends to the analysis of the confectioner's progress in business. A 'special commercial organ' is developed for the production of mince pies, which takes that work out of the hands of 'maids and matrons in private families', where it had traditionally flourished in primitive simplicity. This introduction of 'neck-and-neck trading' into Grimworth, a town not used to 'small profits and quick returns', does not bring the immediate general benefit that some economists might have predicted. The women are not set free 'to add to the wealth of society in some other way', but remain idle, constrained by lack of alternative training and, it goes without saying, by social prejudice against women as entrepreneurs. The confectioner is almost the sole beneficiary; the specialisation does not function as 'the inevitable course of civilization, division of labour, and so forth' (Ch. 2). Rarely does George Eliot write as caustically of greed and its ramifications as in this short story.

Silas Marner (1861) is in some ways mellower, yet certain of the preoccupations of 'Brother Jacob' are carried over into it: theft, deception, exile and prejudice, for example. It was included with 'The Lifted Veil' and 'Brother Jacob' in a single volume in 1877, and, though longer than them, definitely falls into the category of short fiction. Many of its scenes are treated very economically; there are only a few didactic asides. We know it was very rapidly composed.[14] Even where the narrative pace is leisurely, as with the Rainbow Inn scene (Ch. 6), suspense is heightened by leaving Silas Marner at the bar door at the end of the previous chapter, about to make a shattering announcement, which does not occur until chapter 7, a technique also found in Scott. The narrative soon hurries on, conveying us to the next morning with the whole village already 'excited by the story of the robbery' (Ch. 8). The varied speed with which these strange events are covered, occurring among slow-thinking, untutored inhabitants of obscure places in old times, is curiously skilful.

The narrator also deliberately evokes the primitive and the legendary. Weaving was, in fact, an 'indispensable' trade at that period, but weavers, 'alien-looking men', bent under mysterious burdens and resembling 'the remnants of a disinherited race', are invested with a quality of weirdness.[15] Silas Marner himself, his 'dreadful stare' and 'pale face' associated with his liability to cataleptic fits (Ch. 1), has a dimension of grotesquerie which he never entirely loses. His looks remain against him. His has been a 'strange history', dependent on luck, even when things have gone well for him. The crucial event is the replacement of the stolen gold with the golden-haired infant girl, whom he is able to adopt. The naivety of the characters helps to mediate the sense of the marvellous. Education has no role to play in *Silas Marner*. Even the philosophic narrator, who can point out, for example, that the unwept death of Eppie's mother, 'which, to the general lot, seemed as trivial as the summer-shed leaf, was charged with the force of destiny to certain human lives' (Ch. 14), often effaces herself to let the quaint minds of the story learn and teach their own lessons, which are moral and humble.

Silas Marner and his village friend Dolly Winthrop agree that the proper deduction from their experiences is that they should trust in the unseen good which in due course brings out 'the rights' of things and secures for people the gift of family loyalty: 'Since the time the child was sent to me and I've come to love her as myself, I've had light enough to trusten by' (Ch. 21). This belief in a Providence which caters for loving relations is a kind of Wordsworthian wise passiveness, and suffices too for Nancy Cass, who accepts that there must be some 'high reason' for her childlessness (Ch. 17), as also for the trusting marital relationship which she enjoys with Godfrey; she advises her husband to resign himself 'to the lot that's been given us' (Ch. 20). Such limited understanding is again observed to be sufficient for personal happiness in the matter of Silas's refusal to improve his domestic conveniences by the addition of a grate and oven; 'he loved the old brick hearth as he had loved his brown pot—and was it not there when he had found Eppie? The gods of the hearth exist for us still; and let all new faith be tolerant of that fetishism, lest it bruise its own roots' (Ch. 16). But to be tolerant of beliefs which express a generally defensive optimism is not to endorse them as explanatory myths.[16] Nancy Cass's refusal to adopt children and, more unobtrusively, Silas Marner's disinclination to marry are unendorsed.

A faith of which the narrator of *Silas Marner* is disapproving is reliance on luck or the taking or risks by gambling on an undeserved stroke of good fortune. The Cass family in the first part of the tale is particularly prone to this form of pretentiousness. The father's interest in cock-fighting doubtless depends on the excitement of betting; the uncle's disgust when the luck turns against him at cards extends to a world 'where such things could happen' (Ch. 13); the son Dunsey's reliance on his own luck ('you must keep me by you for your crooked sixpence') lands him literally in the pit, dead; and his elder brother Godfrey's preference for trusting to 'casualties' rather than to 'his own resolve' (Ch. 13) results in his missing his one chance of the love of a child of his own. Favourable chance *may*, of course, resolve difficulties which have been occasioned by shirking and shortcomings, but to 'worship' it is to invite disaster (Ch. 9). Life contains both laws of consequences and random events. Marner's cataleptic fits occur unpredictably, allowing, for example, William Dane to cheat him with impunity, but also the infant child to reach the shelter of his house. Molly's death was predictable, but its location near Silas's cottage, was not. The coincidence enabled Godfrey to conceal his first marriage from Nancy and Silas to gain a new purpose for living. Events may seem to turn out right in the end, but the poetic justice felt by some readers as gratuitous[17] is actually not total. Nancy could be wished better luck than a childless marriage, as her sister Priscilla indicates fairly (Conclusion), and William Dane deserved to be tracked down and exposed. Life's complexities appear in these ragged edges which the formula of the neatly-ended plot cannot contain.

Though the story of *Silas Marner* encompasses both pathos and sentiment, the tone can be unsparing when it comes to the faults of our 'rural forefathers', those flushed and dull-eyed people without the 'higher sensibility that accompanies higher culture' (Ch. 13). There is a radical undertone in the presentation of the squirearchy and the backward pre-industrial village which brings the story closer to Crabbe than to George Eliot's favourite Goldsmith. Henry James's admiration for the display of the 'grossly material life of agriculture England' in the days of 'full-orbed Toryism' in *Silas Marner* is justified.[18] Even Dolly Winthrop, with her refusal to 'speak ill o' this world' in case she offends the powers above, lets slip that 'if there is any good to be got, we've need on it i' this world—that we have' and adds 'what wi' the drink, and the quarrelling, and the bad illnesses, and the hard dying, as I've seen times and times, one's thankful to hear of a better' (Ch. 10). The story cannot, therefore, be truly said to be 'comfortably'[19] set among squires and weavers in the 'rich central plain' of England; it is set rather in 'what we are pleased to call Merry England' (Ch. 1), and that includes places characterised by inefficient farming and social immobility.

The exercise of authority based on land-ownership is noted with much harsher sarcasm in *Silas Marner* than in *Adam Bede*. The whole Cass family is sharply portrayed. The men's weaknesses are traced to an inner and outer cause, the lack of a presiding female presence at the Red House and their unchallenged assumption of superiority, with resulting casualness, indecisiveness and treachery. The New Year dance scene brings a shift of perspective. It is the first scene presented through a female consciousness, that of Nancy Lammeter. We are drawn to Nancy through her concern for her less pretty sister and through the malice of the two town-bred Miss Gunns, who regard her dialectal speech as vulgar and her dispensing with servants as a form of ignorance. When the narrator tell us that Nancy 'had the essential attributes of a lady, high veracity, delicate honour in her dealings, deference to others, and refined personal habits' (Ch. 11), she is successfully protecting the character's virtue against snobbery, that of the Miss Gunns. But Godfrey Cass cannot be protected from the snobbery to which he himself contributes. The class barrier thus erected proves too high for Godfrey to cross at the end. Yet the 'hereditary ease and dignity' of the Cass family is for Godfrey 'a sort of reason for living' (Ch. 3); and Dunsey Cass, whose dull mind is stimulated only by cupidity, is still to be thought of as a 'young gentleman', to whom walking is a bewilderingly unwanted 'mode of locomotion' (Ch. 4). Snobbery is perhaps hardly the word for the unquestioning arrogance of these Cass men, who are used to 'parish homage' (Ch. 9). The squire believes he has 'the hereditary duty of being noisily jovial' (Ch. 11), yet despite his self-possession and authoritativeness of voice, he is indecisive in handling his sons, following faulty indulgence with 'sudden fits of unrelentingness' (Ch. 8). In view of Godfrey's own moral weakness in not acknowledging his child when it turns up ('he had only conscience and heart enough to make him for ever uneasy under the weakness that forbade the renunication', Ch. 13, the renunciation of Nancy Lammeter, that is), his emergence sixteen years later as squire himself, one of Silas Marner's 'betters', those 'tall, powerful, florid men, seen chiefly on horseback', is highly ironic. His daughter's preference for 'working folks, and their houses, and their ways' (Ch. 19) strikes us as perfectly understandable after what we have read,[20] quite apart from her affection for Aaron. Godfrey Cass's view of what is good for his daughter is vitiated by his sense of social superiority; he has the unjustifiable impression 'that deep affections can hardly go along with callous palms and scant means' (Ch. 17). His punishment is to fear that Eppie thinks him worse than he is; she may suspect him of having acted unjustly towards her mother (Ch. 20). But Eppie, wishing to hold to her own, is not critical of class deference as such. The 'charter of Raveloe' which the New Year's Eve dance at the Red House seems to renew, confirming the social hierarchy—'what everyone had been used to' (Ch. 11)—is not to be challenged by her. The character who comes nearest to questioning the system of hereditary privilege is Aaron. When Eppie baulks at having lavender in her planned garden for the characteristic reason that lavender is to be found only in 'gentlefolks' gardens', Aaron points out that cut slips of it are just thrown away, a fact which sets him thinking about the more equal distribution of goods in society; 'there need nobody run short o' victuals if the land was made the most on, and there was never a morsel but what could find its way to a mouth' (Ch. 16). At a time when communications were so poor, such radical thought remains 'untravelled' (Ch. 1), left in the air, as it were. The possibility of organised political protest is perhaps glanced at in the sight of men and women streaming from a large factory 'for their mid-day meal' which meets Silas and Eppie instead of the old Lantern Yard chapel and its familiar surroundings, now 'all swept away', when they visit the northern manufacturing town years after he had left it. But the main point is still the uninformed state of rural people: we recall that 'those were not days of active inquiry and wide report' (Ch. 13). Poor communications leave Raveloe in its ravelled, tangled state.

But despite its fixed responses and hostility to strangers, the rural community *is* able to offer the disillusioned immigrant Marner a stability which is not available in the town. Significantly, he is able to exercise economic independence in Raveloe, since he is no longer working for a wholesaler-dealer. Too honest to drive 'a profitable trade in charms' and herbal remedies (Ch. 2), he accumulates wealth almost automatically and remains unpersecuted, though at first isolated. The local inability to explain his peculiarities or to suggest a context in which they could have arisen gives him a kind of negative protection, the robbery notwithstanding. When Eppie's needs furnish him with a purpose for earning, he begins to respond more positively to his human surroundings.

Marner's salvation through parenthood is by no means a simple matter, however. His repressed, self-doubting personality retains much of its surprising quality throughout the tale. The special closeness of his friendship with William Dane, which led to the Lantern Yard brethren calling them David and Jonathan may be a clue; it prepares us for his reluctance to attempt to win his fiancée's 'belief in his innocence' (Ch. 1) after the lots point to his supposed guilt. Under the shock of betrayal by his friend, Marner retreats from women into impulsive industriousness as the weaver of Raveloe. In comparing him with the spider at his unrelenting work George Eliot is able to impress us with the *harmlessness* of a figure usually associated with miserliness, with its harmlessness but not exactly with its innocence. He draws out the gold coins 'to enjoy their companionship', bathing his hands in them, and thinks of the half-earned ones 'as if they had been unborn children' (Ch. 2). The gold has fashioned him into correspondence with itself by its 'hard isolation'. The sexual implications of his obsession are specially detectable when he discovers the loss of his gold; he passes 'his trembling hand all about the hole' and shakes 'so violently' that he lets fall his candle (Ch. 5). The point is clinched in the corresponding scene where he fingers the foundling; with his heart beating violently he touches, not 'hard coin with the familiar resisting outline', but 'soft warm curls' (Ch. 12). Marner's insistence that he keep the child comes from a need deep within himself and represents self-recognition. Uttered abruptly 'under a strong sudden impulse', unintended, but like a revelation, the claim refers to himself, a 'lone thing', as he says, partly 'mayed', but able now to relate to another 'lone thing'. The scene in which Godfrey Cass, the real father, watches Silas as he lulls the child combines a Wordsworthian width of view with a psychological force that is George Eliot's own; the child is soothed:

> into that wide gazing calm which makes us older human beings, with our inward turmoil, feel a certain awe in the presence of a little child, such as we feel before some quiet majesty or beauty in the earth or sky—before a steady-glowing planet, or a full-flowered eglantine, or the bending trees over a silent pathway. The wide open blue eyes looked up at Godfrey's without any uneasiness or sign of recognition: the child could make no visible,

audible claim on its father, and the father felt a strange mixture of feelings, a conflict of regret and joy, that the pulse of that little heart had no response for the half-jealous yearning in his own, when the blue eyes turned away from him slowly, and fixed themselves on the weaver's queer face, which was bent low to look at them, while the small hand began to pull Marner's withered cheek with loving disfiguration. (Ch. 13)

The final oxymoron in this passage not only secures the scene from an excess of sensibility, but also establishes the peculiarity of the new situation which is taking shape, the one-parent family with the stepfather in the female role. There are many tactful, supportive touches for Silas Marner's determination to maintain this (for him) liberating role. Dolly Winthrop, for instance, admits, 'I've seen men as are wonderful handy wi' children'. Silas insists on taking full responsibility, on learning the ways of rearing and fending for them both; 'she 'll be *my* little un'. Though Eppie's development brings him new links with his neighbours, with nature, 'with the whole world', it also reinforces his individuality. The reasons why Marner takes Eppie with him on most of his journeys to the farmhouses is not to make new ties, but to keep her out of Dolly's hands; he does not always adhere to Dolly's welcome suggestions. Eppie is brought up on Silas' own system of 'downy patience', not punishment. He bears the burden of her misdeeds 'vicariously' (Ch. 14), a humanist version of the atonement doctrine which allows for indications of the man's psychological satisfaction, but first he even tries to teach her by himself before sending her to a dame school. He does not conceal from Eppie that she is an orphan and adopted, but rears her 'in almost inseparable companionship with himself', a process which yet allows her transfer to the protection of another (Aaron) when time weakens the father's earning capacity: 'I like to think as you'd have somebody else besides me' (Ch. 16). Marner's sincerity here is the proof of his intensity. And Eppie responds in kind, she can own nobody nearer than him: 'We've been used to be happy together every day, and I can't think o' no happiness wi'out him' (Ch. 19). Aaron seems to enter this symbiotic world mainly to see it through to its logical end. The tale ends with 'a peculiar sort of family marriage'[21] in which Dolly stands in temporarily as a partner for Silas to make up 'the four united people' before returning to her actual husband, the wheelwright. Silas has not so much given Eppie away as gained his 'larger family', to accommodate which his property has been improved at Godfrey Cass's expense (Conclusion). The story thus contrives to combine a universally acceptable moral of pure, healing love with a penetrating and tolerant study of a rather unusual character, Silas Marner.

Notes

1. *The Art of the Novel: Critical Prefaces by Henry James*, intro. R. P. Blackmur (New York: Scribners, 1934), p. 233. James states that, with the anecdote, his effort was to follow a 'little situation' from 'its outer edge in, rather than from its centre outward'. See also pp. xxviii–xxix, 181 and 221.

2. *Letters*, vol. II, p. 407. George Eliot's Journal, 6 December 1857.

3. Of Trollope's series of Barchester novels, which present more consistent scenes of clerical life than do George Eliot's tales, only *The Warden* (1855) precedes *Scenes of Clerical Life*.

4. U. C. Knoepflmacher, in *George Eliot's Early Novels: The Limits of Realism* (Berkeley and Los Angeles, Calif.: University of California Press, 1968), p. 56, argues that George Eliot idealises Milly Barton excessively as an 'angelic mate', dropping irony and indirection in favour of hortatory sentimentality. T. A. Noble, whom Knoepflmacher aims to refute, is surely nearer the mark in defending George Eliot's sure 'sense of reality' in this tale's scenes of pathos (see his *George Eliot's Scenes of Clerical Life*, New Haven, Conn.: Yale University Press, 1965, pp. 113–15).

5. George Eliot, *Scenes of Clerical Life*, ed. T. A. Noble (Oxford: Clarendon Press, 1985), p. 9, n. 8.

6. Dianne F. Sadoff, *Monsters of Affection: Dickens, Eliot, and Brontë on Fatherhood* (Baltimore and London: Johns Hopkins University Press, 1982), pp. 66–67. The daughter, encouraged by the dying mother to replace her, 'reaps the structural rewards of familial desire' as substitute wife and housekeeper. Hence George Eliot's first story 'obscures its sexual meaning'. See also S. Marcus, 'Literature and Social Theory: Starting in with George Eliot', in *Representations: Essays on Literature and Society* (New York: Random House, 1975), pp. 183–213.

7. T. A. Noble's view (*op. cit.*, p. 134) that in this tale the 'foreign background seems thrown in simply for glamour and romance' excludes both the humour and the tension which George Eliot derives from the situation of the aristocratic English family's adoption of an alien child, a theme which still exercised her as late as *Daniel Deronda* (1876).

8. 'To a Mouse, On turning her up in her Nest, with the Plough, November, 1785', ll. 7–12.

> I'm truly sorry Man's dominion
> Has broken Nature's social union,
> An' justifies that ill opinion
> Which makes thee startle,
> At me, thy poor, earth-born companion,
> An' *fellow-mortal!*

R. Burns, *Poems, Chiefly in the Scottish Dialect* (Kilmarnock: John Wilson, 1786), pp. 138–39.

9. George Eliot assured her publisher that everything in 'Janet's Repentance' was 'softened from the fact…. The real town was more vicious than my Milby; the real Dempster was far more disgusting than mine', *Letters*, vol. II, p. 347. Letter to John Blackwood, 11 June 1857.

10. The manuscript of 'Janet's Repentance' contains several cancelled and dropped passages, which coarsen the behaviour of the people of Milby in the 1820s and 1830s; e.g. 'Drunkenness was indulged in with great candour' (*ed. cit.*, p. 204). The mitigating effect of the alterations also serves to bring the present and the past closer together in the narrator's implied view.

11. G. H. Lewes (*Letters*, vol. II, p. 378. Lewes's letter to John Blackwood, 23 August 1857) accepted that the story of Tryan's past misdemeanour was a 'hacknied episode'; yet it does explain Tryan's ability to make what T. A. Noble calls the 'imaginative identification upon which the fullest sympathy depends' and thus to express 'the practical side of Christian ethics' (*op. cit.*, p. 90).

12. *Letters*, vol. III, p. 41. Letter to John Blackwood, 31 March 1859. K. M. Newton observes that recent George Eliot criticism regards 'The Lifted Veil' as 'an integral part of her *oeuvre* and not as a strange anomaly.' See his *George Eliot* (London: Longman, 1991), pp. 25 and 28, n. 40.

13. Henry James, review of 'George Eliot's Newly Published Tales', i.e. 'The Lifted Veil' and 'Brother Jacob', *The Nation*, XXVI (25 April 1878) p. 277, reprinted in A. Mordell (ed.), *Literary Reviews and Essays by Henry James* (New York: Grove Press, 1957), p. 291. James Diedrick discerns the influence of German novellas like Gottfried Keller's in the grotesque images and 'detached and harshly ironic style' of 'Brother Jacob', which in its turn anticipates the presentation of Gwendolen Harleths's 'grotesque alter-egos' in *Daniel Deronda*; see his 'George Eliot's Experiments in Fiction: "Brother Jacob" and the German *Novella*', *Studies in Short Fiction*, vol. XXII (Fall 1985), pp. 464 and 468.

14. *Letters*, vol. III, p. 371. Letter to J. Blackwood, 12 January 1861; the story came across other plans 'by a sudden inspiration'; it was finished in four months, *ibid.*, p. 387. Letter to John Blackwood, 11 March 1861. Several critics have commented on the economy of means in the composition of *Silas Marner*. R. Speight, in *George Eliot* (London: Arthur Barker, 1954), p. 66, says, 'one feels that she has put into it exactly the right weight of writing', and L. Haddakin, in 'Silas Marner', in B. Hardy (ed.), *Critical Essays on George Eliot* (London: Routledge & Kegan Paul, 1970), p. 64, remarks, 'when you turn back to the book itself you are surprised by its brevity'.

15. John Blackwood, George Eliot's publisher, reported a conversation which he had had with her shortly after *Silas Marner* was published, in which she said that the work had sprung 'from her childish recollection of a man with a stoop and expression of face that led her to think that he was an alien from his fellows', *Letters*, vol. III, p. 427. John Blackwood's letter to Mrs John Blackwood, 15 June 1861.

16. Still the most severe analysis of George Eliot's underlying theme in *Silas Marner* is Richard Simpson's in 'George Eliot's Novels', *Home and Foreign Review*, III (October 1863), pp. 522–49. He argued that the tale contained an ironic apology for Providence in a 'specious defence of the truth' which was achieved by 'planting opinions' which George Eliot wished to eradicate. The irony consists in 'making Marner's conversion depend altogether on human sympathies and love, while he, simple fellow, fails to see the action of the general law of humanity, and attributes every thing to the "dealings" which regulate the accidents', p. 529. See D. Carroll (ed.), *George Eliot: The Critical Heritage* (London: Routledge & Kegan Paul, 1971), p. 229.

17. David Cecil, arguing that there is 'no inherent reason in the nature of things why a morally-feeble man should not beget twenty children', regards Godfrey Cass's discontent as 'a gratuitious piece of poetic justice imposed on him by the arbitrary will of his creator'. *Early Victorian Novelists: Essays in Revaluation* (London: Constable, 1934), p. 323.

18. Henry James, 'The Novels of George Eliot', *Atlantic Monthly*, vol. XVIII (October 1866), p. 482.

19. The suggestion of I. Taylor in her *George Eliot: Woman of Contradictions* (London: Weidenfeld and Nicolson, 1989), p. 175.

20. Q. D. Leavis in her wide-ranging introduction to the Penguin English Library edition of *Silas Marner* (Harmondsworth: Penguin, 1967) stresses George Eliot's 'complete emancipation from restrictive ideas of class' as well as her penetrating criticisms of its causes and manifestations. When the Casses retire helpless and humiliated in Ch. 19, Q. D. Leavis goes so far as to say 'we feel impelled to cheer', pp. 32–33. Sally Shuttleworth in 'Fairy Tale or Science? Physiological Psychology in *Silas Marner*', in *Languages of Nature: Critical Essays on Science and Literature*, ed. L. Jordanova (London: Free Association Books, 1986), pp. 250–88, argues that George Eliot is 'far from confirming organicist theories of social or economic development' in *Silas Marner*, 'yet requires an image of essential social order' to show Silas and Eppie as 'participants in an integrated community' at the close; hence it is a 'fundamentally divided' text, pp. 273 and 285.

21. L. C. Emery, in *George Eliot's Creative Conflict: The Other Side of Silence* (Berkeley and Los Angeles, Calif.: University of California Press, 1976), p. 71; she finds in the ending evidence of a disguised Oedipal wish with Silas perhaps representing 'the return of the repressed', p. 77.

HENRY ALLEY

Silas Marner *and the Anonymous Heroism of Parenthood*

Since Henry James, critics have seen *Silas Marner* as the culmination of a phase.[1] At the same time, however, it signals the beginning of Eliot's closer examination of how traditionally masculine and feminine traits might be successfully combined and how such a combination might lead to the proper raising of children who, in turn, would also acquire the balance. In the fiction that precedes *Silas Marner*, George Eliot dramatizes intense conflicts between the sexes, between husband and wife, brother and sister, lover and lover. The corollary to this struggle is an effort, on the part of the protagonists, to develop, side by side, both male and female characteristics within themselves; feminine susceptibility must be complemented by male detachment. But in all cases, the tradition of heroic chivalry, with its attendant evils of predominance and subordination, is exchanged for a newer, more freeing vision. There are precursors to Silas, in Mr. Irwine of *Adam Bede*, with his quiet attendance to his family and his flock, Mr. Tryan of *Scenes of Clerical Life*, and in Philip Wakem, who "nursed," as U. C. Knoepflmacher puts it, "Maggie's internal conflicts" (*George Eliot's Early Novels*, 228).

Maggie's struggles alone dramatize the desire to defy convention and acquire that worldliness normally reserved for polite gentlemen. Eliot offers no sustained resolution until, paradoxically, we reach the even remoter world of Raveloe, where Silas must become both mother and father to Eppie, and

From *The Quest for Anonymity: The Novels of George Eliot.* © 1997 by Associated University Presses, Inc.

embody, as a character, the education that in *The Mill on the Floss* was reserved for the reader alone. In this sense, *Silas Marner* could be called an idyll, in exactly the way Freidrich von Schiller defined the form, one which holds all in a "dynamic calm" (146) and yet "display[s] that pastoral innocence even in creatures of civilization and under all the conditions of the most active and vigorous life" (153). In the spirit of the pastoral, *Silas Marner* charms away tensions that, in the more conventionally realistic works, would have led to tragic consequences[2], and the novel also prepares the way for the larger inner solutions which the four works of Eliot's later phase were to explore.

Implicitly and with an understatedness that has been frequently praised, *Silas Marner* shows how the enlightened raising of children—a part of the "active and vigorous life"—crucially depends on the balancing of male and female within the parent. In this case, the competent father is the man who can be both protective and sympathetic, who can know the value of the single-minded masculine world which provides one's bread and yet can withstand the challenges of being "moithered" (180)[3] in the female world of sustenance and care. Conversely, the antihero is the displaced father, the man, who, for one reason or another, fails to heed the call to develop his nurturing powers. For thematic emphasis, Eliot makes this foil the natural father, in contrast to the true father who has acquired the role through patient performance and love. In achieving the wider vision, which leads, ultimately, to anonymous heroism, one father succeeds and the other fails. Jennifer Uglow, when writing of this challenge, says that "the two men are therefore tested by the way they respond to an inarticulate plea in the shock of the moment" (154).

In *Silas Marner*, the covenant between apparent opposites[4] is made obtainable to those who are willing to be humble and teachable. This is true not only of the covenant between man and woman but also between past and present, individual and society—and the man and woman within the self. The iconographic symbol of Oedipus and Antigone at Colonus, which, as mentioned earlier, perhaps best explains this kind of union, also unites the three-novel sequence of *The Mill on the Floss*, *Silas Marner*, and *Romola*. Each presents a father who loses power and must endure his daughter's guidance— an experience which, paradoxically, strengthens him and makes him a new sort of parent. Such a yielding and such a renewal of energy are critical to our understanding of both the biographical Marian Evans, who saw the nursing of her father as a "worship for mortals" (*Letters* 1: 284) and the literary George Eliot, who offers an ideal of parental balance. In her novels, it is only through such a symbiosis of dependency and independence that the child herself can grow into power. In writing to Blackwood concerning the proofing of *Silas Marner* (3: 398), Eliot was particularly vehement about "quite the worst error," a one-letter misprint in Eppie's vehement retort to Godfrey: "And it'd be poor work for me to put on things, and ride in a gig, and sit in a place at church as 'ud make them as I'm fond of think me unfitting company for 'em. What could *I* care for then?" (234). The printer had put in "them" just before the question mark—which shifted the whole meaning away to the finer "things." What the one letter correction meant was exactly this: if Eppie could not care for the covenant that she and Silas-Aaron-Dolly embodied, she would not have the power to care for anything.

While a number of critics have pointed out the balance of male and female as an ideal in the novel, we have yet to see, closely and in a most explicit way, how Eliot introduces the concept of anonymity, as obtained through this bridging of the genders, which is in turn symbolic of Silas's reentry into the community as a whole. At the opening of the novel proper, Silas is seen as traditionally masculine and bound, by work, to his loom. As he grows through the child, however, he learns to see himself as a mother as well and as an anonymous contributor to the world as a whole.

Surely this transformation does not occur overnight. Prior to his coming to Raveloe, Silas is presented as a reformulation of Philip Wakem, struggling to preserve a sensibility that is more feminine than masculine. Paralleling the Philip-Tom friendship, Silas's adoration of William Dane (William Waif in the original manuscript) gives way to "strong," "masculine" defensiveness once the initial trust is broken.[5] It is as though Silas perceived William as the waif who needed both love and worship, and then underwent a kind of dreadful disillusionment of motherhood. Unlike Philip, however, Silas is given time to recover and to recover the lost side of himself. After secluding himself away, Silas learns to trust men once more, once he has discovered that his reputation is less important than his anonymous dedication to what he holds dear.

The dramatic metamorphosis occurs through Silas's recollections of his mother and sister. The William Dane crisis, combined with the zeal of Lantern Yard, causes him, initially, to discard his mother's "bequest" (57) of healing herbal knowledge and dedicate his life to the invulnerable loom. When Eppie suddenly appears on his hearth, however, we witness a return to the "remedial"[6] memories of his mother and what he knew of her in his sister:

> Could this be his little sister come back to him in a dream—his little sister whom he had carried about in his arms for a year before she died, when he was a small boy without shoes or stockings? (168)

Thus, *Silas Marner* is not simply the story of a withered man whose wounded sensibility is restored through love of a child but the story of an incomplete man, one as incomplete as Philip Wakem or Tom Tulliver, whose female self is reawakened through the raising of a daughter. It is important to note, as David Carroll does (*Silas Marner*, 153), that Eppie enters through "the chasm in his consciousness" (ch. 12, 167). Thus Silas undergoes a complete loss of self before embracing the female part of himself. This change, symbolized by the catalepsy, shows Silas letting go of his egoistic concerns and welcoming not only Eppie but his little sister, who passed away, and who was the only one, most likely, who appreciated and acknowledged his heroic tenderness. The memory of boyhood returns to Silas with the point that whatever credit he received for his efforts as a brother, came from an unseen Good, one closely linked with Dolly's higher "Them." The two "chasms of consciousness" which preceded this inner revolution have, of course, been the perfect preparation. Silas had to lose his good standing at Lantern Yard as well as his Raveloe treasure trove before he could secure the anonymous heroism which would secure Eppie.

Eppie, then, must be named for Silas's mother and sister, since she draws together those memories of womanly care and healing that are to be the wellspring of the life of the present and are to be the models for this special form of parenthood. If Hepzibah means "my delight in her," surely Silas is delighting in the new fullness of his psyche as well as in Eppie herself and in a world no longer connected with trophies and recognition.

Once Silas begins attending to Eppie and his mind starts "growing into memory," he also recalls his mother's lore and looks "for the once familiar herbs again" (ch. 14, 185).[7] The search is made possible also because Silas has given up his own resentment over the Salley Oates incident, an incident that had involved, once again, a concern with reputation and external recognition. With his new goals of motherhood and anonymous heroism, he is able to transcend a sulky disposition and move on to the very thing that symbolizes an enlightened pity and therefore his own regeneration. Jennifer Uglow writes that "they [the herbs] become part of his own healing, knitting together his broken spirit and soothing his wounded memory" (152).

Silas's psychic change is heightened, or better, facilitated, by the frequently noted fairytale quality of the Raveloe society. Often in Eliot, modernization can be seen to hasten the tensions between man and woman—as if to move through time were to advance further and further from an Edenic sexual harmony. Thus Raveloe, although remote and out of date, encourages Silas not only in his adoption of Eppie but also in his pursuit of the dual roles that must come with it. We are in an ideal world where the past easily connects with the present and the ways of woman harmonize with the ways of man, even in the halves of a single nature. On the other side of the universe is St. Ogg's, where all exists in division. Maggie cannot connect the world of the fabled past with her present and therefore cannot unite conflicting characteristics within herself. Although Silas makes some of the same errors as Maggie, as well as those of Tom and Philip, redemption arrives for him—and speedily—because in Raveloe, the past is always restorative, and its bearing upon the present is readily felt:

> The thoughts were strange to him now, like old friendships impossible to revive; and yet he had a dreamy feeling that this child was somehow a message come to him from that far-off life: it stirred fibres that had never been moved in Raveloe—old quiverings of tenderness—old impressions of awe at the presentiment of some Power presiding over his life; for him imagination had not yet extricated itself from the sense of mystery in the child's sudden presence, and had formed no conjectures of ordinary natural means by which the event could have been brought about. (ch. 12, 168)

Unlike many of Eliot's protagonists, Silas finds the powers of memory to be completely at his disposal as he reenters society. The past returns with ease and leads directly to a sense of rightness and devotion. Just as Raveloe, with its powerful traditions, has no trouble connecting the past with the present, so Silas, in belonging to its charmed context, can reach, almost effortlessly, that part of his personal history which he most requires. As Silas recovers his old affections for his mother and sister, as well as his compassionate religious zeal, he becomes the tender boy "without shoes or stockings" again, and therefore, motherlike, can press Eppie to him "and almost unconsciously [offer] hushing tenderness" (168). He is no longer "himself" because he has lost his identity to a universal parenthood, and because of this change, his anxiety over whether the old "Silas" will survive on his gold disappears. He is on his own way to achieving anonymous heroism because he has embraced a faith in the unseen. The moment of change is altogether convincing since we are in a novel of charmed psychological transformation, where error, though still possible, can be rectified or bypassed at the right moment.

At the same time, however, Silas's growth into a special brand of "motherhood"[8] does not loosen his hold on the world of masculine work, and it is as if Eliot wishes to emphasize the point that her protagonist stays simultaneously in both worlds. As Gillian Beer writes, "Silas is a weaver, deliberately set *across* the stereotype of the woman weaving" (126, emphasis hers). The subsequent conflict is small, however, since, in Raveloe, as opposed to St. Ogg's, harmony is also possible between traditionally male and female duties. In doing what is surprising for a man, Silas elicits the sympathy of the community:

> Silas Marner's determination to keep the "tramp's child" was matter of hardly less surprise and iterated talk in the village than the robbery of his money. That softening of feeling towards him which dated from his misfortune, that merging of suspicion and dislike in a rather contemptuous pity for him as lone and crazy, was now accompanied with a more active sympathy, especially amongst the women. (ch. 14, 178)

The mothers' representative is, of course, Dolly Winthrop, but in an important way, she takes Raveloe's eccentricity one step further in denying the supposedly impassable gulf between masculine labor and childrearing. Although some critics might argue that mother figures are conspicuously missing from the novel—and therefore Eliot is once again concentrating solely on the transformed male, while ignoring the psychically balanced woman—Dolly should be seen as a distinct reply. She also is an anonymous hero because she acknowledges the delicacy and the challenge of the tasks facing Silas. Frequently she encourages and often embodies the many strong "masculine" attributes which enable Silas to earn his bread while raising Eppie at the same time. Like Mr. Irwine of *Adam Bede*, she suggests a heroic perception and breadth of vision which the other characters must quest for until the novel is finished. Thus, it makes sense that she is, in some ways, the commander, advisor, and teacher of the protagonist. In the dialogue of chapter 14, while the difficulties of combining childrearing with the pursuit of one's trade are always acknowledged, compromises are found: the rather alarming prospect of leashing Eppie to the loom so as to keep her from hurting herself is balanced by Dolly's proposal of "my little chair, and some bits o' red rag and things for her to play wi'; an' she'll sit and chatter to 'em as if they was alive" (181). This exchange between Dolly and Silas, along with the solution of prospective conflict in roles, foreshadows, crucially, the novel's ultimate harmonizing of both male and female and also shows a mutual celebration of what no exterior point of view could appreciate.

During Silas's subsequent raising of Eppie, the difficult balance between severity and permissiveness, so elusive to the parent is, once again, achievable. Eppie is not spoiled because psychology serves the idyllic laws of the pastoral. Eppie can grow into perfection, even while her doting father lacks the will of the conventional male to discipline her. Because Eppie is loved, with a father's true, balanced love, she can grow into the best of children:

> Perfect love has a breath of poetry which can exalt the relations of the least-instructed human beings; and this breath of poetry had surrounded Eppie from the time she had followed the bright gleam that had beckoned her to Silas' hearth; so that it is not surprising if, in other things besides her delicate prettiness, she was not quite a common village maiden, but had a touch of refinement and fervour which came from no other teaching than that of tenderly nurtured unvitiated feeling. (ch. 16, 206)

Thus, even though "Eppie was reared without punishment" (189), there is to be no ensuing nemesis, as there is in the history of Gwendolen Harleth, since in Raveloe, making the child the center of attention cannot lead to problems. It is poetry that dominates the life of Silas and his adopted daughter.

Surely Eliot had this in mind when writing her often-quoted letter concerning the composition of the novel. "I have felt," she wrote, "all through as if the story would have lent itself best to metrical rather than prose fiction, especially in all that relates to the psychology of Silas" (*Letters* 3: 382). Not only is the psychological transformation of Silas a charmed process, as in a verse romance or idyll, but so are the effects: love, even doting love, is beneficent without qualification. In the "Notes on Form in Art," which was quoted earlier, Eliot speaks of "rhythms & images" forming a "natural history of mind" (435). Here the meter of the changing idyllic landscape lays before us the unique and dynamic process of Silas's male and female mind, as well as its quest toward the anonymous heroism of parenthood. Healing is made visible and believable through a dense imagery and rhythmic sentences that invoke a protected but poetically heightened world—in this case, in a prose context. We will see this again when Eliot adapts another German poet and playwright—Goethe—to the healing medium of the novel *Middlemarch*.

Although Silas's case seems to be the special one, the one reserved for a "legendary" world rather than a realistic one, Eliot is quite consistent in fulfilling Schiller's call for a work that could be idealized and yet apply to the actual world of the reader.[9] The strategy is multiple; it is achieved first through a series of direct editorial links, between Silas's experience and the experience of "modernday" people; it is achieved, by extension, through the negative example of Godfrey Cass. Also the peculiarity of Silas's case presents a balance. He belongs and yet does not belong, and he is given a variety of suggested identities, with which the reader might possibly identify; he is compared to an artist, a storyteller,[10] and a scholar. The resulting bridge[11] means that Raveloe itself has a more realistic presence than, say, Sidney's Arcadia or even Austen's Highbury. David Carroll, in writing of *Silas Marner's* double nature as both tale and novel, captures again this tenuous balance, saying that "the reader is constantly being reminded that amidst the fictional complexity there is a simple story with its own narrative logic" (*George Eliot and the Conflict of Interpretations*, 141), so that both magic and narrative explanation of the fictional "reality" are accepted.

Silas's example, of course, becomes most applicable to the reader's experience when he tries to become both mother and father to Eppie. By contrast, Godfrey Cass heightens the achievement, when he proves unable to follow his more vulnerable instincts. Unlike Silas, who has distinct memories of a mother and sister to guide him, Godfrey has only "an essentially domestic nature" (ch. 3, 81)—which another family, the Lammeters, must work to save. Thus, at the crucial[12] moment, Godfrey condemns and isolates himself, making Silas's sympathetic response all the more desirable—much more so than the original scheme proposed by Eliot, the isolated "metrical" treatment, devoid of contrast, would have done. Like Arthur Donnithorne and Adam Bede in his initial phases, Godfrey stands as the rejected heroic model. He has all the trappings of a "big muscular frame" (76), but, consistent with Eliot's sustained irony, he is not yielding enough to rise to the level of true heroism, and he is too concerned with what reputation will bring in order to come close to anything like true parenthood.

With the force of a musical recapitulation, chapter 19 holds important links with the opening of the book, dramatizing Silas initially in crisis "when the keenness of the susceptibility makes external stimulus intolerable" (225). Silas then defeats the crisis and defends his right of parenthood in a combined effort to keep his dual sensibility whole and yet counter Godfrey with "a touch of parental fierceness" (231). Godfrey, for his part, clings to his code of proprietorship and represents, quite predictably, the Letter of the Law. It is quite clear that he has started to pursue the title of "father" in a mechanical and conventionally masculine attempt to head off the anonymity of dying without an identified heir. If the child is father to the man, then in Wordsworthian terms, this scene shows Godfrey to be morally illegitimate.[13]

In the heated debate between the father-by-blood and the father-by-love, we expect Silas to be more awkward and less articulate than he is, and we are pleasantly surprised to find the true parent winning even on Godfrey's argumentative territory. The full force of this scene depends partly on the reader's dawning awareness of the extent of Silas's growth. Eppie surprises as well, in her moving reply to Godfrey's offer, showing herself the rightful heir to the transformed Silas, a protector of his anonymous heroism, in full line with the role that Dolly Winthrop has served all along: "And he took care of me and loved me from the first" (234). In making this affirmation directly to her legal father, she proves, more than could any shy country maiden, to be a true integrater also of masculine and feminine ways. Consistent with the power shift that Eliot was careful to assure in correcting the galley proofs, Eppie's "What could I care for then?" prepares the way for her vision of taking care of Silas: "I've always thought of a little home where he'd sit i' the corner, and I should fend and do everything for him" (234). She will become an unrecognized hero as well. Thus, the scene allows the reader to see Eppie's character in a new light, and as Dianne Sadoff notes, when comparing Silas Marner with Felix Holt, there is a "redemption first of father, then of daughter" (72).

Because Godfrey is the shallower character, he is left to find his equilibrium in a more external way; he must turn to Nancy's feminine wisdom and higher moral nature in order to reach the balance that Silas finds within. In this sense, Silas is, morally, miles ahead of Godfrey, since he sought Dolly's tutelage first and demonstrated the full fruits of his education when the moment came to defend himself and his home. Appropriately, then, Godfrey cannot share in the joy of Eppie and Aaron's wedding, since he has been the absent father during the crucial years of her childhood and adolescence; yet even his salvation can be anticipated in the new peace he finds with Nancy, after the confrontation with Silas.

The "rainbow" at the conclusion of the novel, then, spans the polarity of male and female as it unites symbolically the other crucial opposites that Eliot has dramatized. Presumably, Aaron will live on to sustain Silas's example of the nurturing parent, when he openly declares his plan that his father-in-law live with them. Further, Aaron's being a gardener suggests, symbolically, that he has a caring hand in all matters. Of him, Silas says, "He's his mother's lad" (ch. 16, 209), defying the patriarchal tradition while, ironically, suggesting how much Aaron is like himself. Decidedly he has let go of the self who was an isolated achiever, finding his "living memorial" in another man—and woman. In providing this reconciliation along with the struggle of an ultimately triumphing "legitimate" parent, Eliot has opened up her definition of heroism. For Silas transcends the narrower examples of Dinah Morris, who attended to Hayslope and Stoniton but only with a certain limited piety, and Mr. Irwine, who was large-souled but confined to the outer reaches of the novel. Silas's heroism also transcends *The Mill on the Floss*, where heroism must occur as an implied aggregate of the best qualities of several characters, once the instructive narrator has pointed them out. In *Silas Marner*, heroism is thus discovered to be a revelation of both the male and female nature, as embodied in enlightened parenthood, which seeks no rewards. This is true not only because the old codes of chivalry are emphatically transformed, but also because true heroism exists as a harmony between man and woman within the individual soul, whether of man or woman, and the harmony may be passed on—bequeathed—not as a name but as a nurturing condition. For this reason, the penultimate scene of Eppie attending Silas to the vanished Lantern Yard must overshadow the wedding. It is indeed a reformulation of Antigone helping Oedipus "see" Colonus, but it is also, more generally, a scene of a man letting go of his hard, masculine past that, most fortunately, only temporarily excluded the woman within. He has yielded to the anonymity that has been planned for him. We begin to understand that Silas's catalepsy and "chasm[s] in consciousness" were really only a beneficent forewarning of his growth in soul. Anxiety over individual survival has yielded to faith in a collective identity, and in the tradition which Aaron and Eppie will sustain. Thus, at the end of the novel, when Silas speaks of the mysterious disappearance of Lantern Yard, he ushers in a new code when he says "I doubt it'll be dark to the last."

> "Well, yes, Master Marner," said Dolly, who sat with a placid listening face, now bordered by grey hairs; "I doubt it may. It's the will o'Them above as a many things should be dark to us; but there's somethings as I've never felt i'the dark about, and they're mostly what comes i' the day's work. You were hard done by that once, Master Marner, and it seems as you'll never know the rights of it; but that doesn't hinder there being a rights, Master Marner, for all it's dark to you and me."
>
> "No," said Silas, "no; that doesn't hinder. Since the time the child was sent to me and I've come to love her as myself, I've had light enough to trusten by; and now she says she'll never leave me, I think I shall trusten till I die." (ch. 20, 241)

Surely Dolly's "Them" must acknowledge the deeds of heroism "which have no great name on earth," because they were done for their own sake— in the enlightened dark, so to speak, rather than by the light of external reward, and surely Dolly's "Them" must suggest that the Divine Ones above must be both genders.

NOTES

1. In his characteristically approving-disapproving manner, James writes, "To a certain extent, I think *Silas Marner* holds a higher place than any of the author's works. It is more nearly a masterpiece; it has more that simple,

rounded, consummate aspect, that absence of loose ends and gaping issues, which marks a classical work" (46). F. R. Leavis, clearly following up on James's observation, presents *Silas Marner* as closing "the first phase of George Eliot's creative life" (47).

2. I am indebted to Donald F. Stone, who, in *The Romantic Impulse in Victorian Fiction* (218–20), points out the strong applicability of Schiller's definition.

3. Of this word. Q. D. Leavis writes, "a Midlands and northern dialect word meaning 'broken into very small flakes,' used of breaking up curds and whey if the flakes are small, and hence metaphorically, to mean 'worried', 'bewildered', but with a vivid particularity these words lack, of course" (*Silas*, 262, note 2).

4. U. C. Knoepflmacher tells how, in view of its tensions, *The Mill on the Floss* ends where *Silas Marner* begins, how "Earth and water, fixity and motion, tradition and change, at odds in *The Mill on the Floss*, coalesce with this wanderer's return to the lands denied to Tom and Maggie" (*George Eliot's*, 233).

5. In writing of George Eliot's conception of sympathy, Elizabeth Ermarth notes that it is "Silas's 'trusting simplicity' [that] likewise makes him vulnerable to a rapacious friend" (100).

6. See *Letters* 3: 382.

7. As Brian Swann writes in another study, "Silas Marner and the New Mythus," "Eppie is that striven-for particle Silas lost in his mother and little sister, the feminine part of him" (108).

8. In her article "The Question of Vocation: From *Romola* to *Middlemarch*," Susan M. Greenstein writes, "*Silas Marner* makes clear that not all work is worthy of the sacrifice of the affections or leads to the salvation predicated in the motion of a secular vocation. Silas's labor had to be redeemed and transformed through a service to which it could be subordinated. And the primary form of service in George Eliot is maternal" (502). Although Greenstein goes on to show how Silas's love for Eppie leads "him to stretch his understanding in order to make every maternal effort for her well-being" (502–3), her main point is that the maternal life, in Eliot, is usually at odds with the "nurture of one's genius" (503). *Silas Marner*, however, supplies the appropriate counterexample, as long as "genius" is seen as having certain anonymous properties.

9. See Schiller, *Naive and Sentimental Poetry*, 146.

10. For the artistic comparison, see Knoepflmacher (*George Eliot's*, 257) and Swann, *Silas Marner* (103). The storyteller is suggested in the sentence "he worked far into the night to finish the tale of Mrs. Osgood's tablelinen" (64, punsurely intended).

11. In *George Eliot and Community*, Suzanne Graver writes, "Because Silas begins as an outcast and has a 'strange history,' the narrator carefully solicits our sympathy for uncommon experience but maintains a certain distance between the author and the reader lest the overture become too overbearing" (286–87).

12. Carroll, in his analysis of the parallels between the two men, writes, "George Eliot wants us to locate the crucial difference, to discover for ourselves the razoredge between potential salvation and damnation" (*Silas Marner*, 178). This statement, which makes Godfrey overly culpable, finds its reply in Bruce K. Martin's "Similarity Within Dissimilarity: The Dual Structure of *Silas Marner*" (479–89), which presents him as a victim. In addition, as an interesting twist, Alexander Welsh, in *George Eliot and Blackmail*, observes, "For those tempted to scorn someone who has been unable to make the two halves of his life meet, Godfrey Cass suffices as a target. To yield to this response, however, is curiously to side with the much more despicable Dunstan Cass" (165–66).

13. As John R. Reed and Jerry Herron have shown, this particular kind of tension fascinated and absorbed Eliot throughout her career as a novelist.

EFRAIM SICHER

George Eliot's 'Glue Test': Language, Law, and Legitimacy *in* Silas Marner[1]

I.

Chapter six of George Eliot's novel, *Silas Marner*, is set, it will be recalled, in the public house called *The Rainbow*, a name suggestive of the biblical covenant and the Christian prefiguration that situates grace in Nature, in contrast to the destructive deluge in *The Mill on the Floss*.[2] It seems a locus of the pastoral that Oliver Goldsmith had thought lost forever,

> [...] where nut-brown draughts inspired,
> Where grey-beard mirth, and smiling toil retired,
> Where village statesmen talked with looks profound,
> And news much older than their ale went round.

The entire chapter consists of the conversation among the villagers in the pub on diverse topics that range from Mr. Lammeter's cow to the existence of ghosts, and it is neatly framed by the apparition at the beginning of chapter seven of Marner himself. His ghostly appearance and the diabolical explanation given for it by some of his listeners hints at the preternatural and questions of belief. But the whole episode is more entertaining than serious in the gentle fun it pokes at the ignorance and superstitions of country folk. In his 1881 obituary of George Eliot, Leslie Stephen spoke of the quaint charm of this rustic humor for a cultivated intellect that raised it above the

From *The Modern Language Review* 94, part 1 (January 1999). © 1999 by the Modern Humanities Research Association. Revised especially for this volume.

picturesque.[3] The episode is usually taken as a splendid example of Realism in George Eliot's careful recording of rustic speech, an ideal application of Wordsworth's strictures in "The Preface" to *The Lyrical Ballads*. This misses the point made by Q.D. Leavis that Wordsworth's aesthetic justification of the rustic has been transformed into a *moral* obligation,[4] and it is an ethics of reading exercised by extension of that sympathy which George Eliot believed, as she argued in her essay "The Natural History of German Life," was essential to a true realism in portrayal of such scenes.

I believe, however, that there is a topic of conversation in chapter six which suggests there is something more subtle and intellectual going on under the surface. Obviously the ground is being seeded for Silas Marner's organic growth back into community, and the story of Cliff is allegorical of the consequences of manic obsessions and non-conformism to class stratification (we are reminded that old Lammeter, like Marner, came from a bit North'ard). Marner's catalepsy is a catastrophic break which allows a Wordsworthian transition to another state.[5] The ritualistic mode of the telling renders it ballad-like, a Rime which the cataleptic Marner, ancient before his time, cannot tell. His story, like Coleridge's, is one of "severance, loss, and expiation,"[6] of alienation from Nature, and of guilt for an unnatural sin, something that made Coleridge's "strange, striking thing" suitable reading for Captain Donnithorne, though he dismisses the rest of *Lyrical Ballads* as "twaddling stuff" and unfortunately later fails to read to the end of another exemplary text, *Zeluco*.[7] This is in response to Mrs. Irwine's comment about not liking people's eyes, so that Coleridge's Ancient Mariner with his mesmeric gaze can be taken as exemplary for the extension of sympathy through literature. But the tale told by Mr. Macey, like Coleridge's ballad, also self-consciously concerns interpretation in language and law.[8] The *Rainbow* is the place where Marner expects to find the "powers and dignities [sic] of Raveloe" so that he can proclaim the theft of his gold. It is, then, the site of judicial and legal authority, as well as representing a community of interpretation and covenant, one that must give meaning to language and hence to Law, which is a linguistic construction that reads interpretively the texts and codes governing moral judgment.

Mr. Macey recites the oft-told story of Mr. Lammeter's marriage ceremony, during which the rector put the questions "contrariwise" and transposed the genders of husband and wife. The question is what makes a marriage legally binding? Is it the utterance of the marriage vow or the inscription of words in a parish register? Does language determine binding relations or is the text governed by Law? As Mr. Macey recalls saying to himself,

"Is't the meaning or the words makes folks fast i' wedlock?" [...]
But then, when I come to think on it, meanin' goes but a little
way i' most things, for you may mean to stick things together and
your glue may be bad, and then where are you? And so I says to
mysen, 'It isn't the meanin', it's the glue.' (*Silas Marner*, p. 101)

The answer to this doubtful exercise in semantics, decided by the parson,
that the glue is inscription in the written text, the registry, questions the
meaning of its meaning—we have only Mr Macey's word that parsons and
doctors are authoritative interpreters of the Law, and he deduces this from
the fact that they seem to know everything by heart!

It is, however, an answer that engenders other questions besides the
relation of "form" to "substance."[9] What is the glue in conjugal union if it is
not the letter of the law? Is Marian Evans any less married to George Lewes
for not having said the right words at a ceremony according to law? Or to
put it in terms of speech act theory, is the utterance of the marriage vow
descriptive, imperative or performative? J.L. Austin, in his 1955 lecture
series *How To do Things With Words*, thought it performative, but effective
only in as much as it was instrumental in law and uttered according to due
form and ceremony. That the wrong words were said (a mistake was made—
one of Austin's examples of infelicity) or the fact that the union is bigamous
does not, however, necessarily render the statement nonsensical, but it may
make it ineffective, effective in an undesirable manner or subject to social
judgment ("shame" in Austin's parallel example of the misnamed ship).[10] In
Silas Marner, of course, bigamy is contemplated, but not committed, by
Godfrey.

The same example of the marriage vows in speech-act theory prompts
J. Hillis Miller to ask a further question: can a literary text lay down the law
by synecdochal example, or is the story it tells no more authoritative or
readable than that fragmentary performative?[11] Discussing Sam Weller's
Valentine card and Pickwick's trial for breach of promise, Miller follows
Derrida in arguing that this performative gains its efficacy from its
iterability.[12] Miller's use of such examples attempts to disprove Austin's
contention that poetry cannot be a performative speech act and to show that
intentionality cannot always be controlled by the speaker. These are,
however, examples of Dickens's own deconstruction of the fiction of legally
binding language seen in several examples of the abuse of the marriage laws
in Doctors' Commons in *Pickwick Papers*, as well as in *David Copperfield*.
Another example of a performative in *David Copperfield*, "Barkis is willing,"
is an unorthodox marriage proposal, but there is no question about its

efficacy or intention. Rather the point is that, while connectivity is the glue which sticks sentences and texts together, it is not so easy to understand how connectivity is effective in law when the uttered formula is an utterly arbitrary signifier. The question which Eliot seems to be asking is, what is the glue in conjugal union in such conditions? What is the glue in our text if not language? And what moral authority does it then exert? For example, what is its binding authority when the author is no longer regarded as legitimate? Indeed, what happens when the authority of scriptural law is itself questioned?[13] And, finally, how can language prescribe gender? Both Marner and the author undergo gender switches, the former as a male mother, the latter as a female pseudonymous novelist. The choice of her lover's first name as her pseudonym and the example of George Sand have been duly noted, and feminist critics have seen the choice as an attempt to subvert the gender codes of patriarchal discourse and legitimize a relationship which inevitably would ruin a woman's reputation.[14] Prior to 1858, a married woman had no property rights and therefore no claim to copyright of her works, so that the author's marital status (having said the right words at a ceremony) was very much relevant to the question of legal authorship, while the preservation of anonymity together with the concealment of gender protected the lawfulness of her work, in the sense of transgression of social, moral and religious codes and of libel laws. When authorship was claimed by someone else, George Eliot was forced into exposure, and the lawfulness of her authority as author came into question.

Few critics have taken the episode in *The Rainbow* too seriously, though U.C. Knoepflmacher understands the "glue" to be in a general way representative of the reconciliation of opposites, the worldly and the otherworldly, fable and reality, which the novel tries to reconcile.[15] My claim is that it is precisely George Eliot's anxiety about the legitimacy of the author, as well as her own legitimacy, especially following the revelations about the author of *Scenes of Clerical Life* (a theme reflected elsewhere in the disgrace of Hetty or Maggie), that explains the hitherto neglected concern in *Silas Marner* with the "glue test" of language. To apply the "glue test" to Eliot's own text would offer a rereading that confirms the familiar doctrine of sympathy but in a way which opens up unexpected metafictional concerns and reflections of autobiographical anxieties.

II.

While it might be unwise to speculate about identifications of the author, both Mary Magdalene and Mary-Ann are "sinful" women, and Molly is, of course, Mary, though she is legally married to Godfrey; she does, however, symbolically fall. These transformations and contiguities bring into consideration the fact that Marian Evans was a "fallen woman" living with a man not legally her husband. As we know, she did not do this to spite social approbation, nor because she believed in sexual freedom, but because she saw no other option for a woman in that particular legal situation: George Lewes was debarred from divorce because he had condoned his wife's extramarital relations.[16] Women who were satisfied with "light and easily broken ties [..] do not act as I have done—they obtain what they desire and are still invited to dinner," Marian Evans wrote to Cara Bray on 4 September 1855 (*Letters* II, p. 214). In the same letter she asserts her characteristic view that two individuals could differ about the marriage laws and could each believe their understanding of morality to be "good"; this view understands the coexistence of a plurality of moral standards and beliefs to be a reality of life—it is public opinion and prejudice which pronounces the relationship "immoral." Feuerbach's definition of a truly moral and religious marriage as a free bond of love sacred in itself in *The Essence of Christianity* (which she had recently translated) and, more arguably, Comtean attitudes no doubt influenced Marian Evans's thinking.[17] In an oft-quoted letter to her brother, Marian Evans conceded that her marriage was "not a legal one," but both partners regarded it "as a sacred bond" (13 June 1857, *Letters* II, p. 349). Feuerbach's "bond," which was exemplary of all moral relations, is certainly relevant to the "glue test" in *Silas Marner*, and a rereading of that novel might suffice to reveal on different levels a hidden debate over the laws governing human relations that may reflect personal anxiety concerning legitimacy.

There is a glue that holds the story together, the glue of interpersonal feelings, and it brings about the cohesion of Silas with Eppie and of Silas through Eppie with Nature and community. These are the "remedial influences of pure, natural human relations" described in George Eliot's letter to John Blackwood of 24 February 1861 (*Letters* III, p. 382). This glue would also be the cohesion which Marian Evans sought at the time of writing the novel, when she was stigmatised and isolated because she was living with a married man, and her publisher was fearful of the effect on sales when the identity of George Eliot was exposed publicly as a woman whose sexual relations were irregular, a double secret that Alexander Welsh has found to be projected in personal shame and guilt in both the author's correspondence and fiction.[18]

Marian Evans's letters provide rich material for a Freudian interpretation of her gloomy state of mind at this time: she complains of "mental depression"; she is unsettled by house moves and has lost her pen (letter to Sara Hennell, 20 December 1860, *Letters* III, pp. 364-365). This emotional stress is confounded by the strained relations with her brother, loss of a sister, the fear of disclosure of the authorship of her novels and her dependence on her writing for ready cash. In the letter to her publisher John Blackwell of 12 January 1861 that speaks of the inception and conception of the novel, she complains of slowness and timidity in her writing, attributing it to physical weakness and worry "about houses and servants and boys" (*Letters* III, pp. 371-372), as well as to the move to London, whose "depressing influence" she thought largely responsible for her "*malaise*" (letter to Mrs. Richard Congreve 16 February 1861, *Letters* III, p. 379). Eliot's Journal and correspondence for February 1861 speak of illness and discomfort, as well as a lack of faith in her future as a writer. These were, she admitted, "fat grievances," that possibly indicate psychosomatic symptoms of her anxiety that she and/or George Lewes might fail in their writing careers. Clearly, such anxieties had to be remedied through her writing, through a reclamation of her "lost pen"—the claim for phallic authority inscribed in a male pen-name[19]—and the legitimacy of authorship, so that her own rupture from society and from her father might be repaired in terms of Freud's recognition of the need for synthesis in therapeutic cohesion (glue) into the social fabric.[20]

The need for cohesion and its remedy through writing has been diagnosed by psychoanalysts who conclude that *Silas Marner* was written out of a sense of alienation, depression, and mourning for the loss of the countryside. "The familiar bulwarks of intensive intellectual activity as a defence against depressive anxiety suddenly gave way with the eruption of the inspired story."[21] The analysis reads *Silas Marner* as a "parable of self-creation" that implies an "evolution of the mind from a two-dimensional adhesive existence" to a more meaningful cohesion in society.[22] In her essay on George Eliot, on the other hand, Virginia Woolf understood it was the union with Lewes which released the springs of creativity, rather than writing which unblocked the effects of social exclusion caused by that illicit relationship.[23]

Significantly, George Eliot wanted to publish *Silas Marner* now because it belonged to a series of successive "mental phases," and publication in order of composition would allow her to distance herself "from that thorough identification with them which gave zest to the sense of authorship," as she wrote to Blackwood on 24 February 1861 (*Letters* III, p. 383). It was earlier in this letter that she spoke of "remedial influences" as the focus of her story. This working through of trauma looks back to childhood memory, in a story about an itinerant weaver—an "alien class"—carrying a burden, just when Marian Evans mentions reminders she has been getting of "Coventry distress" (letter to Sara Hennell of 8 February 1861, *Letters* III, p. 377). These reminders referred to the collapse of the ribbon industry which led to unemployment and a strike in summer 1860. Her Coventry friend Charles Bray, a ribbon manufacturer, was involved in efforts to help the unemployed weavers. It was Charles Bray who was closely associated with her earlier traumatic rift with her father when she abandoned her religious beliefs in 1842, another "Coventry distress," so that the weaver's burden could be that of the bogey-man of childhood or a burden of repressed trauma. What better way to work through that trauma too than by telling the story of an itinerant "disinherited" weaver who suffers traumatic severance and loss of faith and who must go through phases of reintegration in a Midlands village where he is alienated and isolated?

Moreover, both the rift from community and the severance from nature are mended in the novel through the adoption of a child. This coincides with Marian Evans's adoption of George Lewes's boys, whom she encouraged to call her by the name of mother ("Mutter"). There are, of course, several examples in George Eliot's novels of family structures that are dysfunctional or supplemented by the addition of a child, which may or may not have to do with Marian Evans's rupture with her father and brother or a desire to bear children,[24] and we can see in the claim for authorship (a literary and legal paternity) also a claim for maternity by a childless social outcast.[25]

The image of procreation in George Eliot's description of the story's conception and in similar descriptions of writing as pregnancy elsewhere in Marian Evans's correspondence connects with the theme of surrogate parenthood. Seen together with the tension between the desire to nurture and to depend on a strong masculinity (her father, her brother, George Lewes), this has yielded a Lacanian analysis of the Law of the Father in the tensions between literal and figural language: the daughter relates to the father in the way the son does to the mother in Lacan's understanding of child development, and the awareness of sexual difference gives rise to desire, the expression of lack, and to symbolic language.[26] In such a view, the reclamation of phallic authority—the lost pen mentioned above—would be made a signifier for the loss expressed by nostalgia for the countryside and for the lack of maternal love by the signing of the author's name as a male progenitor, author of her work. It is surely no coincidence that Eppie appears on the eve of Circumcision.[27]

After completing *Silas Marner*, Marian Evans wrote to her friend Clementia Doughty (the wife of the Radical politician Peter Alfred Taylor who had supported Marian Evans when rumors circulated in June 1856 about her relationship with George Lewes) in terms which show that the meaning of naming and words was to be determined by personal feelings and responsibilities, not any contractual code of law and language:

> For the last six years I have ceased to be "Miss Evans" for anyone
> who has personal relations with me—having held myself under
> all the responsibilities of a married woman. (6 April 1861, *Letters*
> III, p. 396)

In asking not to be addressed by her maiden name, Marian Evans is, in effect, proposing her own answer to the "glue test," though her own rift with society and her family was not healed until she married John Cross legally, in a church ceremony. In fact, she lived by the rule of not being bound by social conventions and expressed her freedom from "unnatural" relations by "renouncing all social intercourse" except with those who accepted her sexual status, so that she would not be obliged to reciprocate visits with those whose legal and linguistic discourse did not accept it (letter to Clementia Doughty of 8 April 1861, *Letters* III, p. 398).

David Carroll, who has also noticed a philosophical debate in *The Rainbow*, suggests that its central thesis is the opposition of natural and unnatural relations and that it prepares for the rejection of Godfrey's claim of biological rights to Eppie in favor of Marner's emotional claim of paternity,[28] which seems to me similar to Marian Evans's claim on George Lewes's boys. That argument, like the parable of Nathan in II Samuel 12 when the prophet chastised David for his immoral relations with Bathsheba, is an argument from nature (Silas cites the Biblical passage when he says of Eppie that "we eat o' the same bit, and drink o' the same cup"). Repentance, however, doesn't help Godfrey, who like David has lost a child. "Repentance," Silas tells Godfrey, "doesn't alter what's been going on for sixteen year. Your coming and saying 'I'm her father' doesn't alter the feelings inside us" (*Silas Marner*, p. 231). The legitimacy of a paternity that arises from natural sympathy thus outweighs any "duty" to what Nancy calls a "lawful father" (*Silas Marner*, p. 234), and it recognises a human bonding unknown in Godfrey's language and experience or in Law. That exercise of human sympathy is the aim of what David Carroll calls the novel's "rustic hermeneutics,"[29] and this is what is offered as the binding glue that matches the cohesion which Marian Evans herself desired at the time of writing.

III.

By way of further evidence for the significance here of "glue," one need look no further than that salutary fable, "Brother Jacob," contemporaneous with *Silas Marner* (it was conceived in Florence in 1860 and published under this title in 1864). The brother theme is here too: the "false" brother (Faux) who goes to the bad is David, a false messiah and false friend to Jonathan (his elder brother), just as Silas is betrayed by his "Jonathan" (*Silas Marner*, p. 57),

William Dane. This is a disruption of patriarchal authority in the Biblical narrative, as Kristin Brady has pointed out,[30] in that in the Bible it was Jonathan who invoked Saul's displeasure and Jacob who tricked his father Isaac into blessing him as the first-born; here, however, the role reversal suggests guilt in the son and not fault in the father. Like Geoffrey who cannot free himself of Dunstan, David cannot shake off his idiot brother Jacob, who has exchanged his Biblical staff for a more dangerous pitchfork; the struggle over the birthright ends with the latterday Esau being exposed as a dishonest rascal who has deceived his mother (parental duty having made her as blind as Isaac to true identity).

In relating how Jacob sticks to his brother after being offered sticky candies, the narrator describes the idiot's "adhesive fingers." In reality, of course, Marian Evans was the one cast off by her brother Isaac and she was in danger of being cut off from her birthright (held in trust) because of her liason with George Lewes (contrary to Isaac's wishes, like Esau's liason with Canaanite women). Marian Evans might have dearly wished her brother to reappear in her home and stick to her, but such adhesion is blocked by the guilt associated with the reappearance of David's brother Jacob (the return of the repressed) in his sweet-shop towards the end of the tale. This guilt over the theft of his mother's guineas, which threatens forfeiture of inheritance and social status, may hint at sexual transgression in the Freudian symbol of the tin (a jewel box) which David was trying to get into a hole (comparable with the gold that is hidden away by Silas and later found with Dunstan's body in a hole). In the anti-Midas transference of the golden guineas into the sticky lozenges, Jacob sticks to David at the end of the story so that the guilt also sticks to him. This is, however, still adhesion and not cohesion, as in synthesis, and the "rainbow" opening of the shop promises no true community as in *The Rainbow*—on the contrary, it draws the village women away from domestic care into the alienating "division of labor" in the industrial production of mince-pies (unlike Marner's progression from factory to cottage loom). The parable is barely relieved by ironic humour and is not graced by the workings of sympathy. Yet the musings on Providence and how "wonderfully" things come about anticipate the more subtle treatment of Nemesis in *Silas Marner*.

Whereas in "Brother Jacob" marriage was thwarted and the moral decline into middle-class shopkeeping halted, *Silas Marner* concludes with a rejection of the cash nexus in social law. Eppie's choice—like Esther's in *Felix Holt*—is a free-willed decision to forego the privilege awarded her by birth in the deterministic code of social inheritance. This would be another transformation of the response to the inheritance plot we see in *Oliver Twist* or *Wuthering Heights*, where property rights do not square with natural rights and legitimacy.[31] The home which Eppie and Silas set up in their cottage and garden is a restoration of edenic happiness and an ideal light comparable to the *Evening Star* in Wordsworth's *Michael*, something which suggests that the separation of man from Nature is reversible.[32] The relevance of the episode in *The Rainbow* is underscored by the fact that Silas Marner enters amid supernatural rumors after a ritual narrative about a wedding ceremony; unlike Coleridge's hero, however, Marner does not interrupt the wedding, and marriage is consummated at the end of the novel by Aaron and Eppie, a marriage of a priest of nature (the messianic gardener) with a christological figure and harbinger of a secular redemption. The wedding is followed by a celebration in the *Rainbow* yard, where Silas earlier reentered the covenant of community, the site of the natural organism which is the ideal form of the novel itself. This matching of form to content is part of the argument for natural growth and bonding which is familiar from George Eliot's metaphorical description of the genesis of her story as unfolding from a "millet seed of thought" (letter to John Blackwood, 12 January 1861, *Letters* III, p. 371).

IV.

To say that George Eliot's fiction is a parable of personal or social cohesion is to refute J. Hillis Miller's conclusion in his reading of *Adam Bede* that the glue or "cement of society" is a cynical lie when it is the fiction that "my ugly, stupid neighbour is lovable."[33] We should note that it is Mrs. Irwine who cannot love ugly neighbors, while Mrs. Poyser, who holds a worldly view of human prosperity, thinks Dinah is going "against Scripture" on this point. Adam Bede acts out Dinah's exposition of sympathy and demonstrates that it is feelings which stick us together. The Dutch genre realism of chapter seventeen rests, in fact, on the "secret" of human feelings, for which religion is mere form and upon which it is the task of Art to act, for if it does not "enlarge men's sympathies, it does nothing morally," as Marian Evans wrote in response to the narrow-minded hypocrisy which excluded her from society (5 July 1859, *Letters* III, p. 111).

For J. Hillis Miller the choice between charity and cynicism is impossible, and the Biblical commandment to love one's neighbor is ultimately unreadable because it remains a performative speech act divorced from the certainty of its fulfillment. In Miller's view, Eliot's claim to the truth of narration relies on ethicity as an emotive force and on the subjective, therefore arbitrary, displacement of value-systems through catachresis, through a figurative language borrowed from Scripture, which borrows it from Nature, thus effecting a multiple displacement.[34] That is a recognition similar to Freud's in *Civilization and its Discontents* that the cultural super-ego was too demanding of the ego and ignored human psychology, particularly the limits of control over the id, thus causing unhappiness, neurosis and revolt; the commandment to love your neighbor as yourself is impossible to fulfil because it overinflates the value of love and puts anyone following the precept at disadvantage to the rest of society which ignores it.[35]

George Eliot does not merely replace God with the "intersubjectivity" of linguistic structures, a theory J. Hillis Miller has applied to *Middlemarch*; Miller himself acknowledges that the ominiscient narrator in that novel is an application of Feuerbach's "all-inclusive 'consciousness of the species' [..] a divine knowledge, sympathy, and power of judgment which has arisen from the encounters of individual men with their fellows..."[36] Nietzsche's comment on George Eliot in *Twilight of the Gods* that Christian morality was impossible without faith in God moves Miller to conclude that any moral realism in *Middlemarch* is contradictory and therefore unreadable, and that the deconstruction of religious categories or allegorical form leaves George Eliot's humanism empty of real significance.[37] On the contrary, the Biblical commandment to love one's neighbor as oneself posits an ethics of difference between Self and Other in which neither may be denied. George Eliot's narrator is most censorious when Maggie or Dorothea negate the self in selfish acts of self-sacrifice; love for neighbors must recognize self and Other as individual and interdependent within the same social web. To the opposite extreme, Godfrey must learn that the Other is not a convenient means to personal ends.

This is a lesson rather different from Dickens' preaching of compassion and understanding through "Fancy" seven years previously in *Hard Times*. Imprisoned in his loom, the factory weaver Stephen Blackpool can only see "aw a muddle" and cannot be rid of his unwanted wife, unlike Godfrey or Charles Dickens himself, whose relationship with Ellen Ternan created scandal but did not endanger his moral authority or his authorship, even though almost killed with her in the train accident mentioned in the Postscript of *Our Mutual Friend*. In the end Blackpool does not consummate the desired union with Rachael but dies a martyr in the industrial wasteland of the Old Hell Shaft, his eyes raised to salvation in Heaven. For George Eliot (in "The Natural History of German Life"), Dickens had failed in his representation of the artisan because he had failed in imaginative sympathy.

Eliot recognises Carlyle's "organic filaments" which spin together the torn human tissue with the bond of sympathy in Book 3 chapter 7 of *Sartor Resartus*, and, in keeping with the ideal of Dutch painting in chapter seventeen of *Adam Bede*, England in *Silas Marner* is imagined as a community that has reestablished the bonds of natural feelings. This is neither a real place nor a literary pastoral, but a reversal of history that undoes the alienating effects of industrialisation and urbanisation (the weaver is moved from town to country, from dissenting chapel to Anglican church); it posits an alternative for George Eliot's own time, pointing to an Englishness lost to dispossesion and urban corruption at the end of "Michael."[38]

Because coherence is equated with cohesion in the "community of feeling," the linguistically arbitrary signifiers such as the words of the marriage ceremony and the letters on Dolly's lard-cakes regain coherence in as much as they achieve such cohesion. The ethical model which the novel seeks to construct through the workings of sympathy in the "glue test" stakes a claim for an ideal and therapeutic cohesion in community for Silas, for the author and for the reader.

This is a far more radical solution of social and personal tensions than Tennyson's "Northern Farmer (New Style)" for whom "parputty sticks." Sticking to property rights is, of course, a bone of contention in another George Eliot novel, *Felix Holt*. In chapter 28, Christian tricks Tommy into *sticking* the wrong bills, for a rival contender, a false glue that matches the falsity of property rights as a claim to social, economic, and political legitimacy (which Esther rejects in favor of her love for the true Radical, Felix). The connection of law and language resurfaces in this episode when Christian asks the illiterate Tommy how he came to discover his claim to the Transome estate:

> "It was the regester—the parish regester," said Tommy, with his knowing wag of the head, "that shows as you was born. I allays felt it inside me as I was somebody, and I could see other chaps thought it on me too; and so one day at Littleshaw, where I kept ferrets and a little bit of a public, there comes a fine man looking after me, and walking me up and down wi' questions. And I made out from the clerk as he'd been at the regester; and I gave the clerk a pot or two, and he got it of our parson as the name o' Trounsem was a great name hereabout. And I waits a bit for my fine man to come again. Thinks I, if there's property wants a right owner, I shall be called for; for I didn't know the law then. And I waited and waited, till I see'd no fun i' waiting. So I parted wi' my public and my ferrets—for she was dead a'ready, my wife was, and I hadn't no cumbrance. And off I started a pretty long walk to this countryside, for I could walk for a wager in them days."[39]

A farcical treatment of law and language is Dickens's Cousin Feenix, in *Dombey and Son*, who enters himself as born that morning in the marriage registry and almost marries the bridesmaid. In *Hard Times*, Stephen Blackpool's case is more "grievous," and he wants to know the law that helps him, but the Victorian "self-made man," the banker and industrialist Josiah Bounderby of Coketown, comfortably lunching on chops and sherry, cannot see anything but a disgruntled worker making trouble about something that is none of his piece-work.

Such political constructs of nation, class and gender actually sound more like the false glue described by Isaiah (41:7), in which the idolaters put their faith, than the glue which might mend Sirach's shattered potsherds.⁴⁰ By contrast, the feelings that bond in *Adam Bede* and *Middlemarch* prove more lasting in holding together the social web, and the "glue" which Eliot applies to texts and people, through its testing of ethical action in fiction, reasserts the moral authority of the novel and its author.

NOTES

1. I would like to record my debt for their responses to earlier versions of this essay to Nancy Armstrong; Carol Bernstein; Wayne C. Booth; Leon Burnett; the late Harold Fisch; Chanita Goodblatt; Joseph Glicksohn M.D.; Adam Zachary Newton; Gabriel Pearson; and the late Mark Spilka. In this essay I will be referring to George Eliot, *Silas Marner: The Weaver of Raveloe* ed. Q.D. Leavis (Harmondsworth: Penguin Books, 1967); *Essays of George Eliot.* ed. T. Pinney (London: Routledge, 1963); *The George Eliot Letters*, ed. Gordon S. Haight (New Haven: Yale University Press, 1954).

2. For a discussion of the ambivalence and theological difficulties of the rainbow in Romantic poetry and Victorian art see George P. Landow, "The Rainbow: A Problematic Image," in *Nature in the Victorian Imagination*, ed. U.C. Knoepflmacher and G.B. Tennyson (Berkeley: University of California Press, 1977), pp. 341-69. The choice of an inn is significant if we bear in mind the site of the genesis of Christian mythology in Bethlehem. Eliot may have been thinking of an inn called "The Rainbow," at Allesley, near Coventry, and of the legend that a pot of gold lies at the end of a rainbow.

3. Excerpt in *The Mill on the Floss and Silas Marner: A Casebook*, ed. R.P. Draper (London: Macmillan, 1977), pp. 69-72.

4. "Introduction," in *Silas Marner: The Weaver of Raveloe* ed. Q.D. Leavis (Harmondsworth: Penguin Books, 1967), p. 9.

5. Northrop Frye, *The Secular Scripture: A Study of the Structure of Romance* (Cambridge MA: Harvard University Press, 1976), pp. 102-3.

6. U. C. Knoepflmacher, "Mutations of the Wordsworthian Child of Nature," in *Nature in the Victorian Imagination*, ed. U.C. Knoepflmacher and G.B. Tennyson (Berkeley: University of California Press, 1977), p. 418; Knoepflmacher has commented on the correspondence between Silas Marner and the Ancient Mariner in *George Eliot's Early Novels: The Limits of Realism* (Berkeley: University of California Press, 1968), p. 257.

7. *Adam Bede*, ed. Stephen Gill (Harmondsworth: Penguin Books, 1980), p. 109.

8. See on this David Carroll, *George Eliot and the Conflict of Interpretations: A Reading of the Novels* (Cambridge: Cambridge University Press, 1992), pp. 164-5. For the relevance of Coleridge's ideas on the authority of Scripture to a reconstructed layering of oral and mythical materials in his ballad see Jerome J. McGann, "The Ancient Mariner: The Meaning of the Meanings," in his *The Beauty of Inflections: Literary Investigations in Historical Method and Theory*, corrected paperback edition (Oxford: Oxford University Press, 1988), pp. 143-72.

9. Richard H. Hutton, [unsigned review of *Silas Marner*], *Economist*, 27 April 1861, pp. 455-7; rep. in *George Eliot: The Critical Heritage*, ed. David Carroll (London: Routledge, 1971), p. 177.

10. *How To Do Things With Words* (Oxford: Oxford University Press, 1962). See also Mary Louise Pratt, *Toward a Speech Act Theory of Literary Discourse* (Bloomington: Indiana University Press, 1977). In *Promising Language: Betrothal in Victorian Law and Fiction* (Albany: State University of New York Press, 2000), Randall Craig offers a different approach to the legal aspects of language in, among other texts, *Adam Bede* and *The Mill on the Floss*.

11. *Topographies* (Stanford: Stanford University Press, 1995), pp. 81-3.

12. *Topographies*, p. 118; and see Jacques Derrida, *Limited Inc.* (Evanston: Northwestern University Press, 1988), where Derrida disputes the rights of John Searle's interpretation of speech act theory.

13. See Efraim Sicher, "Rescripting Scripture: George Eliot's 'Ethics of Reading' in *Silas Marner*," *Semeia*, 77 (1998), pp. 243-70. For the context of Victorian debates in law and theology see Jan-Melissa Schramm, *Testimony and Advocacy in Victorian Law, Literature, and Theology* (Cambridge: Cambridge University Press, 2000).

14. Jennifer Uglow, *George Eliot* (London: Virago, 1987), p. 84; Kristin Brady, *George Eliot* (London: Macmillan, 1992), pp. 39-51. For Gillian Beer, George Eliot's writing wreaks a feminist vengeance on patriarchal law through its unfavorable portraits of lawyers and critical view of woman's legal position *(George Eliot* [Brighton: Harvester, 1986]). Joseph Carroll likewise sees here a revision of the patriarchal paradigm in the construction of an ideal androgyny and the merging of gender roles

(*Evolution and Literary Theory* [Columbia: University of Missouri Press, 1995], pp. 279-90). Only Charles Dickens saw through the author's disguise, despite Mrs. Barton's boast in *Scenes of Clerical Life* that she can tailor trousers so that nobody would guess her gender.

15. *George Eliot's Early Novels: The Limits of Realism* (Berkeley: University of California Press, 1968), pp. 254-5.

16. Lawrence Dessner suggests the death of Molly is a kind of wish-fulfillment that Agnes might die, enabling her to legitimize her relationship with Lewes ("The Autobiographical Matrix of *Silas Marner*," *Studies in the Novel*, 11 [1979]: 260-3). Such an interpretation is not borne out by Marian Evans's correspondence, and it would imply some kind of death-wish, killing the self which had brought her shame through her sexual desire, rather than undercutting the hypocritical standards by which the fallen woman was judged.

17. See Susan E. Hill, "Translating Feuerbach, Constructing Morality: The Theological and Literary Significance of Translation for George Eliot," *Journal of the American Academy of Religion* 65, 3 (1997): 635-52; James McLaverty, "Comtean Fetishism in *Silas Marner*," *Nineteenth-Century Fiction* 36 (1981-82): 318-36; Valerie R. Dodd, *George Eliot: An Intellectual Life* (New York: St. Martin's Press, 1990); Terence R. Wright, *The Religion of Humanity: The Impact of Comte's Positivism on Victorian Britain* (Cambridge: Cambridge University Press, 1986). Elizabeth Deeds Ermath has traced Eliot's notion of sympathy to Feurbach and Comte in "George Eliot's Conception of Sympathy," *Nineteenth-Century Fiction* 40, 1 (1985): 23-42.

18. Alexander Welsh, *George Eliot and Blackmail* (Cambridge MA: Harvard University Press, 1985), pp. 113-31. Welsh believes that G.H. Lewes was instrumental in stage-managing the selling and marketing of "George Eliot" and skillful in exploiting the secret of authorship, while, in a different vein, Nina Auerbach has posited the theory that Lewes' stage-managership was essential to Marian Evans's transformation into fiction of her personality, an acting out of roles, including that of Fallen Woman, according to a written script (*Romantic Imprisonment: Women and Other Glorified Outcasts* [New York: Columbia University Press, 1986], pp. 253-67). Both these views presume a certain conscious cynicism in the presentation of illegitimacy. On the contrary, Geoffrey and Katherine Tillotson believe this rich material in the correspondence would have attracted a Trollope or Henry James but was not used by George Eliot (*Mid-Victorian Studies* [London: Athlone Press, 1965], p. 68).

19. Sandra M. Gilbert and Susan Gubar have described the prevalent Western metaphor of the pen for the fathering of creativity, an authoring

of patriarchal authority, in *The Madwoman in the Attic* (New Haven: Yale University Press, 1979), but this image of the pen as penis has become confused with the Lacanian notion of the phallus as a symbol of woman's lack; see Toril Moi, *Sexual/Textual Politics* (London: Methuen 1985); and Jane Gallop, *Reading Lacan* (Ithaca: Cornell University Press, 1985).

20. I am grateful to Alan Flashman M.D. for directing my attention to Freud's remarks on synthesis and analysis in his paper of 1919, "Lines of Advance in Psycho-Analytic Therapy," in *The Standard Edition of the Complete Psychological Works of Sigmund Freud* (London: Hogarth, 1958), vol. XVII, pp. 167-73. The description of Marian Evans's mood as "gloomy" is my own, but it is a pun that neatly suggests the desired remedy: cohesion into community. Incidentally, the phrenologist George Combe, who had earlier diagnosed Marian Evans's "Amat[iveness]" as "rather small," revised his analysis in light of her relations with George Lewes and concluded that this was a case of "mental aberration" (Gordon S. Haight, "George Eliot's Bastards," in *George Eliot: A Centenary Tribute*, ed. Gordon S. Haight and R.T. van Arsdep [Totowa, NJ: Barnes and Noble, 1982], pp. 4, 9). Her friend Charles Bray's analysis of a cast of Marian Evans's head was perhaps nearer the mark when he noted that "the social feelings were very active, particularly the *adhesiveness*" and that she was "not fitted to stand alone," but required someone stronger and male to lean upon (ibid., p. 3; my emphasis).

21. Meg Harris Williams and Margot Waddell, *The Chamber of Maiden Thought: Literary Origins of the Psychoanalytic Model of the Mind* (London: Routledge, 1991), p. 155.

22. *The Chamber of Maiden Thought*, p. 154. See Peggy Fitzhugh Johnstone's study of the therapeutic reworking of aggression into creativity in George Eliot's novels, *The Transformation of Rage: Mourning and Creativity in George Eliot's Fiction* (New York: New York University Press, 1994). Johnstone develops the Freudian analysis proposed in Laura Emery's *George Eliot's Creative Conflict: The Other Side of Silence* (Berkeley: University of California Press, 1976) and explores the pre-Oedipal development of the author. She concludes that Marian Evans's changes of name and her self-creation as an author coincide with anniversaries of bereavement and loss. Themes of betrayal in *Silas Marner*, for instance, reflect a working through of the pain caused by separation from maternal attachment or by the estrangement from her family, particularly Isaac and Chrissey. Laura Emery and Margaret Keenan deduce from Johnstone's evidence of early traumatic loss that the writing of the novel performed a "therapeutic intervention," forcing the author to work through childhood losses, just as Silas Marner's

acknowledgment of loss of his symbolic children, the gold guineas, allows the healing process to begin and to lead to reconciliation ("'I've been robbed!': Breaking the Silence in *Silas Marner*," *American Journal of Psychoanalysis* 59, 3 [1999]: 209-23). A tentative Jungian analysis of the father-daughter relationship in *Silas Marner* is offered in Terence Dawson, "'Light Enough to Trusten By': Structure and Experience in *Silas Marner*," *Modern Language Review* 88, 1 (1983): 26-45; however, Dawson's argument rests on the centrality of Nancy to the plot and structure of the novel. See also Ruby Redinger, *George Eliot: The Emergent Self* (New York: Knopf, 1975).

23. *Collected Essays* (London: Hogarth Press, 1968), volume I, p. 199.

24. See Rosemarie Bodenheimer's discussion of the relationship of the author's biography with her fiction, *The Real Life of Mary Ann Evans: George Eliot, Her Letters and Fiction* (Ithaca: Cornell University Press, 1994), pp. 203-8. Bodenheimer shows how the gain of motherhood in adoption of Lewes's boys might be reflected in the adoption by Silas of Eppie, but also (in the case of Thornton and Herbert) points to the parallel of the unmothered Cass boys who are in danger of wasting their lives in immorality and debauchery; the relationship of life and fiction is further complicated by the story of Nancy's childlessness, which Bodenheimer understands to be morally connected with the childless author's repressed anxieties and unfulfilled desires. Such autobiographical correspondences adduce projection of self from correspondence that is itself, as Bodenheimer calls it, an "epistolatory performance" of issues that were exercising Marian Evans' mind. Gordon S. Haight has pointed out a real-life prototype for Eppie's adoption in the adoption by the childless Charles and Cara Bray of Bray's natural daughter in 1846 ("George Eliot's Bastards," in *George Eliot: A Centenary Tribute*, ed. Gordon S. Haight and R.T. van Arsdep [Totowa, NJ: Barnes and Noble, 1982], p. 7). Jenny Bourne Tayloe prefers to see Eppie as a device to legitimize Marner's male motherhood and thus subvert the class, gender and ideological constructions of the foundling that were shifting in the Victorian period ("Representing Illegitimacy in Victorian Culture," in *Victorian Identities: Social and Cultural Formations in Nineteenth-Century Literature*, ed. Ruth Robbins and Julian Wolfreys [London:Macmillan and New York: St. Martin's, 1996], pp. 119-142).

25. On George Eliot's role as a literary mother and its relevance for a reading of *Silas Marner* see Sandra M. Gilbert, "Life's Empty Pack: Notes Toward a Literary Daughteronomy," *Critical Inquiry*, 11 (1984-1985): 355-84. On Eliot's self-creation as a woman writer see also Deirdre David, *Intellectual Women and Victorian Patriarchy* (Ithaca: Cornell University Press, 1987).

26. Margaret Homans, *Bearing the Word: Language and Female Experience in Nineteenth-Century Women's Writing* (Chicago: Chicago University Press, 1986), pp. 179-82.

27. This strengthens the circumstantial evidence of Eliot's autobiographical circumscription (to adapt a Derridean pun from his "Circumfession," reproduced as the parallel text of *Jacques Derrida*, by Geofrey Bennington and Jacques Derrida [Chicago: Chicago University Press, 1993]). See Derrida's theory of "phallogocentrism" in *Margins of Philosophy*, trans. Alan Brass (Brighton: Harvester, 1982), as well as his comments on circumcision as the signature of absence in Nietzsche and Joyce, in *A Derrida Reader: Between the Blinds*, ed. Peggy Kamuf (New York: Columbia University Press, 1991), pp. 365-6, 571, 589-90.

28. David Carroll, "Reversing the Oracles of Religion," in *The Mill on the Floss and Silas Marner: A Casebook*, ed. R.P. Draper (London: Macmillan, 1977), pp. 212-13.

29. David Carroll, *George Eliot and the Conflict of Interpretations: A Reading of the Novels* (Cambridge: Cambridge University Press, 1992), pp. 140-66.

30. *George Eliot* (London: Macmillan, 1992), pp. 107-8.

31. See on this Bernard Semmel, *George Eliot and the Politics of National Inheritance.* (Oxford: Oxford University Press, 1994), pp. 23-26; and see also the discussion of naming, property and propriety in *Wuthering Heights* in Patricia Parker, *Literary Fat Ladies: Rhetoric, Gender, Property* (London: Methuen, 1987), pp. 155-77.

32. On the poetic context of this theme see U.C. Knoepflmacher, "Mutations of the Wordsworthian Child of Nature," in *Nature in the Victorian Imagination*, ed. U.C. Knoepflmacher and G.B. Tennyson (Berkeley: University of California Press, 1977), pp. 419, 421.

33. J. Hillis Miller, *The Ethics of Reading* (New York: Columbia University Press, 1987), pp. 79-80.

34. *The Ethics of Reading*, p. 72.

35. *The Standard Edition of the Complete Psychological Works of Sigmund Freud* (London: Hogarth, 1958), volume XXI, p. 143. In the *Interpretation of Dreams*, Freud reports the case of a patient who identifies with Adam Bede as an example of split personality that reveals hidden sexual desires (*The Standard Edition of the Complete Psychological Works of Sigmund Freud* [London: Hogarth, 1958], volume IV, p. 290); this is another example of Freud's view of the "impossibility" of religious ethics that is relevant to Eliot's own situation.

36. *The Form of Victorian Fiction* (Notre-Dame IN: University of Notre-Dame Press, 1968), pp. 84-5.

37. *Victorian Subjects* (Durham: Duke University Press, 1991), pp. 84-5, 234-35 For a rebuttal of Miller's Nietzschean position see David Parker's reading of *Middlemarch* in his *Ethics, Theory and the Novel* (Cambridge: Cambridge University Press, 1994), pp. 77-106.

38 David Gervais, *Literary Englands: Versions of "Englishness" in Modern Writing* (Cambridge: Cambridge University Press, 1993), p. 5.

39 *Felix Holt: The Radical*, ed. Peter Coveney (Harmondsworth: Penguin Books, 1972), p. 378.

40 The Hebrew Bible employs the root *dvk* ("glue"): both for the cleaving of man and woman and cleaving to God. Eliot, who had a polyglot bible, might possibly have been aware of this.

Chronology

1819	Born as Mary Ann Evans on November 22 in Arbury, Warwickshire, England to Robert and his second wife, Christiana Pearson.
1828	Attends Miss Wallington's Boarding School in Nuneaton.
1832	Attends the Misses Franklin's School in Coventry.
1836	Mother dies.
1837–47	Returns to be father's housekeeper.
1841	Father retires and they move to Foleshill, Coventry. Becomes part of the freethinking intellectual circle of Charles and Cara Bray and Charles Hennell.
1842	Leaves orthodox Christian faith, causing four-month estrangement from her father.
1846	Publishes her translation of David F. Strauss's *The Life of Jesus, Critically Examined.*
1849–50	Father dies. Travels with Brays to Europe, staying in Geneva for eight months.
1850–51	Meets John Chapman, editor of the *Westminster Review.* Becomes assistant editor of the publication; contributes articles and reviews to this and other publications. Lives with Chapman and his wife in London. Meets Herbert Spencer, who does not return her affection.
1853	Meets George Henry Lewes.

1854	Intimately involved with Lewes and will remain so for the rest of his life; the two travel to Germany and will travel to Europe many times in the next 20 years. Publishes her translation of Ludwig Feuerbach's *The Essence of Christianity*.
1857	*Scenes of Clerical Life* published in *Blackwood's Edinburgh Magazine*; assumes pseudonym George Eliot. Informs her brother Isaac of her relationship with Lewes, and he refuses any further communication with her.
1858	*Scenes of Clerical Life* published.
1859	*Adam Bede* published.
1860	*The Mill on the Floss* published.
1861	*Silas Marner* published.
1862	*Romola* begins to appear in serial form in *Cornhill Magazine*.
1863	*Romola* published.
1866	*Felix Holt* published.
1868	*The Spanish Gypsy*, an epic poem, published.
1869	Thornton, son of Lewes, dies.
1871–72	*Middlemarch* published.
1874	*The Legend of Jubal and Other Poems* published.
1875	Death of Bertie, another child of Lewes.
1876	*Daniel Deronda* published.
1877	Working on *Impressions of Theophrastus Such*, a series of essays. Lewes dies on November 30.
1879	Completes and publishes Lewes's *Problems of Life and Mind*. John Blackwood, Evans's publisher, dies.
1880	Marries 40-year-old John Walter Cross, her financial advisor, on May 6. Brother Isaac communicates with her for the first time since beginning of her relationship with Lewes. Evans dies on December 22.

Contributors

HAROLD BLOOM is Sterling Professor of the Humanities at Yale University and Henry W. and Albert A. Berg Professor of English at the New York University Graduate School. He is the author of over 20 books, including *Shelly's Mythmaking* (1959), *The Visionary Company* (1961), *Blake's Apocalypse* (1963), *Yeats* (1970), *A Map of Misreading* (1975), *Kabbalah and Criticism* (1975), *Agon: Toward a Theory of Revisionism* (1982), *The American Religion* (1992), *The Western Canon* (1994), and *Omens of Millennium: The Gnosis of Angels, Dreams, and Resurrection* (1996). *The Anxiety of Influence* (1973) sets forth Professor Bloom's provocative theory of the literary relationships between the great writers and their predecessors. His most recent books include *Shakespeare: The Invention of the Human*, a 1998 National Book Award finalist, and *How to Read and Why*, which was published in 2000. In 1999, Professor Bloom received the prestigious American Academy of Arts and Letters Gold Medal for Criticism.

PHILIP FISHER is Reid Professor of English at Harvard University. He has written and edited books on literature, including *The Vehement Passions* and *Still the New World: American Literature in a Culture of Creative Destruction*.

MERI-JANE ROCHELSON teaches English at Florida International University. She is a co-editor of *Transforming Genres: New Approaches to British Fiction of the 1890s*.

ELIZABETH DEEDS ERMARTH has taught English at the University of Maryland. She is the author of *George Eliot* in Twayne's English Authors Series, and has written other books about literature.

HAROLD FISCH has taught at the Institute for Literary Research at Bar-Ilan University. He is the author of *Biblical Presence in Shakespeare, Milton & Blake: A Comparative Study*.

ANGUS EASSON has been Professor of English at the University of Salford. He is the author of *Elizabeth Gaskell* and has also been the editor for books of Dickens and Gaskell.

KERRY MCSWEENEY is Molson Professor of English at McGill University in Montreal. He is the author of *Middlemarch* for the Unwin Critical Library. He also has written numerous other books on both classic and contemporary authors.

PATRICK SWINDEN has taught English Language and Literature at the University of Manchester. He has written and edited numerous books, including *George Eliot: Middlemarch*.

TERRENCE DAWSON has taught at the National University of Singapore.

ALAN W. BELLRINGER has taught at the University of Wales, Bangor. Aside from his book on George Eliot he has written several others, including *Henry James*.

HENRY ALLEY is the author of *Umbrella of Glass* and *The York Handbook for the Teaching of Creative Writing* as well as other books.

EFRAIM SICHER has taught at Ben-Gurion University of the Negev. He has written books on Jewish literature.

Bibliography

Alley, Henry. "*Silas Marner* and the Balance of Male and Female," *VIJ: Victorians Institute Journal* 16 (1988): pp. 65-73.

Arthurs, Caroline. "*Silas Marner*; the Uncertain Joys of Fatherhood," *English: The Journal of the English Association* 37, no. 157 (Spring 1988): pp. 41-47.

Auster, Henry. *Local Habitations: Regionalism in the Early Novels of George Eliot.* Cambridge: Harvard University Press, 1970.

Bamlett, Steve. *The Scene of a Great Future: George Eliot, America, and Political Economy.* In Taylor, Neil. *America in English Literature.* London: Roehampton Institute of Higher Education, Southlands College, 1980.

Barrat, Alain. "George Eliot's Mixed Vision of Human Progress in *Silas Marner*: A Pessimistic Reading of the Novel," *Cahiers Victoriens et Edouardiens: Revue du Centre d'Etudes* 35 (April 1992): pp. 193-200.

Barrett, D. *Vocation and Desire: George Eliot's Heroines.* London: Routledge & Kegan Paul, 1989.

Beer, Gillian. *George Eliot.* Key Women Writers Series. Brighton, England: Harvester, 1986

Breen, Margaret Soenser. "Silas Marner—George Eliot's Male Heroine," *George Eliot Henry Lewes Studies* 28-29 (September 1995): pp. 1-15.

Brown, Kate E. "Loss, Revelry, and the Temporal Measures of *Silas Marner*: Performance, Regret, Recollection," *Novel* 32, no. 2 (Spring 1999): p. 222-49.

Carpenter, Mary Wilson. *George Eliot and the Landscape of Time: Narrative Form and Protestant Apocalyptic History*. Chapel Hill: University of North Carolina Press, 1986.

Carroll, David R., ed. *"Silas Marner." George Eliot: The Critical Heritage*. London: Routledge & Kegan Paul, 1971, pp. 168-95.

Carroll, David R. *"Silas Marner*: Reversing the Oracles of Religion," *Literary Monographs* 1 (1967): pp. 165-200.

Cohen, Susan R. "'A History and a Metamorphosis': Continuity and Discontinuity in *Silas Marner*," *Texas Studies in Literature and Language* 25 (1983): p. 410-26.

Crehan, Stewart. "Scandalous Topicality: Silas Marner and the Political Unconscious," *Victorian Newsletter* 92 (Fall 1997): pp. 1-5.

Dessner, Lawrence Jay. "The Autobiographical Matrix of *Silas Marner*," *Studies in the Novel* 11 (1979): pp. 257-82.

Draper, R. P., ed. *George Eliot:* The Mill on the Floss *and* Silas Marner. Casebook Series. London: Macmillan, 1977.

Dunham, Robert H. *"Silas Marner* and the Wordsworthian Child," *Studies in English Literature* 16 (1976): 645-59.

Emery, Laura, and Margaret Keenan. "'I've Been Robbed!': Breaking the Silence in *Silas Marner*," *The American Journal of Psychoanalysis* 59, no. 3 (September 1999): pp. 209-23.

Gilbert, Sandra M. "Life's Empty Pack: Notes toward a Literary Daughteronomy," *Critical Inquiry* 11 (1985): pp. 355-84.

Hawes, Donald. "Chance in *Silas Marner*," *English: The Journal of the English Association* 31, no. 141 (Autumn 1982): pp. 213-18.

Higdon, D. L. "A Bibliography of George Eliot Criticism 1971-1977," *Bulletin of Bibliography* 37, no. 2 (1980).

Holloway, John. "George Eliot." In *The Victorian Sage*. London: Macmillan, 1953.

Johnstone, Peggy Fitzhugh. *The Transformation of Rage: Mourning and Creativity in George Eliot's Fiction*. New York: New York University Press, 1994.

Knoepflmacher, U. C. "George Eliot." Ford, G., ed. *Victorian Fiction: A Second Guide to Research*. New York: Modern Language Association of America, 1978.

————. *George Eliot's Early Novels: The Limits of Realism*. Berkeley, Calif.: University of California Press, 1968.

————. "Unveiling Men: Power and Masculinity in George Eliot's Fiction." Todd, Janet, ed. *Men by Women: Women and Literature*. New York: Holmes, 1981.

Levine, G. L. *An Annotated Critical Bibliography of George Eliot*. Brighton, England: Harvester Press, 1988.

Lovesay, Oliver. "Tigresses, Tinsel Madonnas, and Citizens of the World: The 'Other' Woman in George Eliot's Fiction." In Button, Marilyn Demarest, ed. *The Foreign Woman in British Literature: Exotics, Aliens, and Outsiders*. Westport, CT: Greenwood, 1999, pp. 117-26.

Marshall, William H. "A Selective Bibliography of Writings about George Eliot, to 1965." *Bulletin of Bibliography* 25, nos. 3-4 (1967).

Martin, Bruce K. "Similarity Within Dissimilarity: The Dual Structure of *Silas Marner*." *Texas Studies in Literature and Language* 14 (1972): 479-89.

Masters, Donald C. "George Eliot and the Evangelicals." *Dalhousie Review* 41 (1962): p. 505-12.

McCaw, Neil. *George Eliot and Victorian Historiography: Imagining the National Past*. London: Macmillan Press Ltd., 2000.

McLaverty, James. "Comtean Fetishism in *Silas Marner*." *Nineteenth Century Fiction* 36 (1982): pp. 318-36.

Milner, Ian. "Structure and Quality in *Silas Marner*." *Studies in English Literature* 6 (1966): pp. 717-29.

New, Peter. "Chance, Providence and Destiny in George Eliot's Fiction." *English: The Journal of the English Association* 34, no. 150 (Autumn 1985): pp. 191-208.

Newton, K.M. "George Eliot as Proto-Modernist," *Cambridge Quarterly* 27. no. 4 (1998): 275-86.

Pangallo, Karen L. *The Critical Response to George Eliot*. Westport, CT: Greenwood Press, 1994.

Parsons, Coleman O. "The Authority of the Past in George Eliot's Novels." *Nineteenth Century Fiction* 21 (1966): pp. 131-47.

Preston, John. "The Community of the Novel: Silas Marner." Comparative Criticism: A Yearbook 2 (1980): pp. 109-30.

Quick, Jonathan R. "Silas Marner as Romance: The Example of Hawthorne." Nineteenth Century Fiction 29 (1974): pp. 287-98.

Rignall, John, ed. Oxford Reader's Companion to George Eliot. Oxford: Oxford University Press, 2000.

Robertson, Linda K. "The Role of Popular Medicine in The Mill on the Floss, Silas Marner, and Felix Holt." The George Eliot Fellowship Review 13 (1982): pp. 33-37.

Sandoff, D. F. Monsters of Affection: Dickens, Eliot, and Brontë on Fatherhood. Baltimore: Johns Hopkins University Press, 1982.

Semmel, Bernard. George Eliot and the Politics of National Inheritance. New York: Oxford University Press, 1994.

Shuttleworth, Sally. "Fairy Tale or Science? Physiological Psychology in Silas Marner." In Jordanova, L. J., ed. Languages of Nature: Critical Essays on Science and Literature. New Brunswick: Rutgers University Press, 1986.

Simpson, Peter. "Crisis and Recovery: William Wordsworth, George Eliot, and Silas Marner." University of Toronto Quarterly 48 (1978): pp. 95-114.

Swann, Brian. "Silas Marner and the New Mythus." Criticism: A Quarterly for Literature and the Arts 18 (Spring 1976): 101-21.

Thale, Jerome. "George Eliot's Fable for Her Time." College English 19 (1958): pp. 141-46.

Thomson, Fred C. "The Theme of Alienation in Silas Marner." Nineteenth Century Fiction 20 (1965): pp. 69-84.

Woolf, David. An Aspect of Fiction: Its Logical Structure and Interpretation. Ravenna: Long, 1980.

Acknowledgments

"*Silas Marner*" by Philip Fisher. From *Making Up Society: The Novels of George Eliot*: 99-110. © 1981 by the University of Pittsburgh Press. Reprinted by permission.

"The Weaver of Raveloe: Metaphor as Narrative Persuasion in *Silas Marner*" by Meri-Jane Rochelson. From *Studies in the Novel*, v. 15.1 (Spring 1983): 35-43. © 1983 by North Texas State University. Reprinted by permission of the publisher.

"George Eliot's Conception of Sympathy" by Elizabeth Deeds Ermarth. From *Nineteenth-Century Fiction* 40, no. 1 (June 1985): 23-42. © 1985 by The Regents of the University of California. Reprinted by permission.

"Biblical Realism in *Silas Marner*" by Harold Fisch. From *Identity and Ethos: A Festschrift for Sol Liptzin on the Occasion of His 85th Birthday*, edited by Mark H. Gelber: 343-358. © 1986 by Peter Lang Publishing, Inc. Reprinted by permission.

"Statesman, Dwarf and Weaver: Wordsworth and Nineteenth-Century Narrative" by Angus Easson. From *The Nineteenth-Century British Novel*, edited by Jeremy Hawthorn: 17-29. © 1986 by Edward Arnold (Publishers) Ltd. Reprinted by permission.

"*Adam Bede* (1858) and *Silas Marner* (1861)" by Kerry McSweeney. From *George Eliot (Marian Evans): A Literary Life*: 62-79. ©1991 by Kerry McSweeney. Reprinted by permission.

"Epilogue: Part 2 of *Silas Marner*" by Patrick Swinden. From Silas Marner: *Memory and Salvation*: 106-115. © 1992 by Twayne Publishers. Reprinted by permission of the Gale Group.

"'Light Enough to Trusten By': Structure and Experience in *Silas Marner*" by Terence Dawson. From *The Modern Language Review* 88, part 1 (January 1993): 26-45. © 1993 by The Modern Humanities Research Association. Reprinted by permission of the publisher.

"George Eliot's Shorter Fiction, including *Silas Marner*" by Alan W. Bellringer. From *George Eliot*: 63-79. © 1993 by Alan W. Bellringer. Reprinted by permission.

"*Silas Marner* and the Anonymous Heroism of Parenthood" by Henry Alley. From *The Quest for Anonymity: The Novels of George Eliot*: 71-81. © 1997 by Associated University Presses, Inc. Reprinted by permission.

"George Eliot's 'Glue Test': Language, Law, and Legitimacy in *Silas Marner*" by Efraim Sicher. From *The Modern Language Review* 94, part 1 (January 1999): 11-21. © 1999 by the Modern Humanities Research Association. Reprinted by permission of the publisher.

Index